T0316323

The Impact of New Health Imperatives on Educational Policy and Schooling

Currently a great deal of public discourse around health is on the assumed relationship between childhood inactivity, young people's diets, and a putative steep rise in obesity. Children and young people are increasingly being identified as a population at 'risk' in relation to these health concerns. Such concerns are driving what might be described as new 'health imperatives' which prescribe the choices young people should make around lifestyle: physical activity, body regulation, dietary habits, and sedentary behaviour. These health imperatives are a powerful force driving major policy initiatives on health and education in a number of countries in the Western world. Schools in particular have been targeted for the implementation of a plethora of initiatives designed to help children and young people lose weight, become more active and change their eating patterns inside and outside school.

Addressing these issues requires an innovative theoretical approach. Neither the fields of 'eating disorders' nor 'obesity research' has addressed these issues from a sociological and pedagogical perspective. The contributors to this edited collection draw on a range of social theories, including Michel Foucault and Basil Bernstein to interpret the data collected across three countries (Australia and New Zealand, United Kingdom) and from a range of primary and secondary schools. Each chapter addresses various aspects of the relationship between health imperatives as constituted in government policies, school programs and practices, their recontextualisation in school practices and the impact of this on the subjectivities of children and teachers.

This book was originally published as a special issue of *Discourse: Studies in the Cultural Politics of Education.*

Jan Wright is a Professorial Fellow in the Faculty of Social Sciences at the University of Wollongong, Australia, and a member of the Early Start Research Institute. Her research draws on feminist and poststructuralist theory to critically engage issues associated with the relationship between embodiment, culture and health. Her most recent work has focused on the recontextualisation of health imperatives in various pedagogical sites, including school and the media, and on the consequences of these imperatives for the subjectivities of children, young people, teachers and parents. She is co-editor of *Biopolitics and the 'Obesity Epidemic': Governing Bodies* (Routledge, 2009) with Valerie Harwood, *Young People, Physical Activity and the Everyday* (Routledge, 2010) and co-author with Michael Gard of *The 'Obesity Epidemic': Science, Ideology and Morality* (Routledge, 2005).

Valerie Harwood is an Associate Professor in the Faculty of Social Sciences at the University of Wollongong, Australia, and a Future Fellow with the Australian Research Council. Her research interests include the production of knowledge on child and youth psychopathology, critical disability studies, youth exclusion and practices of medicalisation in schools. This work is engaged in the critical analysis of issues that impact on inclusion in education. Research projects include work with Indigenous young people and education, and the investigation of socio-economic status and place in educational disadvantages. Her most recent book, co-authored with Professor Julie Allan, is *Psychopathology at School: Theorizing Mental Disorders in Education* (Routledge, 2014).

The Impact of New Health Imperatives on Educational Policy and Schooling

Edited by
Jan Wright and Valerie Harwood

Routledge
Taylor & Francis Group

LONDON AND NEW YORK

First published 2015
by Routledge
2 Park Square, Milton Park, Abingdon, Oxon, OX14 4RN, UK

and by Routledge
711 Third Avenue, New York, NY 10017, USA

Routledge is an imprint of the Taylor & Francis Group, an informa business

British Library Cataloguing in Publication Data
A catalogue record for this book is available from the British Library

ISBN 13: 978-1-138-80241-4

Typeset in Times New Roman
by RefineCatch Limited, Bungay, Suffolk

Publisher's Note
The publisher accepts responsibility for any inconsistencies that may have
arisen during the conversion of this book from journal articles to book chapters,
namely the possible inclusion of journal terminology.

Disclaimer
Every effort has been made to contact copyright holders for their permission to
reprint material in this book. The publishers would be grateful to hear from any
copyright holder who is not here acknowledged and will undertake to rectify
any errors or omissions in future editions of this book.

Contents

Citation Information

The chapters in this book were originally published in *Discourse: Studies in the Cultural Politics of Education*, volume 33, issue 5 (December 2012). When citing this material, please use the original page numbering for each article, as follows:

Chapter 1
Editorial: Policy, schools and the new health imperatives
Valerie Harwood and Jan Wright
Discourse: Studies in the Cultural Politics of Education, volume 33, issue 5 (December 2012) pp. 611–616

Chapter 2
Embodying policy concepts
John Evans and Brian Davies
Discourse: Studies in the Cultural Politics of Education, volume 33, issue 5 (December 2012) pp. 617–634

Chapter 3
Beyond school boundaries: new health imperatives, families and schools
Emma Rich
Discourse: Studies in the Cultural Politics of Education, volume 33, issue 5 (December 2012) pp. 635–654

Chapter 4
'Emboldened bodies': social class, school health policy and obesity discourse
Laura De Pian
Discourse: Studies in the Cultural Politics of Education, volume 33, issue 5 (December 2012) pp. 655–672

Chapter 5
Health imperatives in primary schools across three countries: intersections of class, culture and subjectivity
Jan Wright, Lisette Burrows and Emma Rich
Discourse: Studies in the Cultural Politics of Education, volume 33, issue 5 (December 2012) pp. 673–692

Chapter 6
Neither good nor useful: looking ad vivum in children's assessments of fat and healthy bodies
Valerie Harwood
Discourse: Studies in the Cultural Politics of Education, volume 33, issue 5 (December 2012) pp. 693–712

Chapter 7
The medicalisation of food pedagogies in primary schools and popular culture: a case for awakening subjugated knowledges
Rosie Welch, Samantha McMahon and Jan Wright
Discourse: Studies in the Cultural Politics of Education, volume 33, issue 5 (December 2012) pp. 713–728

Chapter 8
Teachers' talk about health, self and the student 'body'
Lisette Burrows and Jaleh McCormack
Discourse: Studies in the Cultural Politics of Education, volume 33, issue 5 (December 2012) pp. 729–744

Please direct any queries you may have about the citations to
clsuk.permissions@cengage.com

Notes on Contributors

Lisette Burrows is an Associate Professor in Physical Education Pedagogy at the School of Physical Education, University of Otago, New Zealand, where she has taught for over 20 years. Her research is primarily focused on understanding the place and meaning of health and physical culture in young people's lives. Health and Physical Education curriculum, issues around inclusion of young people with disabilities and critical obesity work are also part of her research agenda. She predominantly draws on poststructural theoretical resources in her writing and teaching.

Brian Davies is Emeritus Professor of Education in the School of Social Sciences, Cardiff University, Wales. Since the publication of his book *Social Control and Education* (1976) he has taught and written widely on social theory and research, educational policy and pedagogic practice. His co-edited books include, with Joe Muller and Ana Morias, *Reading Bernstein, Researching Bernstein* (Routledge/Falmer, 2004); with John Fitz and John Evans, *Education Policy and Reproduction* (Routledge/Falmer, 2005); with John Evans, Emma Rich and Rachel Allwood, *Education, Disordered Eating and Obesity Discourse: Fat Fabrications* (Routledge, 2008); with Gabrielle Ivinson and John Fitz, *Knowledge and Identity: Concepts and Applications in Bernstein's Sociology* (Routledge, 2011); and with John Evans, *New Direction in Social Theory, Education and Embodiment* (Routledge, 2013).

Laura De Pian is a Lecturer in Sport and Social Sciences at the University of Bath, UK. Her teaching and publications to date involve critical engagement with obesity and health discourse, teachers' enactment of health policy and pedagogy in schools and young people's embodied learning through health education. Her interests in these areas pertain to issues of diversity and social class in particular, as well as innovative methods to engage young people in research.

John Evans is a Professor of Sociology of Education and Physical Education at Loughborough University, UK. He teaches and writes on issues of equity, education policy, identity, and processes of schooling. He has authored and edited a number of papers, books and special editions in the Sociology of Education and Physical Education. The most recent of these being, with Emma Rich, Brian Davies and Rachel Allwood, *Education, Disordered Eating and Obesity Discourse* (Routledge, 2008), with Brian Davies, *New Direction in Social Theory, Education and Embodiment* (Routledge, 2013). He is founding Editor of the international journal, *Sport, Education and Society*.

Valerie Harwood is an Associate Professor in the Faculty of Social Sciences at the University of Wollongong, Australia, and a Future Fellow with the Australian Research

Council. Her research interests include the production of knowledge on child and youth psychopathology, critical disability studies, youth exclusion and practices of medicalisation in schools. This work is engaged in the critical analysis of issues that impact on inclusion in education. Research projects include work with Indigenous young people and education, and the investigation of socio-economic status and place in educational disadvantages. Her most recent book, co-authored with Professor Julie Allan, is *Psychopathology at School: Theorizing Mental Disorders in Education* (Routledge, 2014).

Jaleh McCormack is a doctoral graduate of the School of Physical Education, Sport and Exercise Sciences at the University of Otago, New Zealand. Jaleh has worked in research, policy and advocacy roles focused on current issues facing children and families in New Zealand. Her doctoral thesis critically examined discourses that contribute to positioning parents as responsible for the shape of their children's bodies.

Samantha McMahon is a Research Fellow in the School of Education, Faculty of Social Sciences at the University of Wollongong, Australia. Her research interests include the medicalisation of child behaviour, pre-service teacher epistemology, inclusive education and teacher education. Her PhD thesis was a study of preservice teachers' knowledge of challenging behaviour.

Emma Rich is a Senior Lecturer in the Department of Education at the University of Bath, UK. Her work draws on the sociology of education, pedagogy, the body and physical culture to explore how learning about and through the body (body pedagogies) take places in relation to different physical cultures, spaces and sites. In recent years, research projects have explored issues such as moral panic over obesity, eating disorders and education and surveillance of young people's bodies. She is co-editor of *Debating Obesity Critical Perspectives* (2010), *The Medicalization of Cyberspace* (Routledge, 2008) and co-author of *Education, Disordered Eating and Obesity Discourse: Fat Fabrications* (Routledge, 2008).

Rosie Welch is a Lecturer in the Faculty of Social Science, University of Wollongong, Australia, and is a Research Fellow for a project examining social inclusion in higher education. Her research focus has involved biographical narrative methods, bio-politics and pre-service primary teachers' subjectivities in relation to health and the body. Rosie's current research and teaching interests lie in social geography and pedagogies of health, yoga and creative dance.

Jan Wright is a Professorial Fellow in the Faculty of Social Sciences at the University of Wollongong, Australia, and a member of the Early Start Research Institute. Her research draws on feminist and poststructuralist theory to critically engage issues associated with the relationship between embodiment, culture and health. Her most recent work has focused on social constructions of youth, particularly in the context of public health imperatives and schooling. Her most recent publications include *Biopolitics and the 'Obesity Epidemic': Governing Bodies* (Routledge, 2009) co-edited with Valerie Harwood, *Young People, Physical Activity and the Everyday* (Routledge, 2010), co-edited with Doune Macdonald and *The 'Obesity Epidemic': Science, Ideology and Morality* (Routledge, 2005), co-authored with Michael Gard.

INTRODUCTION

Policy, schools and the new health imperatives

Obesity is a 'derogatory' word, says NICE

Doctors tasked with tackling the country's obesity crisis have been told to avoid using the word obese, because it could be considered 'unhelpful' or even 'derogatory' (Adams, 2012).

The above newsprint quote is one of several that appeared in the British media in response to the draft guidelines by the UK National Institute for Health and Clinical Excellence (NICE). These draft guidelines, designed to address health services in local communities, include a discussion of the term 'obese', and advocate not using the term with patients, instead using terms such as 'healthier weight' (NICE, 2012). Debate about using 'obese' is between, on the one hand, those who advocate being upfront about obesity with the obese person, and on the other, those who propose that harm that may be done through using the term. What has been overlooked by both camps is that, as the papers in this special issue will variously argue, the outcry over obesity is a much more complex issue, and that there are very real and to us, disconcerting effects of the widespread obsession with obesity as a major public health issue.

This contemporary 'obsession', we argue, reveals much about how weight and health are understood in this contemporary moment. As Gard and Wright (2005) state:

We are concerned that discussion (both popular and scientific) about the consequences of increasing numbers of overweight and obese people may be just as misguided as talk about why it is happening … [W]e explore the possibility that the dire predictions and sheer intensity of 'obesity talk' has more to do with preconceived moral and ideological beliefs about fatness than a sober assessment of existing evidence. (p. 3)

Despite these misgivings, governments in the UK, New Zealand and Australia have made and are continuing to make substantial investments in policies, strategies and research to address the perceived risk of obesity and related health issues. One of the main foci of current public health discourse is the relationship between childhood inactivity, young people's diets and a putative steep rise in obesity. This focus drives major policy initiatives on health, and schools in particular have been targeted for the implementation of a plethora of initiatives geared towards helping children and young people lose weight, become more active and change their eating patterns in and outside school. Such concerns are driving what might be described as the 'new health imperatives', which prescribe the choices young people should make around lifestyle: physical activity, body regulation, dietary habits and sedentary behaviour. These imperatives share a number of distinctive features that separate them from other health discourses. Health imperatives around 'eating well', exercising regularly and monitoring our bodies carry powerful moral overtones and as such are very difficult to resist or contest. Young people (and their guardians, including schools) are implicitly held personally responsible and accountable for the prevention of obesity and related health problems, by knowing and avoiding relevant 'risk' factors.

Despite the sheer range and volume of initiatives associated with these health imperatives, we know relatively little of how such imperatives are being 'recontextualised', that is to say, received, interpreted and reconfigured within schools. Nor do we have evidence of how they may be regulating school policy and practice, and impacting on young people's and teachers' understandings of health, identities and 'human rights'.

Addressing these issues requires an innovative theoretical approach. Neither the field of 'eating disorders' nor of 'obesity research' has addressed these issues from a sociological and pedagogical perspective. The research reported in this Special Issue was designed to do this. The contributors draw on a range of social theorists, including Michel Foucault and Basil Bernstein to interpret the data collected across three countries (Australia, New Zealand and the UK) and from a range of primary and secondary schools. Each paper in this special issue will address various aspects of the relationship between the health imperatives as constituted in government policies, school programmes and practices, their recontextualisation in school practices and the impact of this on the subjectivities of children and teachers.

The new health imperatives are tied to moral and ideological beliefs about fatness, as well as to ideals about medical and scientific understanding of concerns such as diagnosis and treatment. These ideals are evident both in the depiction of the health-obesity binary and in the ready subscription to medically orientated ways of recognising and dealing with obesity. Yet as the papers in this special issue demonstrate, paradoxically it is not obesity that the new health imperatives pick up on, but rather a particular configuration that *health-is-without-obesity* – which is to say that a key way to represent health is via a lack of obesity. One of the consequences of this attention is that other ways of interpreting health are elided, or even, to press the point, put out of commission. In putting forward this provocative statement we are not suggesting that government policies, for instance, are taking obesity to be the yardstick by which health is measured, but rather, that the very focus on obesity is having unplanned biopedagogical effects on our societies' children and young people. Children, for example, are being taught new ways to conceptualise health and are forming different relationships with food. What is all too frequently overlooked, however, are the very real and to us, damaging effects of attention on obesity. The papers each take up different aspects of these effects and the influence of the new health imperatives.

The papers in this issue all arise from a joint international project involving teams from Australia, the UK and New Zealand. Research in Australia was funded by an Australian Research Council Linkage International Social Science Collaboration (2007–2010), in New Zealand by an Otago University Grant and in the UK by an Economic and Social Research Council. The studies involved research in nine primary schools and six secondary schools in each of the three countries, with a range of schools represented (government funded and independent) and from a range of socio-economic areas. Our methods were primarily qualitative, involving surveys, interviews and observations. In total, we collected survey data from 2636 children and young people. Interviews were also held with a sample of students from each school site as well as with key teaching staff.

Overview of papers in this issue

The papers in this special issue begin with three papers from the UK team, followed by four papers from the Australian and New Zealand researchers. In some of the papers research across all three countries is reported, while others, such as De Pian (UK) and Welch, McMahon and Wright (Australia and New Zealand) focus on specific country settings. The first of the three papers from the UK team is by Evans and Davies. In this paper, the authors make a strong case for the influence of policy on body pedagogies and outline how policy is mediated into effect by the in situ processes of pedagogic and corporeal devices. Evans and Davies describe how work on Bernstein's economic and symbolic codes can be used to analyse the ways in which policy becomes recontextualised into the everyday discourses – and subjectivities of schools and the people who inhabit them. This means, as they explain:

> ...registering the embodied effects of both symbolic and economic control, for we know that policy making is 'a multidimensional and value laden activity that exists in context' (Fitz, Davies, & Evans, 2006, p. 2) always configured by both discursive and economic resource to reflect national and, or, local purposes (Evans & Davies, see this issue).

To examine these processes, Evans and Davies describe how corporeal and pedagogic devices influence emplacement, enactment and embodiment. As they explain, a sensitive use of Bernstein's work allows for a nuanced analysis of the effects of policy, and particularly how these are embodied.

Rich's paper examines how the moral panic about obesity has given rise to a range of policies and interventions in school contexts geared towards monitoring and regulating the lives and bodies of children and young people. The paper draws on an analysis of interviews with school staff from the UK schools to argue that these policies and practices reflect forms of surveillance which can derive from the school but reach beyond it into public (family) spaces. Such policies and practices can be understood as part of a surveillant assemblage of bodies where biopedagogical flows move via power relations across and between families and schools in ways that are profoundly marked by social class. The paper particularly engages with the theorisation of surveillance, biopedagogies and assemblages and the relations between these.

De Pian's paper picks up on the ways that the new health imperatives become embodied. The paper describes how children from middle-class primary schools in England developed *troubled bodies, emboldened bodies* or *insouciant bodies* in relation to the policies, curriculum and pedagogies they encountered in their school environments. De Pian's paper offers an analysis of how social class intersects with the take up of the imperatives and the very real effects that the current policy on health-obesity is having on the lives of children.

The next four papers pay particular attention to the research in Australia and New Zealand. The impact of the health imperatives described above seems increasingly to have an impact on young children. Wright, Burrows and Rich cite evidence that suggests that younger and younger children are talking in very negative and disturbing ways about themselves and their bodies. It is in this context that they examine the impact of the new health imperatives on the young children attending UK, Australian and New Zealand primary schools. Through an analysis of interviews conducted with primary aged children, they demonstrate how for the children interviewed, across the three countries, the ways they engaged with health messages were mediated by family relations and by the ways schools took up and transacted health imperatives, which were themselves mediated by class and culture. The extent to which many of these messages were congruent with each other and the certainty with which the children talked about health as related to eating 'good' food and exercising, they argue, points to the ubiquity of the obesity discourse and its related translation into policy, media and school syllabuses and practices in the UK, Australia and New Zealand. The narratives of two of the girls interviewed are examined in greater depth to illustrate how the children's negotiation of health messages was always and inevitably mediated by body shape and size (that is, by the sense of their own corporeality in time, place and space) and importantly by class, culture and gender.

The paper by Harwood takes up the issue of how children and young people 'see' health. In this paper, Harwood argues that the children and young people in our research in each of the countries placed significant emphasis on what they saw of bodies in order to determine health. While this may not at first glance appear strange, Harwood's analysis suggests that a problem of significance is occurring because these assessments rely on visual analysis of the surfaces of people – such as their shape, and this alone can signify good or ill health. These are, Harwood argues, evidence of the influence of the new health imperatives on children's and young people's understanding of health.

Welch, McMahon and Wright begin with a kindergarten song to illustrate how times have changed in relation to what counts as healthy and unhealthy food. Where once butter, bread, eggs, syrup and cream (as French toast) might have been understood as a nourishing breakfast, this combination of foods would now be banished from the 'nutritional' breakfast menu. Welch and her colleagues demonstrate in their paper how primary school children interviewed for the Australian study were well aware of this dichotomy between healthy and unhealthy, good and bad foods. The children reiterated meanings that associated eating as a practice of 'risk; and 'temptation' in ways that reflected the nutrition-based knowledge of food circulated in popular culture and health programmes. Of consequence in this account are the effects that the new health imperatives had on children's and young people's perceptions of food and their own behaviour. Welch et al. argue that the children's talk about food suggests a need to be constantly alert to temptation and feelings of guilt when they succumbed. They also argue that medico-scientific notions of 'healthy' food close down other ways of thinking and acting towards food and conclude the paper by exploring some of the subjugated knowledges about food that provide alternative ways of knowing.

New Zealand has recently implemented a new primary health education syllabus, which 'affords a newfound flexibility around what is taught and how it is taught'. On one hand this could be viewed as good news but this all depends on the values, pedagogical and content knowledge that primary teachers bring to such a value-laden subject. Burrows and McCormack draw on interviews with three teachers, collected as part of an ethnographic study of two New Zealand primary schools, to explore the personal health dispositions and knowledge that the teachers draw on to make decisions about how to teach about health. On the basis of their analysis of these interviews, Burrows and McCormack argue that the teachers' perceptions of their students' health needs, their understanding of the role of schools in ameliorating children's health problems and the pedagogical choices made were intimately linked to their lived histories of 'health', their understandings of their own and others' bodies and their personal convictions about what, for them, constituted a 'healthy' life. While the ubiquitous nature of health discourses, particularly those linked to obesity, might at first glance, invoke notions of a shared agenda and a uniform commitment to improving children and young people's health, their analysis points to the *diverse* ways in which teachers constitute their role as health and physical educators, 'care' about students and teach health and physical education curricula.

The special issue concludes with a Review Essay by Meg Maguire of Evans, Rich, Davies and Allwood's book, *Education, disordered eating and obesity discourse: fat fabrications*. The research described in this book is one of the main motivations for the studies reported in this Special Issue. The book examines the damaging health consequences of an ubiquitous obesity discourse, which has shaped government policy, cultural processes and school practices, for a group of young women who have been diagnosed with eating disorders. As Maguire says in the conclusion, 'What this book does is to take seriously the need to listen, and listen hard and then *act* differently'. In their different ways this is what all of the authors in this Special Issue seek to effect with their research. Each study makes visible the ways in which the obsession with obesity has effects for the ways schools act on children and young people, and in turn for how children and young people come to understand themselves, their health and their bodies. We argue that schools, governments and health researchers would do well to reflect on their role in promoting the new health imperatives and consider the value of acting differently.

References

Adams, S. (2012, May 8). Obesity a 'derogatory' word, says Nice. *The Telegraph*. Retrieved May 10, 2012, from http://www.telegraph.co.uk/health/healthnews/9252311/Obesity-a-derogatory-word-says-Nice.html

Fitz, J., Davies, B., & Evans, J. (2006). *Educational policy and social reproduction: Class inscription and symbolic control*. London: Routledge.

Gard, M., & Wright, J. (2005). *The obesity epidemic: Science, morality and ideology*. Oxford: Routledge.

National Institute for Health and Clinical Excellence (NICE). (2012). *Public health draft guidelines, obesity: Working with local communities*. National Health Service. Retrieved from http://www.nice.org.uk/nicemedia/live/12109/59116/59116.pdf

Valerie Harwood and Jan Wright
Faculty of Education, University of Wollongong,
Wollongong, NSW, Australia

Embodying policy concepts

John Evans[a] and Brian Davies[b]

[a]School of Sport, Exercise and Health Sciences, Loughborough University, Loughborough, UK;
[b]School of Social Sciences, Cardiff University, Wales, UK

This article introduces some of the key concepts that we have used in our research to help illuminate the multiple and different ways in which apparently ubiquitous health policies relating to obesity, exercise, diet and health are mediated and shaped both globally and nationally, as well as within regional, school and other contexts. The analyses suggest that concepts drawn from the work of Basil Bernstein, if suitably refined and combined with those of other social theorists of policy, may prove particularly useful when investigating the constantly shifting relationships between discourse, knowledge and bio power and the pedagogical and policy processes that occur within and between relationships of this kind. The article foregrounds the importance of concepts *emplacement, enactment* and *embodiment* and the transactions they represent. Taken together these concepts add nuance and sophistication to understandings of relationships between discourse, policy, in situational activity, subjectivity and actor differences without, however, being sufficient to explain why health education policies, pedagogies and the subjectivities they affect/effect, are configured in particular ways in specific national, regional or school settings. Achieving this, we suggest, requires that we further explore how these surface features of policy (emplacement, enactment, embodiment) are shaped, structured and regulated *in situ* by underlying processes involving the intersection of the *pedagogic* and *corporeal* devices.

Introduction

Over recent years, along with colleagues in the UK, Australia and New Zealand, we have been concerned to address how the lives of teachers and young people have been influenced and shaped by 'obesity discourse' (the articulation of 'health' largely in terms of assessed weight, diet and exercise levels) as it is recycled through formal and informal policies, pedagogies and practices of schools and other social settings including families, peers, the media (e.g. TV, film, websites) and religious institutions. In schools we have studied in the UK[1] we have encountered young people who have variously reported being deeply troubled by the attention given in contemporary culture and health discourse to their bodies' size, weight and shape (see Evans, Rich, Davies, & Allwood, 2008), those who, in contrast, are emboldened and privileged by it (Evans, De Pian, Rich, & Davies, 2011), as well as others for whom it seems not to matter much at all (De Pian, Evans, & Rich, 2008; De Pian, forthcoming). This range of subjectivities and relations to the imperatives of obesity discourse is, we suggest, to be found within schools across all our research sites. Of such relations and subjectivities we have asked a number of inter-related questions:

- How are they brought into play, and to be explained?
- How fluid, malleable and transient are their constitutive characteristics?
- How are specific (national, regional, school and teacher) enactments of bio policy and body pedagogies implicated in the construction and (re)production of embodied subjectivities and relations to obesity discourse?
- What psycho-social purposes, interest and values might these processes serve?
- Do the corporealities of young people, teachers and other adults, shape and/or get shaped by bio polices and body pedagogies as they traverse multiple contexts and sites of social practice, over time?

Broaching questions of this kind offers no small challenge. Like Walkerdine (2009), we take as read that we cannot simply predict the ways in which rhizomatic (multiple, unpredictable, intersecting, seamless) flows of knowledge across and within nation states, including the exercise of bio-power and bio-pedagogies (see Wright, 2009; Wright & Harwood, 2009) relating to health, the body and obesity, will be read, assimilated and embodied by individuals. Nor can we just read (teacher or pupil) subjectivity off from bio political modes of regulation for, as Walkerdine (2009) emphasised, we not only need to know how 'knowledge circulates globally' but also 'how it is picked up and worked with and over differently, in complex intersecting ways' (p. 200). Globalised modes of regulation 'enter into different communities of practice (Lave & Wenger, 1991) [and invoke] different relations of affect' (Walkerdine, 2009, p. 201) as they 'circulate through particular arrangements of time and space' (p. 202). But recognising these complexities is one thing; articulating and explaining them in a way that remains sensitive to individual, local and national differences and acknowledges embodied structure and action, quite another. In this paper, then, we attempt to outline the language and ideas that have allowed us to address such complexities, including the 'constantly shifting relationships between discourse/ knowledge, bio power and the self' (p. 201) to which Walkerdine refers. The concepts proposed (see Figures 1 and 2) are intended to help address the intractable dynamic between biology and culture, the corporal and the corporeal, subjectivity and flows of power/knowledge, and critically, *the pedagogical and policy processes that occur within and between relationships of this kind* (Evans, Davies, & Rich, 2011).[2]

Cultural sensitivities

Some years ago, Broadfoot (2001) wrote that, in an increasingly international world characterised by a 'knowledge economy', it was little surprise that the relative success of national educational systems in terms of their production of 'human capital' should become an explicit concern of policy-makers. Comparative studies had, she says, become fashionable because they were considered to 'provide a kind of educational laboratory in which it is possible to elucidate the impact of different classroom practices' (p. 261). While we may have little to show from these studies, it is perhaps unsurprising that 'health', one particular form of social capital, should also have become a major concern of policy-makers in recent years and a matter for international comparison facilitated by a reduction of 'health' to a measurable/

manageable commodity in terms of individuals' or populations' obesity level or 'weight', as defined by body mass index. Policy-makers' obsession with 'weight issues' and national obesity standards, especially when reported as international league tables comparing 'their' nation's/populations' collective girth size, has been remarkable. Faced with apparently incontrovertible evidence from obesity research and a plethora of reports defining 'their' nations' (ill) health (e.g. Evans & Rich, 2011; Foresight Commission, 2007) many governments have charged schools and other state agencies with responsibility for safeguarding children's well-being by ensuring that they eat the right foodstuffs, exercise sufficiently and either lose, or reach, 'ideal weight'.

The limitations of such obesity statistics are well documented (e.g. Evans, Rich, & Davies, 2004; Gard, 2011; Gard & Wright, 2005) and we ought to be equally aware of the dangers of making crude generalisations based on them across countries, regions and cultures. Those of us in Physical Education and Health might echo concerns of Brennan, Green, Klenowski, and Zynger (2008) as to the ways in which data on certain educational performances, for example, from the OECD Programme for International Student Assessment, have been used and abused by politicians and Governments internationally, as they either laud or lambast their educational establishments. Obesity statistics, divorced from consideration of their locus of origin have the potential to be used and abused in much the same way and to similar ends. Broadfoot (2001) has reminded us, 'In any educational encounter there is a complex network of contextual factors at work' (p. 261), including levels of inequality and socio-economic and political resources that require consideration when making comparative assessments of performance data. From this perspective, the reference point for the success of any educational strategy, whether concerned with performance in education, health or sport, should be seen to depend in major part on levels of resourcing available to nations, regions, schools and teachers, including those that teachers and students themselves bring to the 'learner encounter' in the way of embodied cultural predispositions. Like Broadfoot, we have thus been fundamentally concerned to register ways in which teachers' and pupils' needs, interests and abilities and other embodied dispositions 'interrelate with and are affected by the various cultural settings they experience, at home, at school, in their peer group and elsewhere' (p. 264). But how are we to articulate and describe such complex relationships? How are we to read, analyse and interpret data generated within different countries, regions, schools and classrooms in ways that do not do symbolic violence to the meaning systems, cultures and practices from which they arise (Manathunga, 2009)? How are we to conceptualise these relationships in a way that acknowledges 'the global' or national as well as 'local', agency and structure, biology and culture, and the pedagogical and policy processes that affect teachers' and young people's lives? In what follows we foreground some of the concepts and ideas that have allowed us to begin to address issues of this kind.

Symbolic and economic control: a political economy of health

If we are to understand how and why some people, populations or communities fall ill, or are defined as being at risk of being unwell in different contexts, we need pay as much heed to the political economy of health as to its cultural politics (Evans & Davies, 2010; Wright, Macdonald, & Groom, 2003). In Bernstein's (1990, p. 134) terms this means addressing both the fields of *economic* control and *symbolic* control and relationships between them. The field of symbolic control relates to:

> ...the means whereby (embodied) consciousness is given a specialised form and distributed through forms of communication which relay a given distribution of power and dominant cultural categories.

and analysing 'the set of agencies and agents that specialise in discursive codes which they dominate' has been at the forefront of our concerns. In our work (Evans & Davies, 2004; Evans, Davies, & Rich, 2009; Evans, Rich, Davies, & Allwood, 2008a), we have been particularly concerned to document how certain codes (we have termed them body 'perfection codes', Evans & Davies, 2004) in terms of inherent principles and selected meanings in health education discourse influence and regulate ways of relating, thinking and feeling towards the body and specialise and distribute forms of consciousness, social relations and dispositions. Perfection codes have their social bases outside formal education in the economic interests of business, industry and the media and the medical and health fields. Unlike other educational codes (e.g. 'performance' and 'competency', see Bernstein, 1990), they centre on the dynamic between body and nature and biology and culture, on what we refer to as 'relations of' the body rather than 'relations to' or 'differences from' individuals and agencies *out-with* the self. If we were using a more Foucauldian language we would, no doubt, refer to 'relations to one's embodied self'. Such codes often reflect middle class, neo liberal and gendered cultural orientations and value positions (Rich & Evans, 2009a). They regulate consciousness and define subjectivity, and when insensitively expressed in health education curricula and related body pedagogies can badly damage lives, especially those of vulnerable young women (Evans et al., 2008a; Evans, Rich, Davies, & Allwood, 2008b).

Attention to such codes has also driven our concerns with how distributions of economic resource (e.g. within and between schools and families by virtue of social class) determined nationally, regionally and institutionally, regulate the means, contexts and possibilities of discursive resources represented in particular forms of health innovation and with how discursive codes relate to material and other resources and vice versa (Bernstein, 1990). Jamie Oliver's (a popular 'celebrity chef') school dinner series in the UK, for example, highlighted that desirable 'discursive' change in thinking about and attitudes towards school food could not be accomplished unless accompanied by related, structural changes in staffing and training levels and, critically, economic investment to facilitate the provision of 'good food'. Without sufficient attention to and support of the economic exigencies of health, his initiatives have largely failed (The Telegraph, 2012, p. 1). Evidently, health initiatives can no more run acceptably on mere good intention or shifts in consciousness than other curriculum or areas/learning experiences. Merely clarifying or agreeing on prevailing meanings around health and what discursively is considered important, desirable or profane knowledge and action, is not enough. The failure of governments, health educators and teachers in schools to recognise both the economic and discursive elements of health reflects a genuine lacuna in both public health discourse and critical health research.

Given this, attention to the economic field requires us, when making comparisons across countries, regions or schools, to concern ourselves with how the material bases of people's lives, especially their socio-economic resources, help fashion and construct subjectivity. Distributions and levels of income and inequality clearly regulate pupils' access to particular forms of embodied subjectivity and mediate the way in which discursive assemblages or bio-power work within specific school settings, and we have barely begun to elucidate such processes (see De Pian, 2012, forthcoming). There is, indeed, some nascent argument that such refocusing is occurring in wider public health debates and research and that a 'new public health' is rejecting the political individualism which has held individuals responsible for their own health and health education teachers alone as the primary means of altering pupils' health-related behaviours (Fullagar, 2009). In this 'new' view the notion that social or health problems can be solved at the individual level and are individual responsibilities is rejected and instead, the quest is to understand how socio-economic environments determine health (Babones, 2009). Existing levels of social inequality and wide income differentials structurally induce health problems. Wilkinson and Pickett (2009), leading proponents of this view, illustrate that some of the richest countries, for example, the UK, New Zealand and Australia, along with the USA, fare particularly badly on indices of social problems as varied as levels of trust and mental illness, as well as life expectancy, obesity, educational performance, teenage births, homicides, imprisonment rates, social mobility because they are 'less equal societies' (p. 19). These, it is argued, are less healthy social environments in which to live because they 'breed status anxiety, individualism and consumerism, forces which threaten not only the individual health of their members but also the quality of the collective environment in which they must live' (Babones, 2009, p. 4). Problems in rich countries are not caused by the society not being rich enough (or even by being too rich) but, they suggest, 'by the scale of material differences between people within each society being too big. What matters is where we stand in relation to others in our society' (Wilkinson & Pickett, 2009, p. 25). It is the level of income inequality that is to blame. In unequal societies, it is argued, everyone suffers.

Whatever we may think of this perspective (understandably it has its detractors), it refocuses attention on populations and structures, *systemic factors*, 'the bigger picture' in our research. As Wilkinson and Pickett (2009, p. 233) point out, people and governments have been inclined to see health and psychological well-being as dependent on what can be done at the individual level, for example, through the cultivation of individual responsibility, or by providing support in early childhood, or through the reassertion of religious or 'family' values. While these things are important, Wilson and Pickett contend that the best way of responding to harm done by high levels of inequality is to reduce inequality itself, suggesting that 'income distribution provides policy makers with a way of improving the psychosocial well-being of whole populations' (p. 233).

This perspective, focusing both on economic and discursive resources presents a challenge to health researchers and governments alike. It announces that the search for understandings of how health discourses flow across territories and national boundaries and impact upon individual lives over time, has to recognise and adequately conceptualise that health discourses enter socio-political systems already differentiated by economic resource, levels of inequality and weak or strong status hierarchies. The imperatives of obesity discourse are not, then, likely to have the same resonance in cultures, communities or schools where there are low levels of inequality and weak status differentials, as in those with high levels and strong ones. In the latter, where the effects of this discourse are multiplied because pronounced status hierarchies prevail, an emphasis on acquiring 'health' expressed in terms of achieving acceptable weight levels may prove particularly problematic, even psychologically and socially devastating, especially for individuals or populations who do not have the material means, resources or desire to achieve such things. In such contexts individuals and communities, particular classes and/or cultures may, indeed, be consigned to anomic, 'loser', fat and overweight status and positioned in a persistent state of alienation from their and others' bodies. Others, however, may be privileged and emboldened in the very same process (De Pian, 2012, forthcoming).

Policy mediations

Grasping the terminologies and institutional practices of any given national, regional or local education system requires a sense of their ideologies, histories, economics, inequalities and the dynamics of power and the control hierarchies that they represent (see Rizvi & Lingard, 2010). It means registering the embodied effects of both symbolic and economic control, for we know that policy-making is 'a multidimensional and value laden activity that exists in context' (Fitz, Davies, & Evans, 2006, p. 2) always configured by both discursive and economic resources to reflect national and/or local purposes. For such very good reasons we cannot assume that globalised health discourse has either homogenising or predictable effects. For example, neo liberalism has dominated political culture in all our research settings and has shaped both the vocabulary and syntax of health and educational legislation over many years (Evans et al., 2009). In UK schools, however, we have seen that ubiquitous health imperatives, even when driven and shaped by dominant political ideology, generate very different health curriculum and body pedagogies in different regions and school settings (Evans, De Pian, et al., 2011). Health policies sit alongside policies reflecting a range of national, regional and school centred commitments not all of which resonate comfortably with neo liberal ideals. While obesity discourse and the legislations it generates may appear to be 'the same' on the surface in Australia, New Zealand and England, or in Merthyr, Manchester and Dunfermline, both the process of its delivery and its outcomes and effects are mediated substantially and subtly via different cultures, institutional structures and politico-ideological systems. These are policy-saturated contexts wherein aims of and commitments to health education converge with many other more pressing demands, for example, of literacy and numeracy. Together, such policies form complex assemblages of meaning that 'contour possibilities' for action (Burrows, 2009 and this special issue) shaping curriculum, body pedagogies and the subjectivities of teachers and pupils alike. Such assemblages may display inconsistencies that generate contradictions and tensions of purpose and intent. For example, commitments to equity and inclusion inherent within National Curriculum and other education policy legislation in the UK reflect (at least rhetorically) desires to bring people together and dissipate irrelevant differences. However such measures reverberate badly with the reductive, evaluative and differentiating tendencies of obesity policies centred on manifest body differences nurturing invidious labelling and insensitivity towards those who are not deemed to be of 'correct' weight, size or shape (see Rich, Evans, & De-Pian, 2010).

Our work, then, like that of many others on the policy terrain (Braun, Ball, & Maguire, 2011a; Braun, Ball, Maguire, & Hoskins, 2011b), has highlighted that, if we are to understand how global health imperatives (obesity discourse) impact the lives of young people, we have to interrogate not only how *policy* (imperatives) is *emplaced* in context and *enacted* (as action and performance, consciously/knowingly, unconsciously/unknowingly) but also is *embodied,* i.e. how they affect and effect an individual's sense of being *some-body* in the social world in time, place and space. However, understanding how these intersecting aspects of policy shape pedagogy and subjectivity is not enough, but requires due regard to processes that underlie them, fundamentally, we suggest, the workings of the *corporeal* and *pedagogical* devices (CD/PD). Our understanding of each of these concepts and the intersections they address (represented in Figures 1 and 2) is further outlined below.

Encoding emplacement, enactment and embodiment

Bernstein viewed 'pedagogic communication as a crucial medium of symbolic control' and prospectively set about 'understanding the social processes whereby conscious desires are given specific forms, evaluated, distributed and changed' (Fitz et al, 2006, p. 4). In such quests, 'policy' takes its place as one mode of attempting control of the PD, the internal rules which regulate pedagogic communication and make it possible, acting selectively on potential meanings. As Bernstein (1990) emphasised, its forms of realisation vary with context, are unstable and are not ideologically free. From his perspective, both the linguistic device and the PD provide 'rulers for consciousness', the latter providing the intrinsic grammar of pedagogic discourse (its voice) through its inter-related distributive, re-contextualising and evaluative rules. As mentioned, our research has previously documented how the language and grammar of 'performativity' (celebrating difference, hierarchy, 'objective' measurable 'indices' of health *qua* weight and exercise levels) has provided 'rulers for consciousness', framing and encoding contemporary health discourse (Evans et al., 2008a; Rich & Evans, 2009b) and subsequently how young people think about their bodies in very reductive ways inside and outside schools. Its distributive rules 'specialise forms of knowledge, consciousness and practice to social groups and govern the changing line between the esoteric and the mundane' (Bernstein, 1996, p. 42). For example, they determine who gets what access to health knowledge, as well as the forms it takes and are considered either 'sacred' (valuable, important, high status) or 'profane' (Bernstein, 1996, p. 45) and, in so doing, help perpetuate social class and cultural hierarchies and differences. (Evans et al., 2008b).

We derive our concept of the CD from Bernstein's notion of the PD. As indicated above, in Bernstein's (1990) view, the PD defines the 'voice of pedagogy', constituted by 'a grammar for producing specialised messages (and) realizations, a grammar which regulates what it processes: a grammar which orders and positions and yet contains the potential of its own transformation' (p. 190). Most simply, the PD refers to underlying structures (selected or fought over principles, rules and symbolic resources) which shape school pedagogies (the relay of messages), turn institutional patterns into consciousness, and define the way in which both institutional and individual differences become ways of thinking and acting in the social world. It, therefore, legitimates categories of consciousness. As such it provides, as Bernstein (1996, p. 43) says, a symbolic 'ruler for consciousness'. The concept of PD undoubtedly offers invaluable purchase on the relationships between knowledge selection, organisation, pedagogy and identity but it is essentially a theory of transmission that underplays the role and nature of embodied agency in the activation and realisation of the PD. As indicated in the concepts of embodiment, emplacement and enactment outlined below (see Figure 2), policy discourses, like pedagogical practices, are always and inevitably mediated for individuals through their material (flesh and blood, sentient, thinking and feeling) bodies, their actions and those of their peers, parents/guardians and other adults. As a way of articulating the materiality of the *lived experiences* typically associated with acquiring the attributes required by obesity (or other health) discourse and 'the actual embodied changes resulting from this process' (Shilling, 2005, p. 13), we have been inclined, *pace* Bernstein, to talk of the CD, to focus on the body as not just a discursive representation and relay of messages and power relations external 'to itself' but as a voice 'of itself'. As a material/physical conduit it has an internal grammar and syntax given by the intersection of biology, culture and the predilections of class, which regulate (facilitate and constrain) embodied action and consciousness, including the ways in which discursive messages, such as those conveyed in policy texts (and all other social relations) are read and received. This concept privileges neither biology nor culture and endorses Frank's (2006, p. 433) view that neither 'the experience of embodied health nor the observation of signs of health circulating outside bodies has to trump the other as being the real point of origin. Instead, each is understood as *"making the other possible"*'. How the CD finds expression and is subjectified (given shape, form and definition as 'personality') among relations given by the PD in specific school settings thus becomes our central concern.

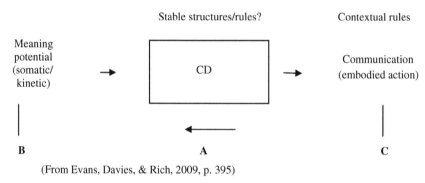

(From Evans, Davies, & Rich, 2009, p. 395)

Figure 1.   Corporeal device.

In Figure 1, **A**, **B** and **C** highlight different but inextricably related aspects of embodied communication, each having distinctive features/qualities and a degree of relative autonomy, though none alone can account for either generative (productive) or constraining (reproductive) elements of embodied action and social reproduction. **A** draws attention to the socio-genetic aspects (potentialities) of corporeality; **B**, the meaning potential of 'the body' brought into play in social context; and **C**, contextual rules and power relations that strongly influence or 'determine' them. In this model, individuals are perceived as physical bodies resourced not just with 'emotions' (Zembylas, 2007), 'desires' (Sykes, 2007) or 'jouissance' (Davis, 2004; Pronger, 2002) but a range and variety of cognitive, affective, social and kinetic capabilities or resources that are always encoded by the device (Evans et al., 2008a). This echoes Zembylas' (2008, p. 4) notion that 'human beings have universal corporeal potential' (**A**), enacted in particular sociocultural and political arrangements that provide them somatic and semiotic meaning (**B**), and that they are always 'socially and culturally specific persons engaged in complex webs of power relations' (**C**). It also announces the body as always both 'being' and 'becoming', capable of action and performance (see Grosz, interviewed by Ausch, Randal, & Perez, 2008). Biology and culture, ontology and epistemology, are inextricably entangled via the interminable dialectics of the CD, clearly denoting a 'structural orientation' but without neglecting the phenomenological/lived body. The CD thus signals a regulative but not a determinative power over the characteristic experiences and bodily orientation outcomes of those subject to it. In essence, it describes an intended embedded relation between the three elements which is, however, not guaranteed. The realist impact of the CD is that it both captures a relation between means/experience/outcomes that had happened in the past (but was not guaranteed in the future) and specifies the parameters of a *potential* relation between the three. The CD, then, reminds us of the fundamental processes that underlie and shape policy mediations wherever they occur (across countries, regions and in schools; see Figure 2). It points to culturally encoded human resources that invariably and inevitably are activated by and activate the mechanisms of the PD, including the principles, values, rules and other predispositions that children, teachers and others bring to the school context, are already in place prior to, and will precede, the enactment of particular policies and pedagogies.[3]

We are not alone in endeavouring to deal with the many considerable, social, psychological and epistemological issues to be dealt with when addressing biology/culture relationships of the kind represented in Figure 1 (see Evans et al., 2009). As Thorpe (2011), for example, points out, many sociologists of the body and health and illness are now attempting to 'rethink the relationship between sociology and the biological sciences' (Bury, 1997, p. 199) by 'marrying' the biological and the social in a 'truly embodied fashion' (Newton, 2003; Williams, 2006, p. 13). It might fairly be claimed that '[i]n so doing, material corporeal sociologists (as they have become known)' in the field of health research, 'are making major contributions in linking health and illness' with 'wider structures of power and domination, civilisation and control in society' (Williams, 1998, cited in Thorpe, 2011, p. 3). Attention to the body's materiality has also been reflected in the work of some educational researchers over recent years. James (2000), for example, has revealed that children are understandably hypersensitive to somatic changes occurring to their body, perhaps because they have only limited degrees of control over them. Indeed, much of our and others' work (e.g. Halse, Honey, & Boughtwood, 2008; Wright & Harwood, 2009) endorses James' central finding that children and young people have to come to terms not only with their own constantly changing bodies, the body's generative meaning potential and those of their peers but also with the changing institutional contexts within which meaning is given to these changes. As James (2000, p. 29) points out, 'children's experience of embodiment is the experience of the embodiment of time'. Teacher and other adult embodiments, however, have been rather less well explored.

Our interest here, however, in not in revisiting the vast range of sociological perspectives brought to bear on 'the body in culture' over recent years (e.g. Evans et al., 2009; Thorpe, 2011). Rather, it is in drawing attention to and emphasising the fundamental processes that underlie and shape policy mediations and their expressions as body pedagogies and subjectivities in schools. Critically, relationships between the PD and the CD (encoded, irreducible transactions of biology and culture) help shape and form policies, institutionally and pedagogically and have contingent, not causal, effect. Thus, the outcomes of policy cannot be predicted either within or across different nations, regions or schools. Armed with the above concepts (and due regard for the dynamics represented in Figure 1) we can then begin to explore how policy activates and is activated by embodied and other institutional resources, is given shape when emplaced and enacted *in situ* by intersections of the CD/PD, and how such processes also help reproduce class and cultural differences, hierarchies and relations (Evans et al., 2008a; De Pian, 2012, forthcoming).

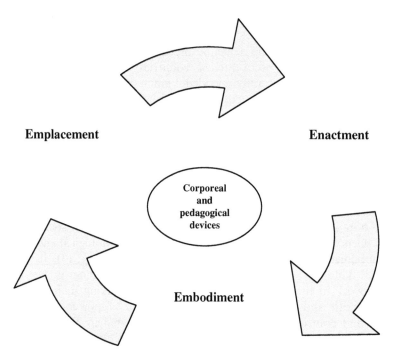

Figure 2. Policy embodied transactions.

Embodied concepts

Figure 2 thus portrays emplacement, enactment and embodiment of policy as on-going and interminable expressions of the underlying intersection of the CD/PD. Our use of the term 'emplacement' (see De Pian, 2012; Evans & Davies, 2011; Evans, Davies, Rich, & De Pian, 2012) has synergies with that of 'context', as used and brilliantly embellished in recent editions of this journal by Braun et al. (2011a, 2011b). They refer to the *situated, professional, material* and *external* elements of context, while others, adopting a critical realist perspective (Edwards, 2011), highlight *individual* capacities of key actors; *interpersonal* relationships supporting the intervention; *institutional* setting; and wider *infra-structural factors,* as elements of context. However, for all their sophistication, such definitions, in our view, fall short of capturing the fluid, transient and relational aspects of body-context transactions, better achieved, we suggest, through the notion of emplacement (see Pink, 2011). *Emplacement* signals a body always in 'relation to', transacting either knowingly or habitually with others and objects in time, place and space. If using Bourdieu's terms we might say that bodies are 'constituted in and in relationship to a social space (or field)' (Bourdieu, 1998, p. 1240), such spaces refracting (unequal) distributions of power and resource (Foucault, 1980). Context, in this view, is a representational effect of symbolic transactions between human agents and objects, repetitively forming structures that frame and regulate but never determine or control action that has to be continually achieved. Emplacement, then, allows us to recognise the body as 'part of the ecology of things in progress' (Pink, 2011, p. 354), to see it as an 'organism in relation to other organisms and its representations in relation to other representations'. It recognises not only 'the specificity and intensity of the place event and its contingencies, but also the historicity of processes and their entanglements' (p. 354) within given relations of power, resource and control.

As others and we have demonstrated, obesity discourse enters schools which have very different histories, curricula and purposes, and they serve clienteles who do not have equal access to the levels of (human and economic) resource required to effect desired change in behaviour and thought. It is, therefore, unsurprising that we find diversity of health education practices amongst them. In some schools, for example, teachers' interpretations of pupil and community needs generate health policies that are *reparative*, designed to restore health behaviours thought to be pathological or absent in the wider community; in others, to *enhance* or *enrich* good and privileged behaviours and opportunities considered already present in the family and school (Evans, De Pian, et al., 2011). The diversity of health education curricula and pupil subjectivity produced by apparently ubiquitous obesity discourse when interpolated and recontextualised institutionally in respect of the needs of 'local' or specific clienteles and differential distributions of power and resource, is illustrated in our and other's (e.g. Braun, Maguire, & Ball, 2010, Braun et al., 2011a) work.

Our use of the term '*enactment*' also has resonance with Braun and colleagues' (2010, 2011a) usage announcing 'the interpretive and creative aspects of policies' that are 'translated by diverse policy actors in the school environment, rather than simply implemented' (see De Pian, 2012). As Ball (2006) states, 'policies do not normally tell you what to do, they create circumstances in which the range of options available in deciding what to do are narrowed or changed, or particular goals or outcomes are set' (p. 21). Braun et al. (2010, 2011a, 2011b) use 'enactment' to foreground teachers and other education workers as key actors, rather than merely subjects in policy processes (Armstrong, 2003; Hodgson, Edward, & Gregson, 2007). In this view, policy enactments involve 'creative processes of interpretation and recontextualisation, including 'interpretations of interpretations' (Rizvi & Kemmis, 1987) although the degree of play or freedom for 'interpretation' varies from policy to policy. 'Enactment' thus signals that policies are 'collective and collaborative' processes in which there is interaction and inter-connection between diverse actors, texts, talk, technology and objects (artefacts) which constitute an on-going response to policy, sometimes durable sometimes fragile, within networks and chains (Ball, Maguire, Braun, & Hoskins, 2011; Maguire, Hoskins, Ball, & Braun, 2011). Policy, therefore, is not 'done' at one point in time in our schools; it is always a process of 'becoming' and always embodied, as indicted in Figure 2.

The concepts of emplacement and enactment, however, even when embellished to capture a stronger sense of subjectivity and agency (Ball, Maguire, Braun, & Hoskins, 2011), in our view, remain incomplete to the extent that they understate the embodied, agentic and corporeal aspects of policy processes. Perhaps in a way that is unique to health legislation, teachers and pupils are expected not just to enact or emplace policy but 'become' its embodiment (see De Pian, 2012; Wrench, 2011), their manifest actions in and outside schools (exercising, eating the 'right' food) being representative of what policy-makers and others expect individuals and populations to become. The concept 'embodiment' brings such processes to the fore though, once more, if perceived reductively (or independently of emplacement and enactment) conjures up images of stasis and permanence belying the developmental, transient and performative aspects of its 'becoming' in relation to time and place and space. Most simply we might say that embodiment refers to a certain mode of being in one's body (Benhabib, 1991) though, with Sykes (2011), we prefer Weiss's (1999) broader view, seeing it as a fluid process involving biological, social and psychic processes. For Sykes, embodied subjectivity refers to 'the intersections between the body, the unconscious and identity...constructed within a normative gender-sex system (Benhabib, 1991; Prosser, 1998), that is racialised (Eng, 2001) and overvalues productive, thin bodies' (see Sykes, 2011, p. 6). The concept of embodiment, then, signals that bodies are both material and corporeal objects configured through discourses and discursive practices that are themselves refractions of – enacted and emplaced – power relations. Therefore, we might anticipate that, in Wrench's (2011, p. 148) terms, in 'spaces, such as PE and sport' and health, the [teacher's or student's] body becomes 'an essential conduit and effect of the nexus between discourse and power relations', all visceral manifestations, we would suggest, of differential distributions of authority and control.

Taken together then, the concepts of emplacement, enactment and embodiment certainly add nuance and sophistication to understandings of relationships between policy, institutional activity, subjectivity and actor differences. But our claim here is that they are not sufficient to explain why health education policies, body pedagogies, and the subjectivities they affect/effect, are configured in particular ways in specific national, regional or school settings. Achieving this, requires that we further explore how these surface features of policy (emplacement, enactment, embodiment) are shaped and structured *in situ* by underlying processes involving the intersection of the PD (Bernstein, 1990) and CD (Evans, Davies, et al., 2011). Figures 1 and 2 but allude to the complexities of such relationships. It goes without saying that further empirical investigation is now required if we are to better understand how health public discourse and associated policies materialise in specific contexts and their effects on the lives of individuals and populations therein.

Conclusion

If nothing more, the above analyses remind us that we need a sociological way of conceptualising policy *origins*, for example, the production of globalised obesity discourse, say through the workings of the World Health Organisation or other agencies and individuals in the primary research field, among obesity researchers, *processes* and *destinations*, that allows us to stay in touch with their complexity and scope, while also retaining the view that appropriate languages of description are possible that connect and compare empirical and theoretical work. Such language is, of course, to be found in a variety of perspectives some represented in this and previous special editions. However, Bernstein's (1990) analyses of the structure of pedagogic discourse, suitably refined to embrace a stronger sense of embodied agency with the notion of the CD, not only help us make cross cultural comparisons but also understand how assemblages of meaning around health are shaped through various sites of practice to form the body pedagogies that regulate consciousness and young people's lives. Such concepts and the empirical data they attend, announce not only the intersections of biology and culture and the inseparability (unity) of agency and structure but also the multiple ways in which state and school policies and associated 'body pedagogies' are shaped and help deliver 'health education' in ways that reproduce class and cultural hierarchies and differences (see De Pian, 2012; Evans et al., 2012).

There is, of course, as others have stated, 'no "just nice"', no definitive account of educational policy or pedagogy and its effects; there are only more or less adequate ones from some perspectives, for given purposes'. And coherent, culturally sensitive, cross cultural comparisons will certainly not be achieved by conceptually 'flailing around for anything that looks as if it might work' (Ball, 1998, cited in Fitz et al., 2006, p. 2). But Bernstein's work, read sensitively and suitably refined with that of other social theorists, provides a means of achieving this. Indeed, it is these concepts, rather than empirical data itself, that facilitate communication and comparison across cultures and contexts. They provide the capacity to read data 'sensitively', to compare how particular discourses are 'made' and encoded at various levels and sites of practice, with given economic and discursive resources and how bodies, whether deemed acceptable or pathological, are brought into being and either privileged or alienated in the process.

How individuals experience the multiple meanings and effects of policy and body pedagogies in relation to the 'proximity' of their own embodied cultural dispositions and abilities and those prevailing over particular terrains in and outside schools, thus, becomes a central concern. Picture the complexity of recontextualising processes (rearticulated as *emplacements, enactments and embodiments*) of health education shaped by intersections of the CD and PD and we might also begin to appreciate how dissonance, dissent and change can occur, and how and where resistance is made possible. Harwood (2009, p. 24) attests that we need focus on modes of subjectification within and across sites and on how individuals constitute themselves in order to emphasise subjecification as an active, embodied process. Again, we would say that Bernstein's concepts, suitably infused with others, allow us to broach these issues, to interrogate the detail of subjectivity and corporality, while viewing schools, communities and countries as layered differentiated spaces subject to economic and discursive resources, in which young people (and their parents) may variously feel empowered or alienated. Whether they do so, of course, depends on the nature of relationships between their corporealities (the activating/activated dispositions of the CD) and those privileged and propelled by the PD. Allegiance to Bernstein thus also helps us avoid an over-determined view of embodiment and subjectification in which individuals are merely the discursive affect/effects of essentially reproductive bio-power and obesity discourse. It presses us to better understand relationships between biology and culture and view 'regulative practices as actions upon the body's experience of itself' (Bergson, cited in Walkerdine, 2009, p. 203). Policy concepts then, properly 'embodied', might begin to provide some better purchase on relationships of this kind, and why some young people are so deeply damaged by obesity discourse in schools, others privileged by it, and others for whom it seems to not matter much at all.

Notes

1. The UK research project, funded by the Economic and Social Research Council, involved a diverse population of young people ($n = 1156$) from across eight schools (three primary, two middle and three secondary) and were representative of the ethnic and social class composition of the UK Midlands county in which the study took place. Our previous research centred the lives and school experiences of some 40 young people suffering from eating disorders, work reported in Evans et al. (2008).
2. We acknowledge Dillabough's (2009, p. 223) argument that theory itself 'impacts on the formation of knowledge about young people' and are acutely aware that the concepts and 'theory', outlined in this article, derived largely from Bernstein, themselves may help constitute a particular view of youth or teacher culture and embodiment. They are not, however, used to 'signal allegiance to particular mentors', or to 'position ourselves in the field' but rather as Dillabough suggests, as a 'mediating device' (p. 223) to assist us to understand and interpret why it is that teachers and young people act, think and speak in the way that they do about their bodies, health and related matters in and outside schools. Our problematic is the corporeality of subjectivity and how we might best illustrate conceptually and empirically the intersections of biology and culture.
3. There are synergies here with Stones (2005) notion of a 'structuration cycle' which centres relationships between external structures (of a context) and internal structures (phenomenological conditions of an individual's mediation of external structures), active agency and outcomes. However, his conceptual frame, like others mentioned in this paper, offers limited means of articulating how such relationships are encoded, shaped and embodied; transactions better captured, in our view, in Bernstein's work via concepts of the PD and CD.

References

Armstrong, F. (2003). *Spaced out: Policy, difference and the challenge of inclusive education.* Dordrecht and London: Kluwer.

Ausch, R., Randal, D., & Perez, L. (2008). *Interview with Elizabeth Grosz.* Retrieved from http://web.gc.cuny.edu/csctw/found_object/text/grosz.htm

Babones, J. (2009). Introduction. In J. Babones (Ed.), *Social inequality and public health* (pp. 1–9). Bristol: The Policy Press.

Ball, S. (2006). *Education policy and social class. The selected works of Stephen J. Ball.* London: Routledge.

Ball, S., Hoskins, K., Maguire, M., & Braun, A. (2011). Disciplinary texts: A policy analysis of national and local behaviour policies. *Critical Studies in Education, 52*(1), 1–14.

Ball, S., Maguire, S., Braun, A., & Hoskins, K. (2011). Policy subjects and policy actors in schools: Some necessary but insufficient analyses. *Discourse: Studies in the Cultural Politics of Education, 32*(4), 611–625.

Benhabib, S. (1991). *Situating the self: Gender, community and postmodernism in contemporary ethics.* Cambridge: Polity.

Bernstein, B. (1990). *The structuring of pedagogic discourse, Volume 1V, class codes and control.* London: Routledge.

Bernstein, B. (1996). *Pedagogy, symbolic control and identity, theory, research critique.* London: Taylor and Francis.

Bourdieu, P. (1998). *The weight of the world. Social suffering in contemporary society.* Oxford: Polity Press.

Braun, A., Ball, S.J., & Maguire, M. (2011a). Policy enactments in schools introduction: Toward a toolbox for theory and research. *Discourse, 32*(4), 581–583.

Braun, A., Ball, S.J., Maguire, M., & Hoskins, K. (2011b). Taking context seriously: Towards explaining policy enactments in the secondary school. *Discourse: Studies in the Cultural Politics of Education, 32*(4), 585–597.

Braun, A., Maguire, M., & Ball, S.J. (2010). Policy enactments in the UK secondary school: Examining policy, practice and school positioning. *Journal of Education Policy, 25*(4), 547–560.

Brennan, M., Green, B., Klenowski, V., & Zynger, D. (2008, 3 December). *The world that made PISA and the world that PISA makes.* Paper BAK081194, presented at the annual AARE Conference, Brisbane.

Broadfoot, P. (2001). Editorial: Culture, learning and comparative education. *Comparative Education, 37*(3), 261–266.

Burrows, L. (2009). Pedagogising families through obesity discourse. In J. Wright & V. Harwood (Eds.), *Biopolitics and the 'obesity epidemic'* (pp. 127–141). London: Routledge.

Bury, M. (1997). *Health and illness in a changing society.* London and New York, NY: Routledge.

Davis, Z. (2004). The debt to pleasure: The subject and knowledge in pedagogic discourse. In J. Muller, B. Davies, & A. Marais (Eds.), *Reading Bernstein, researching Bernstein* (pp. 44–54). London: RoutledgeFalmer.

De Pian, L. (2012). Emboldened bodies: Social class, school health policy and obesity discourse [Special issue]. *Discourse: Studies in the Cultural Politics of Education, 33*(5).

De Pian, L. (Forthcoming). *Embodying policy: Young people, education and obesity discourse* (Unpublished doctoral thesis). Loughborough University, Loughborough.

Dillabough, J.A. (2009). History and the making of young people and the late modern youth researcher: Time, narrative and change. *Discourse: Studies in the Cultural Politics of Education, 30*(2), 213–231.

Edwards, M. (2011). *The impact of school sport partnerships on primary schools: An in-depth evaluation* (Unpublished doctoral thesis). University of Durham, Durham.

Eng, D. (2001). *Racial castration: Managing masculinity in Asian America.* Durham, NC: Duke University.

Evans, J., & Davies, B. (2004). The embodiment of consciousness: Bernstein, health and schooling. In J. Evans, B. Davies, & J. Wright (Eds.), *Body knowledge and control* (pp. 207–217). London: Routledge.

Evans, J., & Davies, B. (2010). Family, class and embodiment: Why school physical education makes so little difference to post-school participation patterns in physical activity. *International Journal of Qualitative Studies in Education, 23*(7), 765–784.

Evans, J., & Davies, B. (2011). New directions, new question? Social theory, education, and embodiment. *Sport, Education and Society, 16*(3), 263–279.

Evans, J., Davies, B., & Rich, E. (2009). Schooling the body in a performative culture. In M.W. Apple, S.J. Ball, & L.A. Gandin (Eds.), *International handbook of research in sociology of education* (pp. 200–213). London: Routledge.

Evans, J., Davies, B., & Rich, E. (2011). Bernstein, body pedagogies and the corporeal device. In G. Ivinson, B. Davies, & J. Fitz (Eds.), *Knowledge and identity: Concepts and applications in Bernstein's Sociology* (pp. 176–191). London: Routledge.

Evans, J., Davies, B., Rich, E., & De Pian, L. (2012). Understanding policy: Why health education policy is important and why it does not appear to work. *British Journal of Educational Research.*

Evans, J., De Pian, L., Rich, E., & Davies, B. (2011). Health imperatives, policy and the corporeal device: Schools, subjectivity and children's health. *Policy Futures in Education, 9*(3), 328–340.

Evans, J., & Rich, E. (2011). Body policies and body pedagogies: Every child matters in totally pedagogised schools. *Journal of Education Policy, 26*(3), 361–381.

Evans, J., Rich, E., Allwood, R., & Davies, B. (2008). Body pedagogies, policy, health and gender. *British Educational Research Journal, 14*(3), 387–411.

Evans, J., Rich, E., & Davies, B. (2004). The emperor's new clothes. Fat, thin, and overweight: The social fabrication of risk and health. *Journal of Teaching in Physical Education, 23*(4), 372–392.

Evans, J., Rich, E., Davies, B., & Allwood, R. (2008a). *Education, disordered eating and obesity discourse: Fat fabrications.* London: Routledge.

Evans, J., Rich, E., Davies, B., & Allwood, R. (2008b). The class and cultural functions of obesity discourse: Our latter day child saving movement. *International Studies in Sociology of Education, 18*(2), 117–133.

Fitz, J., Davies, B., & Evans, J. (2006). *Educational policy and social reproduction.* London: Routledge.

Foresight Commission. (2007). *Tackling obesities: Future choices – Project report.* Department for Innovation, Universities and Skills, Government Office for Science. Retrieved from http://www.foresight.gov.uk/Obesity/Obesity.htm

Foucault, M. (1980). Questions on geography. In C. Gordon (Ed.), *Power/knowledge: Selected interviews and other writings, 1972–1977* (pp. 63–77). New York, NY: Pantheon Books.

Frank, A.W. (2006). Health stories as connectors and subjectifiers. *Health: An Interdisciplinary Journal for the Social Study of Health, Illness and Medicine, 10*(4), 421–440.

Fullagar, S. (2009). Governing healthy family lifestyles through discourses of risk and responsibility. In J. Wright & V. Harwood (Eds.), *Biopolitics and the 'obesity epidemic'* (pp. 108–127). London: Routledge.

Gard, M. (2011). *The end of the obesity epidemic.* London: Routledge.

Gard, M., & Wright, J. (2005). *The obesity epidemic: Science, morality and ideology.* London: Routledge.

Halse, C., Honey, A., & Boughtwood, D. (2008). *Inside anorexia.* London: Jessica Kingsley Publishers.

Harwood, V. (2009). Theorising biopedagogies. In J. Wright & V. Harwood (Eds.), *Biopolitics and the 'obesity epidemic'* (pp. 15–31). London: Routledge.

Hodgson, A., Edward, S., & Gregson, M. (2007). Riding the waves of policy? The case of basic skills in adult and community learning in England. *Journal of Vocational Education and Training, 59*(2), 213–228.

James, A. (2000). Embodied being(s) understanding the self and body in childhood. In A. Prout (Ed.), *The body, childhood and society* (pp. 19–38). Basingstoke: Palgrave Macmillan.

Lave, J., & Wenger, E. (1991). *Situated learning: Legitimate peripheral participation.* Cambridge: Cambridge University Press.

Maguire, M., Hoskins, K., Ball, S., & Braun, A. (2011). Policy discourses in school texts. *Discourse: Studies in the Cultural Politics of Education, 32*(4), 597–609.

Manathunga, C. (2009). Research as an intercultural 'contact zone'. *Discourse: Studies in the Cultural Politics of Education, 30*(2), 165–179.

Newton, T. (2003). Truly embodied sociology: Marrying the social and the biological? *The Sociological Review, 51*(1), 20–42.

Pink, S. (2011). From embodiment to emplacement: Rethinking competing bodies, senses and specialities. *Sport, Education and Society, 16*(3), 343–347.

Pronger, B. (2002). *Body fascism: Salvation in the technology of physical fitness.* Toronto: University of Toronto Press.

Prosser, J. (1998). *Second skins: The body narratives of transsexuality.* New York, NY: Columbia University Press.

Rich, E., & Evans, J. (2009a). Performative health in schools: Welfare policy, neoliberalism and social reproduction. In J. Wright & V. Harwood (Eds.), *Biopolitics and the 'obesity epidemic'* (pp. 157–172). London: Routledge.

Rich, E., & Evans, J. (2009b). Now I am nobody, see me for who I am: the paradox of performativity. *Gender and Education, 21*(1), 1–16.

Rich, E., Evans, J., & De-Pian, L. (2010). Childrens' bodies, surveillance and the obesity crisis. In E. Rich, L.F. Monaghan & L. Aphramor (Eds.), *Debating obesity: Critical perspectives* (pp. 139–164). New York: Palgrave Macmillan.

Rizvi, F., & Kemmis, S. (1987). *Dilemmas for reform.* Geelong: Deakin Institute for Studies in Education.

Rizvi, F., & Lingard, B. (2010). *Globalizing education policy.* London: Routledge.

Shilling, C. (2005). *The body in culture and society.* London: Sage.

Stones, E. (2005). *Structuration theory.* London: Palgrave Macmillan.

Sykes, H. (2007). Anxious identificatioion in *The Sopranos* and Sport: Psychoanalystic and queer theories of embodiment. *Sport, Education and Society, 12*(2), 127–141.

Sykes, H. (2011). *Queer bodies.* New York, NY: Peter Lang.

The Telegraph. (2012). Don't burn Jamie Oliver over school dinners. Retrieved from http://www.telegraph.co.uk/education/7867442/Dont-burn-Jamie-Oliver-over-school-dinners.html

Thorpe, H. (2011, 5 November). *Bodies beyond bo(a)rders: Toward theoretical and transdisciplinary adventures.* Paper prepared for presentation to the North American Sociology of Sport Presidential Panel, University of Waikato, Hamilton.

Walkerdine, V. (2009). Biopedagogy and beyond. In J. Wright & V. Harwood (Eds.), *Biopolitics and the 'obesity epidemic'* (pp. 199–209). London: Routledge.

Weiss, G. (1999). *Body images: Embodiment as intercorporeality.* New York, NY: Routledge.

Wilkinson, R., & Pickett, K. (2009). *The spirit level. Why more equal societies almost always do better.* London: Allen Lane.

Williams, S. (2006). Medical sociology and the biological body: Where are we now and where do we go from here? *Health: An Interdisciplinary Journal for the Social Study of Health, Illness and Medicine, 10*(1), 5–30.

Wrench, A. (2011). *Practicalities, fictions and possibilities: Becoming socially critical teachers of PE* (Unpublished doctoral thesis). University of South Australia, Australia.

Wright, J. (2009). Biopower, biopedagogies and the obesity epidemic. In J. Wright & V. Harwood (Eds.), *Biopolitics and the 'obesity epidemic'* (pp. 1–15). London: Routledge.

Wright, J., & Harwood, V. (Eds.). (2009). *Biopolitics and the 'obesity epidemic'.* London: Routledge.

Wright, J., Macdonald, D., & Groom, L. (2003). Physical activity and young people: Beyond participation. *Sport, Education and Society, 8*(1), 17–33.

Zembylas, M. (2007). Risks and pleasures: A Deleuzo–Guattarian pedagogy of desire in education. *British Educational Research Journal, 33*(3), 331–349.

Zembylas, M. (2008). Trauma, justice and the politics of emotion: The violence of sentimentality. *Discourse: Studies in the Cultural politics of Education, 29*(1), 1–19.

Beyond school boundaries: new health imperatives, families and schools

Emma Rich

Department of Education, University of Bath, Bath, UK

This article draws upon research examining the impact of new health imperatives on schools in the United Kingdom. Specifically, it examines features of emerging surveillant relations, which not only speak to the changing nature of health-related practices in schools but have particular currency for broader under-standings of theorisations of surveillance, and which complicate the view that schools are bounded or territorialised in enacting forms of governance. The article explores how the assemblages through which these biopedagogies are formed constitute emerging interdependent relations between schools and families. The article recognises the presence of *amalgamated* and *extended* pedagogies in schools; approaches within which deliberate attempts were made to ensure whether what students learn in schools was continued beyond the formal school contexts. Among the schools that took part in the research reported in this article, many of them recognised that families constituted a site of learning about health. To this end, there were deliberate attempts to inculcate particular health values and meanings within school and to extend these across other sites of learning such as within the family. The use of surveillant practices utilised to achieve this end is a specific focus of this article and speaks to the broader aspects of what Giroux and others have referred to as 'public pedagogy' which recognise public, popular and cultural spaces as pedagogical sites. The article concludes by suggesting that studies in biopedagogy would benefit not only from a more nuanced understanding of the surveillant forces of pedagogy, but also of the pedagogical flows and forces of what are seen as forms of surveillance.

Introduction

In recent years, approaches to school-based health policy in western society have moved ever closer to particular regimes of accountability and surveillance (Evans, Rich, Davies, & Allwood, 2008; Rich & Perhamus, 2011). In many ways, 'schooling the body' (Kirk, 1993) is not a new phenomenon, as via the codification of certain practices, young people have long been the subject of health interventions that serve to discipline bodies and address what are conceived as social ills and health risks. However, the tendency towards the monitoring of the bodies, lifestyles and health of increasingly younger children and young people, is perhaps reflective of Shilling's (2008) observation of the broader emphasis on body modification in the constitution of subjectivity within postmodern society. Moreover, informed by the field of sociology of health and illness (Bury & Gabe, 2004), in particular, the work on medicalisation (Conrad, 1992) and medical surveillance (Armstrong, 1995), it has been argued that increasingly, everyday activities are placed under scrutiny and regarded as medical issues, thus playing an instrumental role in the broader constitution of deviance and the constitution of certain behaviours as sickness. Therefore certain behaviours are constituted as risky, leading to the classification of everyday behaviours as 'unhealthy' and according to Conrad (2007, p. 151) the classification of otherwise healthy individuals as already of 'potentially ill'. The focus on the 'health' of populations rather than just illness has meant a focus on and investment in early prevention to protect populations against future ill-health. Consequently, increasingly younger children and young people have occupied a more central position in health policy, debates and interventions. These changes have been well documented in the literature examining the current pre-occupation in western society with an 'obesity epidemic' (Burrows & Wright, 2004; Evans & Colls, 2009; Evans et al., 2008; Gard & Wright, 2005; Leahy, 2009; Rich, Monaghan, & Aphramor, 2011; Wright & Harwood, 2009). This article begins by discussing how moral panic about obesity has given rise to a range of policies and interventions in school contexts geared towards monitoring and regulating the lives and bodies of children and young people. The article draws on an Economic and Social Research Council (ESRC) project exploring the impact of new 'health imperatives' (specifically around 'obesity', exercise, diet and health) on the practices and identities of teachers, children and young people in schools. It examines how health-related policies and practices in schools reflect changing forms of surveillance, which might be described as 'deterritorialised' (Osmond, 2010) and produce specific pedagogical flows that reach into public (family) spaces.

Subsequently, I will examine the features of emerging surveillant relations, which not only speak to the changing nature of health-related practices in schools but have particular currency for broader understandings of theorisations of surveillance, and which complicate the view that schools are bounded or territorialised in enacting forms of governance. Rather, it is argued that they form part of an assemblage of surveillance of the body formed with other sites. Specifically, the article explores how the assemblages, through which these biopedagogies are formed, constitute emerging interdependent relations between schools and families. The article recognises the presence of *amalgamated* and *extended* pedagogies in schools; approaches within which deliberate attempts were made to ensure whether what students were learning in schools was continued beyond the formal school contexts. Amongst the schools that took part in the research reported in this article, many of them recognised that families constituted a site of learning about health. To this end, there were deliberate attempts to inculcate particular health values and meanings within school and to extend these across other sites of learning such as within the family. The use of surveillant practices utilised to achieve this end is a specific focus of this article and speaks to the broader aspects of public pedagogy (Giroux, 1998), which recognise public, popular and cultural spaces as pedagogical sites. Surveillance of young people's bodies occurs at the intersection of formalised schooling and broader public (family) pedagogies. This raises a number of questions not only in terms of health education policy and practice, but also for studies in education and/or surveillance in terms of how me theorise. To this end, the article concludes by suggesting that studies in biopedagogy would benefit not only from a more nuanced understanding of the surveillant forces of pedagogy, but also of the pedagogical flows and forces of what are seen as forms of surveillance.

Research design

This article calls on data from a study funded by ESRC exploring 'The Impact of New Health Imperatives on Schools'.[1] The study has investigated how health imperatives and associated curriculum initiatives are operationalised within and across a range of schools located in middle England, while collaborating and collating its findings with parallel studies pursued in Australia and New Zealand,[2] funded by the Australian Research Council (ARC). The methodology was designed to explore the relationships between demographic 'resources' (sociocultural capital), born of age, gender, class, ethnicity and (forms of) schooling; sites and sources of influence on 'body knowledge'; and individuals' relationships to their embodied selves. This research involved a combination of quantitative and qualitative data derived from 1176 questionnaires administered to pupils aged 9–16 years of age in eight schools in Middle England, UK (Table 1) and qualitative data drawn from interviews with 90 pupils and 19 staff (De Pian, Evans, & Rich, 2010). All interview quotes are reported using pseudonyms, school year wherever appropriate and the school type represented by pseudonymn (e.g. school x) referred to in Table 1.

The schools are policy saturated contexts wherein policy on and commitments to health education sit alongside other pressing needs, for example, of literacy and numeracy. Given this, the schools were selected so as to include particular demographics of class and culture pertaining to the region. The data-sets generated a vast wealth of quantitative and qualitative data on a variety of issues around the

Table 1. Schools, descriptions and groups in research sample.

School	Type/description	Groups included in research sample
Bentley Grammar	Large, independent, secondary school for boys (10–18 year olds)	12–13 year olds and 15–16 year olds (years 8 and 11)
Fraser Preparatory	Large, independent, co-ed, preparatory school (4–11 year olds)	9–11 year olds (years 5 and 6)
Grange Park High	Secondary school for girls (11–18 year olds)	12–13 year olds and 15–16 year olds (years 8 and 11)
Huntington High	Large, co-educational, rural state middle school (11–14 year olds). Sample includes	11–14 year olds (years 7–9)
Longcliff High	Large, co-ed, multi-ethnic, state middle school (11–14 year olds)	12–13 year olds (year 8)
Rosehill Primary	Large, co-ed, multi-ethnic, inner city, state primary school (4–11 year olds)	9–11 year olds (years 5 and 6)
Westwood Primary	Very small, co-ed, middle class, rural/ village, state primary school (4–11 year olds)	9–11 year olds (years 5 and 6)
Fielding Community College	Large, co-ed, deprived, multi-ethnic, inner city college (11–16 year olds)	13–15 year olds (years 9 and 10)

body and health, not all of which can be reported here. Instead, the data reported in this article focuses specifically on the interviews with a range of school staff. Semi-structured interviews sought to identify how 'shared' concerns about obesity were variously translated in schools in different cultural, social and policy settings. It was made clear to the school staff that the research was not intending to critique their practice, but instead to explore the following: teacher/staff perceptions of current health issues; their understandings of physical education (PE), health curriculum and physical activity and how this was implemented in terms of policy and practice in their own schools; the health needs and interests of young people and the ways in which these were addressed within their schools.

Surveillant biopedagogies in UK schools

Alarmist concerns about a global childhood obesity crisis (WHO, 1998), brought about by inactive lifestyles, rise in fast food culture, and poor diets, has sustained a variety of initiatives which have sought to alter the lifestyles, health and more specifically, the weight of children and young people. As Wright (2009, p. 1) observes, the 'obesity epidemic' offers one of the most powerful and pervasive discourses influencing ways of thinking about health and the body. As Jutel (2006, p. 2270) argues, the moral panic associated with obesity discourse instils a sense of urgency and disaster that fuels the mongering of 'overweight as a disease category'. As Evans and Colls (2011) note, much of the focus within UK obesity policy is on the control and regulation of children's 'potentially' obese bodies over and above adults. In 2004, House of Commons Health Select committee reported that 'this will be the first generation where children die before their parents as a consequence of childhood obesity' (HOC, 2004, p. 9), thus stressing the need for early intervention. In England and Wales, central Government thus sought joint action from its agencies, the Department of Health (DoH) and the Department for Children, Schools and Families (formerly DfES Department for Education and Skills) to address health matters through policy affecting the whole environment of schools. Subsequently, school curriculum and practice in many countries across western society have been drastically re-shaped by initiatives and policies concerned with tackling a putative childhood 'obesity epidemic' (Burrows & Wright, 2007; Evans et al., 2008; Leahy, 2009; Wright & Harwood, 2009).

In the United Kingdom, many of these initiatives were implemented as part of a Public Services Agreement Target: to halt, by 2010, 'the year-on-year increase in obesity among children under 11' in the context of a broader strategy to tackle obesity in the population as a whole (DoH, 2004). Associated policies and practices became evermore interventionist, from adaptations to school health and Physical Education policy, to the possibility of obese children being removed from their families and placed into social care. In an effort to monitor and regulate childhood obesity, young people were increasingly subjected to a range of techniques of surveillance within schools, which involved not only monitoring their lifestyles in and outside schools (e.g. their food choices, physical activity levels) but more directly the collection of information on their bodies with a view to monitoring and addressing concerns about children's weight fuelled by the construction of obesity as a moral crisis (Gard & Wright, 2005). Various mechanisms of surveillance have since been deployed in schools to monitor children's bodies. These include, but are not limited to fingerprint screening to monitor or report young people's food purchases in school canteens, weighing to determine a Body Mass Index (BMI) classification, pedometers to record the number of steps a child will take, skinfold measurements, heart rate monitors, lunch box inspections and dietary constraints (Rich, Evans, & De Pian, 2011). The National Child Measuring Programme was first rolled out in 2005–2006 (DH, 2006) which has legislated that every year children in reception (4–5 years) and year 6 (10–11 years old) are weighed and measured in school. The collection of BMI data was also rolled out as a monitoring programme in 2006, so that likely future trends or changes in obesity patterns of young people could be monitored (Evans & Colls, 2009). Consequently, as Evans et al. (2008, p. 13) reveal, this obesity discourse has manufactured a renewed focus on 'weight' rather than health. The impact of these disciplinary and regulative practices upon children and young people's developing sense of embodiment has been reported in a growing body of literature (e.g. Beckett, 2004; Burrows & Wright, 2004, 2007; Evans et al., 2008; Rail, 2009). Much of this work has highlighted the disciplinary nature of health discourses within school settings, revealing what Wright and Harwood (2009) describe as 'biopedagogies' and their negative impact on the lives, bodies and identities of young people (Evans & Colls, 2010, 2011; Evans et al., 2008; Gard & Wright, 2005; Halse, Honey, & Boughtwood, 2008; Wright & Harwood, 2009).

The moral panic which has ensued in recent years over concerns regarding a childhood obesity epidemic (perceived or otherwise) and which partly drives these initiatives, underscore how constructed threats to young people's health not only comment upon a health problem but also participate in the constitution of young people and particular 'bodies' as either vulnerable or at risk. Research across various disciplines demonstrates how the status of youth health has been problematised, imagined and endowed with meaning through the construction of 'moral crisis'. Understandings of health concerns are, in this sense, intimately connected to discourses of the body, childhood, youth and responsibility.

The proliferation of initiatives justified on this basis has been the subject of scholarly critique geared towards questioning the justification for and potential effects of the focus on young people (See Evans & Colls, 2011). To this end, work within youth studies examining health issues has also been informed by the growing body of work within surveillance studies engaged with questions about childhood (Steeves & Jones, 2010). In some ways, these obesity policies constitute a broader cultural shift towards increased surveillance which, according to Fotel and Thomsen (2004, p. 1477), is now a 'central characteristic of modern childhood'. Furthermore, it has been claimed that within contemporary neo-liberal cultures of control and fear schools have become hyper-surveilled spaces (Giroux, 2003; Monahan & Torres, 2009) and there has been a concomitant increase in the range of surveillance tools available for parents to monitor their children (Marx & Steeves, 2010). These mechanisms of parental and teacher surveillance over young people essentially tap into broader concerns about the nature of childhood and youth and continue to be justified by the purported need to *protect* children from future *risk*.

> Over the past few decades, the potential to experience that freedom has been restructured and constrained by a wide array of new surveillance technologies [...]. Many schools use closed circuit televisions, fingerprint scanners and Smartcards to keep

an eye on their students as they move through the school throughout the day. (Dowty, 2009; Steeves & Jones, 2010, p. 187)

In this context, obesity policies reflect broader social concerns which underpin efforts to govern the future through a focus on the child (see Steeves & Jones, 2010; Valentine & Holloway, 2002). The constitution of young people as future adults and as 'at risk' thus bring them into politicised discourses which attempt to normalise, govern and regulate their weight, behaviours and lifestyles.

Theorising surveillance

Walkerdine (2009, p. 201) suggests that if we are to develop critical work on biopolitical issues on weight and obesity then we need be cautious of invoking a simple 'relation between the effectivity of biopower and the subject working on the self, or resisting'. Elsewhere, Leahy (2009, pp. 172–173) argues in her work on governmental assemblages of health education 'we need to go beyond the field (biopower and governmentality studies) to engage with more experimental and interdisciplinary perspectives to bring new light to understanding and thinking about biopedagogies'. Taking up these challenges, my specific interest in this article is to better understand the complexities of how surveillance circulates relationally and affectively in school contexts. The uptake of Foucault's work on disciplinary practices has yielded important insights into how self-regulating subjects are produced through obesity discourse. However, as Green (1999, p. 29) observes 'Jeremy Bentham's Panopticon prison design has become the ultimate metaphor for modern surveillance machinery and activity' and this article engages with other theorisations of surveillance. Indeed data collection in schools from the above project revealed a complex flow of surveillant practices and transmission of messages which behove us to question the extent to which current theorisations of surveillance help us to understand the complex relations between power, surveillance and resistance (Dawson, 2006; Fotel & Thomsen, 2004; Lyon, 2002, 2006, 2007; Yar, 2003). Notably school-based surveillance is not simply enacted by the school as institution, but situated in a network of organisations and the circulation of knowledge about childhood, health and obesity. Walkerdine (2009, p. 201) captures this in her reflections on biopedagogies and beyond:

> While the argument in the past has been that subjects are produced through power/ knowledge/desire, this suggests a simple relation between regulation and a subject, which is made at least more complex and problematic by the issues of circulation of knowledge.

This challenge has also been noted in the critiques of panoptican theories, where authors have observed that it does not allow for a full exploration of the nuances and complexities of resistance (Ball, 2005; Green, 1999) and would indicate the limitations of exploring the aforementioned questions through a reliance, on for example, Foucault's concepts of disciplinary practices. Partly born out of this critique, I have thus found it useful to rethink the conceptualisation of the surveillance of children's bodies in schools by drawing upon the growing body of surveillance studies which utilise the concept of an assemblage. Such work challenges the conceptualisation of surveillance as a stable, unified or monolithic entity. Instead, attention focuses on connections formed with other groups, individuals, bodies and institutions, addressing some of the concerns raised by Walkerdine (2009, p. 202):

> ... the communities of practice and of affect ... into which these modes of regulation enter, operate in complex ways so that affect circulates relationally through individual bodies, family bodies, community bodies, in ways that we cannot easily predict using a standard governmentality framework.

Rapid developments in emerging technologies, some of which have been utilised for surveillance purposes, has spawned a range of studies drawing on the concept of 'assemblage' to better understand the complexities of surveillance. Haggerty and Ericson (2000) draw on the works of Deleuze and Guattari to forward their concept of the 'surveillant assemblage'. This offers a useful departure from governmentality towards understanding the 'convergance of what were once discrete surveillance systems to the point that we can now speak of an emerging "surveillant assemblage"' (Haggerty & Ericson, 2000, p. 606). They describe the surveillant assemblage as rhizomatic in character, in that there is no 'centralised structure' which acts to coordinate surveillance. Rather, surveillant assemblages act like rhizome plants, that 'grow across a series of interconnected roots which throw up shoots in different locations' (p. 615). Within the context of health education, calls have already been made to draw upon these theoretical frameworks to advance our understanding of policy and practice. For example, Leahy (2009, p. 173) argues that 'school based health education can be understood as a governmental assemblage in and out of itself with complex linkages and connections to other assemblages'. Leahy offers an insightful account of how various biopedagogical devices are deployed and how they might 'do their work' within classroom settings. Whilst Leahy's work examines a range of biopedagogical devices, this article looks specifically at how 'surveillance' operates within these assemblages and how it comes to bear upon the relationship between schools and other sites of learning, such as family. Following Haggerty and Ericson (2000), we thus need to better understand, through the introduction of the assemblage, the multiplicity and temporal moments of interdependence through which surveillance of weight and the body is (re)assembled. For Leahy (2009, p. 174) this involves 'thinking about the messiness that characterizes contemporary attempts to govern'. It is within rhizomatic networks such as those centered around health that one may find 'once discrete public and private sector informational infrastructures increasingly coming into contact' (Heir, 2003, p. 403). Elsewhere, Clough (2003, p. 360) observes that, the deployment of biopower through control is much more dispersed than its deployment through disciplining:

> The target of control is not subjects whose behaviour expresses internalized social norms but aims at a never-ending modulation of moods, capacities, affects, potentialities, assembled in genetic codes, identification numbers, ratings profiles and preference listings; that is to say, bodies of data and information (including the human body as information and data).

Clough goes on to point 'to the increasing abandonment of socialization and education of the individual subject through interpellation to, and through, national and familial ideological apparatuses' (Clough, 2003, p. 360). Such focus perhaps provides a more complex purchase on how we might conceptualise obesity policy and the way surveillance operates and circulates in schools (Fraser, Maher, & Wright, 2010).

Beyond spatio-temporal boundaries

As outlined earlier, a growing body of work points towards the governing practices of schools and their biopedagogies (Wright & Harwood, 2009) within these spaces. Indeed, in this article one might report what could be read as the disciplinary features of these schools, of the clear instructional and regulative pedagogical practices which they produce in an effort to protect pupils from the risks associated with obesity. However, to limit the analysis to these theoretical lenses can also risk invoking a

> ... kind of determinism implying that there exists an acting 'society', 'social structure' or remote governmental body that acts upon an otherwise homogenous population in a singular and uniform manner. (Heir, 2003, p. 405)

Instead, I want to focus on a particular aspect of surveillance precisely because it speaks to the changing relations of power through which surveillance might be understood. The project data complicates the view that schools, as institutions that can enact a governmental power over its pupils, are bounded or territorialised in that governance. The data revealed how the assemblages through which these biopedagogies are formed, constituted emerging interdependent relations between schools and parents. In terms of the flows of power relations, interdependence emerged in several ways. First, schools in which data was collected employed strategies through which parents, not just children, were the subject of surveillance. Second, in some schools, parents were ostensibly being invited into the decision-making processes concerning health. This is a new process, particularly in the context of health, where parents have not traditionally been involved in the design and delivery of related services (Williams, 2004) are now being enlisted in the fight against obesity. The assemblage functions in such a way that interdependence is formed between school and family context, in an effort to make the surveillance of a child's body or lifestyle practices continuous and total. These dynamics, specifically in relation to health, are what prompted me and others (Leahy, 2009) to examine biopedagogies through alternative frameworks which can account for flows of power relations that cross what might otherwise be seen as professional boundaries or territories. In this sense, one must examine how such assemblages 'persist and propagate through power relations, not just chance networks' (Monahan & Wall, 2007, p. 156). This was perhaps most striking in the research data which revealed that schools purposefully and strategically engaged with parents to ensure that what pupils were learning about health in schools was not disrupted after leaving school. Rather than reflecting territorialised technologies and apparatus of panoptical surveillance located within the school, this would appear to reflect a shift towards what Deleuze refers to as the 'control society' which characterises a –

> ... new modality of de-territorializing power that facilitates the relaxing of surveillance within discrete/bounded biopolitical assemblages so that it is capable of combining with other forces for a more seamless and intensive surveillance that cuts across assemblages

that would otherwise function relatively autonomously using single-minded govern-mental programs. (Osmond, 2010, p. 328)

Some of the schools in the research study endeavoured to create more seamless forms of surveillance through *amalgamated* and *extended* pedagogies in which attempts were made to ensure what pupils were learning or practising in schools was not disrupted after leaving school. This involved the recognition by school staff of a breakdown of discrete surveillance; that an intermittent surveillance would leave space for resistance. Some schools sent home health-related information, and families were expected and sometimes even obliged to engage with biopedagogies and their technologies, in home contexts:

> There [are] not many children nowadays that will eat fruit like there used to be and I think we need to turn that around. We need to turn it around to make sure that children are eating healthy because it is not going to do them any good when they get older at all. But that means to be taught, well hopefully helping parents [...] On the [health] committee so and we sent a letter out to parents on our newsletter saying ... us being healthy schools the suggestion was instead of sweets either fruit or a book for the class [...] Well I think everything where school life is concerned you have to get the parents involved because if you don't the children are not going to ... because if we tell them one thing they are going to go home and the parents are going to tell them another thing. Who are they going to take notice of? The parents. Erm, I think Sally actually spoke to the parents and we had leaflets on how to pack a healthy lunchbox and we had ... afternoons where the parents can come and sample the school dinners and show what you can put into a packed lunchbox. We've actually done, er, things for the parents to come and watch and to be part of as well. So we do try and involve the parents. (Donna Healthy Schools co-ordinator, Rosehill Primary)

The pedagogical force of these forms of surveillance alludes to a form of public pedagogy evident in early work around learning beyond schools. Sandlin, O'Malley and Burdick (2011) observe this historical theme: 'public refers not to a physical site of educational phenomena but rather to an idealized outcome of educational activity: the production of a public aligned in terms of values and collective identity'. Schools, in some ways then, incorporate the pedagogical forces recognised as 'outside curriculum' (Schubert, 2010, p. 71) or what Giroux (1998) refers to as public pedagogy.

Rather than functioning autonomously in a bounded space, school-based biopedagogies were assembled through flows of power relations which facilitated an emerging space in which home and families are expected (sometimes obliged) to engage with school curricular, policy and pedagogy in their home contexts. Such a view reflects Schubert's (1981, p. 186) observation that school curricular (albeit in this case imbued with its surveillant properties) 'must relate to perspectives students acquire from other curricular'. Whilst in the field of public pedagogy, recent studies have alluded to the ways that teachers draw on popular culture in their classroom (Kellner & Share, 2007), less has been written about how teachers and schools incorporate family pedagogies into school policy and practice.

Pupils of various social positioning were differently constituted through discourses within the school contexts and home contexts whilst also experiencing spaces in between, reflecting McCahill and Finn's (2010) observation that 'there is no such thing as a "unitary surveyed child"'. As they argue, the 'social impact that surveillance may have on children's lives is highly dependent upon existing social relations, identities, and cultural traditions' (McCahill & Finn, 2010, p. 288). In this vein, for some teachers, the socio-economic family background of children was seen as a precursory factor for being 'at risk':

> Mainly because I live near quite a few council estates, I go there and nearly every time I'll see someone who is obese walking around and I see lots of teenagers that are obese, and some kids that are obese already and it's probably saying because their Mum and Dad gave them a hard life they think they can live up to it by eating more food and so the food gets out of hand and they become obese because they can't control what they're eating because their emotions get hold of their eating habits. (Melissa, Head of PSHE, Fraser Prep)

Despite the recognition by teachers of sociocultural and socio-economic difference, the capacity to facilitate a more intense form of surveillance was seen to lie in the recognisable 'uniformity' of meaning as to what constituted good health. In this sense, families tended only to incorporate those practices which they could recognise as legitimate (dominant) health practices, as uniformly recognisable as legitimate within other contexts such as medical practices. Various initiatives were thus used by schools to encourage or in some cases enforce a moral obligation towards a mutual/reciprocal responsibility between parents and schools and in the process 'deterritorializes various professionals from their routine spatio-temporal professional boundaries and joins up services across boundaries, as well as across levels of government (planning, delivery and management)' (Osmond, 2010, p. 333).

It is not only children who are surveilled in this process. Parents and guardians are subjected to scrutiny as they are expected to protect the children in their care (Fullagar, 2009). They not only watch the children in their care, but they are also watched, and in this sense surveillance is 'multi-layered and complex' (see McIntosh, Punch, Dorrer, & Emond, 2010). Attempts to re-establish relations between parents/guardians and schools reveal how the de-territorialisation of biopedagogies breaks down traditional school–family boundaries and re-arranges forms of surveillance and flows of regulation oriented towards achieving a more 'totalising' (Haggerty & Ericson, 2000) form of surveillance across different sites. Assemblages of obesity thus play a role in re-establishing surveillance, shifting biopolitical relations which come to re-establish intensive forms of surveillance, which combine a broader cultural shift in guardian/parental expectations, welfare and and biopedagogies. This reflects Osmond's (2010, p. 328) observation that 'Deterritorializing rationalities and techniques are used to breakdown, re-arrange and develop new and more totalising regulatory controls that would not be possible in localised assemblages'.

The continuity of surveillance through networks formed between family and schools renders the boundaries between those constituting and those constituted by biopolitical normalisation far more complicated than that which is understood through panoptican notions of power, discipline and schooling of the body. Nor is this simply the case that schools instruct parents what to do and they follow. Instead, as Osmond (2010) does, we might theorise such relations, 'using Deleuze's conceptualisation of the control society as involving de-territorialising forces that reterritorialise any particular "territorial assemblage" as an "inter-assemblage"' (Osmond, 2010, p. 328).

In this sense, assemblages which constitute meanings associated with parenting and those which shape the practices of schools are not read as territorial or discrete assemblages but in their complex and rhizomatic relations, form an inter-assemblage through which surveillance is intensified. The de-territorialisation of biopedagogies leads to complex relations of power and endeavours to repeat consistent messages across multiple sites within what Osmond describes earlier as inter-assemblages.

The way health education is being read and constituted in these settings cannot be separated from the wider social and moral understandings of particular health conditions and discourses of childhood and youth. This means examining the moral, cultural and political situatedness of images and policies associated with young people and health in addition to those focusing specifically on health or obesity. This point is made evident by the way in which the discourses that frame biopedagogies are multifarious and focus on complex risks and moral crises linked not only to health but to concerns regarding decline in modern parenting skills. In the United Kingdom, government policy on obesity emerged concurrently when public panic had ensued about the protection and vulnerability of young people and the state of parenting. Indeed, many UK obesity-related policies are formed under the Every Child Matters policy.[3] One of the most significant changes brought about by *Every Child Matters* (DfES, 2003) was the shift towards a stronger integration of statutory children's services and the placing of children 'as one of the central subjects in New Labour's social policy' (Williams, 2004, p. 406). To achieve the outcomes established in this and other policies, the focus has been on ensuring that organisations providing services to children, including health professionals and schools, take a more *integrated* approach to care:

> This means that the organisations involved with providing services to children – from hospitals and schools, to police and voluntary groups – will be teaming up in new ways, sharing information and working together, to protect children and young people from harm and help them achieve what they want in life. Children and young people will have far more say about issues that affect them as individuals and collectively. (DfES, 2003)

The centrality of parenting in these political orientations reflects attempts since the advent of New Labour government in 1997 to 'create and occupy a new politico-moral terrain [. . .] to offer a third way to national renewal' (Bullen, Kenway, & Hay, 2000, p. 441). In an effort ostensibly to move beyond the traditional political binaries of left and right, New Labour government 'pushed parenting practice to the centre stage of the social policy curriculum, in line with stated commitments to "support families" and tackle "social exclusion"' (Gillies, 2005, p. 71). As Gillies (2005, p. 84) suggests a 'parenting deficit' has been central to these policies in which crime and anti-social behaviour are linked to 'inadequate childrearing', and 'socially excluded parents are positioned as an abject and dangerous underclass, posing a serious threat to the social fabric'. The combination of these broader anxieties about the nature of youth, and attempts to control them, alongside the shifting focus towards health, rather than just illness, has had significant implications for the way in which imaginings of youth have been critical to contemporary understandings of health and education. Political discourse has explicitly and strategically sought to intervene in the lives of children through a shift towards integrated services in which organisations, institutions and families work closer together. Sylva and Pugh (2005, p. 11) note the shift towards a 'firm focus on families as well as children in the delivery of services' with the advent of a range of policies on children and families (national childcare strategy, Sure Start and Children's Centres):

> We want all schools to become extended schools – acting as the hub for services for children, families and other members of the community. Extended schools offer the community and their pupils a range of services (such as childcare, adult learning, health and community facilities) that go beyond their core educational function. (DfES, 2003, paragraph 2.20)

Driven by a deficit understanding of contemporary parenting, New Labour focused on the need to 'support' parents, creating a range of policies focused on the role of parenting and offering advice on childrearing. Gillies (2005, p. 74) notes that this series of family policies were imbued with paradoxical views of traditional family whilst at the same time drawing on contemporary notions of 'choice', forming 'the basis for a new kind of interventionism, characterized by explicit and implicit attempts to control and regulate the conduct of parents'. In the inter-assemblage between parenting assemblages and school-based pedagogies, attempts to develop an interdependent politico-moral relationship between school and families may ostensibly encourage guardian/parental involvement in the design and delivery of curricula and practice but may actually translate into new relations of power which encourage conformity to biopedagogies. Some schools purposefully involve parents in the construction of policy. It is no coincidence that these schools were of middle class orientation and aware of, what Horvat, Weininger and Lareau (2003) refer to as the network ties that middle class families have access to as a means through which to contest particular school policies or views:

> Well I think everything where school life is concerned you have to get the parents involved because if you don't, the children are not going to ... because if we tell them one thing they are going to go home and the parents are going to tell them another thing. Who are they going to take notice of? The parents. (Donna, Fraser Prep)

Here, schools recognise the need for families to be brought into the discussion on health if governance is to be successful. This reflects Nichols and Griffith (2009, p. 242) observation that 'educational policy is accomplished in the everyday activities (talk and action) of parents and principals as they participate in schooling and, thus, in the textually-mediated relations of governance'. It is precisely at this intersection where the contradictions in the opposing notions of traditional moral duty and negotiation and choice become apparent. Parents are encouraged to be part of the process, to demonstrate agentic opportunity to shape what happens in schools, or indeed in their own homes and thereby 'inculcating parental responsibilities in collaborating with the state to construct their children as educated, disciplined and self-responsible subjects' (Williams, 2004, p. 408):

> So you need to get parents involved in things. We have got a healthy schools committee that involves at the moment, one parent of the school but we do ... we have got a Friends of School R Committee as well which is lots of parents so we discuss it in that as well. We discuss the healthy schools ... So we do involve lots of parents in what we discuss with the children on healthy schools. (Donna, Healthy Schools Co-ordinator, Rosehill Primary)

However, the discourses which constitute the inter-assemblage emphasise the 'politico-moral' (Misra, 2006) obligation to act in a dutiful way within particular parameters not only of what 'good health' is understood to mean but also 'responsible parenting'. As Jess, the PE coordinator of School W, commented, 'parents take the healthy schools seriously – provide healthy snacks all the time' and that this helped with producing 'all-round good people'. In other words, what may be offered up as 'choice' to parents, in the decisions they make regarding their child's health, is actually clearly directed through ethicopolitics in which 'good' parents are constructed as resourceful, agentic and ethically responsible, able to recognise or learn what is best for their children and tailor their behaviour accordingly' (Gillies, 2005, p. 85). In a 'double move of autonomization and responsibilization' (Rose, 2000, p. 1400, cited in Gillies, 2005, p. 77), parents are duty bound to act morally and ethically in relation to normative understandings and intensified expectations of them. These assemblages are also sustained by particular cultural desires and popular forces of the everyday in ways which challenge notions of surveillance as being conducted only by those in an authoritative position. In such assemblages, the impetus is not solely 'located in powerful social actors or elite bodies' but rather 'considerable foundational support derives from popular social grievances . . . various antagonisms directed at a variety of socially constituted risk groups *from below*' (Heir, 2003, p. 400). As Henderson, Harmon and Houser (2010, p. 231) suggest 'mothers surveil one another through interpersonal communication and observation, ranging anywhere from conversations about children's appropriate developmental milestones to a covert, silent monitoring of other moms' disciplining behaviour in public places'. The tendency for parents to survey each other as part of this assemblage and the foregrounding of mother's in this process reflects a broader trend towards 'New Momism' which 'not only revives the intensive parenting ideals that characterized the second half of the twentieth century, but it magnifies the pressure to be perfect' (Henderson, Harmon, & Houser, 2010, p. 232). The assumption that it is mothers' who are central to the school–family relation plays a crucial part in this assemblage and the responsibilisation of mothers and childhood health:

> Well, I tend to . . . I don't tend to do it if it's a one-off thing. As an example I had a child who turned up with a bag of cookies and some other biscuits and nothing else. No sandwich, no pasta, no rice, no fruit, absolutely nothing else at all, so she was basically having biscuits and I . . . she was a child in year 4, so I talked to her about that, and then I looked to see what happened after that. If she had come again with the same sort of lunchbox then I would have asked *her mum* to come and talked her. (Sally, Head teacher, Rosehill Primary)

This is not unique to the issue of health, as historically mothers' have been constituted as playing a particular role in the schooling process. Griffith and Smith (2005) reveal how mothers' work is implicitly and explicitly required by school systems, which come to bear upon the sort of moral assumptions about the role of mothers assumed in the earlier quote.

Cultural pathology of particular families

Surveillance is not just a process of recording or monitoring health, rather as Monahan and Torres (2009, p. 16) note it is a form of 'modern knowledge production, organizational management, and social control' (p. 13). Teachers reported the assessment of risk as attached to particular children and particular families, as understood through particular biopolitical instruments:

> I think in this country at the moment, that parents are not taking enough responsibility for what happens with their children or in life generally, and society ... When I see programmes on television and people can't cook and they don't know how to cook and they get things out of tins and I'm starting to worry greatly about the community and the society we live in and whether or not we're able on our own to live a good healthy life ... I think there's definitely one or two that should take a bit more responsibility because their children are getting fatter and I think it's because they do too much for them as well, they perhaps indulge them. (Jean, Head of PE, Fraser Prep)

It was through the process of sorting that particular groups/families were identified as at greater risk than others involving surveillance techniques of 'translating the "individual" into the logistics of codes and passwords for re-territorialization as a "dividual" within a risk flow and its determinate programme of control' (Osmond, 2010, p. 338).

> [Some pupils] who do diaries with me at the moment – one of them particularly whose family are particularly big, you know, came directly and said I am concerned and they spoke with [another teacher] I think about that, so we suggested a food diary and we're going to look at that. They can talk to our school nurse as well and we can maybe devise, to look at exercise – they both do a fair amount of exercise. (Sarah, Head of personal development, Longcliffe High)

'Affective circulation' (Walkerdine, 2009) of concerns about parental influence on childhood obesity pass through working class parents in ways which reproduce the sort of 'categorical suspicions' (Marx, 1988, quoted in Lyon, 2007) which middle class parents may not experience, as was evidenced in the predominantly working class inner city state primary school, where parents were 'taught' how to pack lunch boxes:

> Erm, I think [another teacher] actually spoke to the parents and we had leaflets on how to pack a healthy lunchbox and we had ... we've had like, erm, afternoons where the parents can come and sample the school dinners and show what you can put into a packed lunchbox. We've actually done, er, things for the parents to come and watch and to be part of as well. So we do try and involve the parents. (Ruth, PE co-ordinator, Rosehill Primary)

Unlike the independent and preparatory schools, these inner city state school staff took a more instructional approach with parents, who were deemed to lack the capital and cultural resources to enact health imperatives. The observation in this paper that families are now recognised as part of the constitution of 'parental deficit' (Gillies, 2005, p. 84) therefore draws upon broader policy discourse described earlier, in which governments pushed inadequate parenting centre stage in discussions about childhood and citizenship.

> Like I said, there are leaflets which we did send out about healthy packed lunchboxes so the parents can see what we expect in the packed lunchboxes and what should be in the packed lunchboxes. (Ruth, PE co-ordinator, Rosehill Primary)

The potential mobilisation of 'network ties' (Horvat et al., 2003) is significant in how pedagogies of health are able to function both within and across school–family relations. Many of the young people in our research study from middle class families made reference to their families having contact with health professionals, personal trainers, doctors and so on. The working class families on the other hand had fewer 'professionals' in their network, and the schools assumed that poorer parents were highly dependent on the school itself for 'proper health care'. However, these class-based differences were seldom acknowledged in this discernment. Rather, the 'political economy of embodiment' (Evans & Davies, 2010), material constraint and cultural preference are subsumed under moral and ethical explanations in which failures to meet health expectations are seen as failures in the ethical regulation of their own bodies and those in their care. This rationalist approach to health assumes that if parents are simply given the correct knowledge, they can then adjust their child's lifestyle or health behaviours accordingly. However, even where parents may undertake ethical and moral reflexivity, this does not mean they may then have the appropriate or sufficient material, sociocultural resources to change the life condition of those in their care. Whilst on the one hand, there is a recognition that some parents many not have the necessary level of reflexivity, and thus need 'educating', those who cannot or who choose not to enact health imperatives are seen as not fulfilling their moral and ethical obligations, thus falling prey to moral surveillance. In these moments, whilst ostensibly acknowledging the limitations particular families face, teachers sometimes re-articulate the parameters, such that it is seen as a moral deviation from the norm (of those who are more able to make such choices). On some occasions, the explanations given by teachers drew on the view that parents choose to disconnect from particular values or morals rather than lacking the material resources to enact health imperatives:

> [Responsibility for obesity is…] everyone's really, parents, government, schools, it's everybody's. I mean they're children and at the end of the day they need guidance. Some are overindulged, others are allowed to just choose what they want to eat and it's the wrong choice, they need guidance through parents, through government initiatives as well. (Melissa, Head of PSHE, Fraser Prep)

Parents are thus constituted through discourses which position them as both victims of, yet also responsible for, the conditions of family health. There is little recognition of the nuances of those who face poverty to the extent that 'the excluded poor are constructed as morally obliged to become part of the included poor for the sake of themselves, their children and the wider community' (Gillies, 2005, p. 86).

Conclusion

The aforementioned research findings reveal the classed nature of these biopedagogies and their recontextualisation in schools. Whilst efforts are made to extend and integrate families and schools in the creation of health education, at least in those schools participating in this research, there is little space in the policy discourse for an approach that incorporates the complexities of health, of their social meaning and significance across class and of the pleasures and desires associated with particular foods. For example, in the Canadian context, McPhail, Gwen, Chapman, and Beagan (2011, p. 306) maintain that –

> …easy conflations among social class, teens' access to fast food as suggested by the discourses of obesogenic environments are troubling in their lack of specificity and

nuance, and their failure to take into consideration the complexity of teens' practices of subjectivity in relation to understandings of healthy eating and fast food consumption.

Within the burgeoning field of public pedagogy, recent studies have alluded to the ways that teachers draw on popular culture in their classroom (Kellner & Share, 2007) to engage students. However, with some notable exceptions (Fullagar, 2009), less has been written about the relationship between teachers and schools and what might be described as family pedagogies. The observation that families are now be recognised as part of a stronger interdependent relationship with schools may be a simple one, but it also draws attention to a more complex dynamic concerning the governance of 'healthy' bodies across different educational sites and through different means. The exploration of health imperatives, school–family relations and surveillance reveals how health education is being reshaped by and shapes complex and fluid power relations. As the data in this article demonstrates, health surveillance is not a practice that relies on a singular meaning. Understandings of health are recontextualised through classed, gendered, sociocultural and economic locations through which health and imaginings of youth are differently understood. The culture of surveillance is such that surveillance biopedagogies are deployed not only by authoritative figures but part of a broader assemblage through which members of family, peer culture and myriad organisations can surveil, revealing itself as transcending temporal and spatial boundaries associated with school life. The politicisation of weight through discourses of obesity, thus, complicates traditional spatio-temporal boundaries, widening the presence of biopedaogies into inter-assemblages between families and schools. It does so in such a way that biopolitical governance is no longer so easily discernable as terrotorialised in particular school or family locations. This reflects Fairclough's (2000) observation that New Labour policies reflected how the traditionally private sphere of the family was being repositioned as public space. In pedagogical terms, this raises a number of questions about the positioning of childhood health 'in the intersections between formalized schooling's means and extrainstitutional ends' (Sandlin et al., 2011). In this sense, it seems we need a much more engaged dialogue between surveillance studies, critical pedagogy and those working within the field of public pedagogy. To do so means establishing a more discerning understanding of both public pedagogy and surveillance to avoid theorising either in a 'totalising' (Savage, 2010, p. 103) way. Doing so means being more specific about surveillance and following Savage (2010, p. 109), examining what makes these public pedagogies 'pedagogical' (Savage, 2010, p. 109) rather than just a form of 'socialisation'.

Finally, whilst this work has registered extended and amalgamated pedagogies and the surveillant aspects of their operationalisation within and across family sites, I would concur with Sandlin et al. (2011) that we need a better understanding of 'learner perspectives' in negotiating these assemblages. Indeed, highlighting the potential for dialogue and overlap in work in surveillance studies and pedagogy, in a similar vein McCahill and Finn (2010, p. 273) argue that 'we know virtually nothing about the "surveilled" as a creative group of "social actors" may negotiate, modify or evade surveillance practices'. Such an approach could work to enrich our understandings of both fields and their relationships but, perhaps more importantly, depart from monolithic understanding of surveillance, health and pedagogy.

Acknowledgements

With thanks to the ESRC for supporting the research on which this article is based (ESRC grant ESRC 000-22-20).

Notes

1. Dr Emma Rich, Professor John Evans, Laura De Pian (RES-000-23-2000).
2. By Professor Jan Wright, Dr Valerie Harwood, Dr Ken Cliff in Australia and Dr Lisette Burrows and Jaleh McCormack.
3. In 2003, the Government published a green paper called *Every Child Matters* (ECM) following the death of Victoria Climbié, a young girl who was horrifically abused and tortured, and eventually killed by her great aunt and the man with whom they lived in England. This awful event led to extensive public discourse and concern about protection of young people and the role of children's services. Tapping into these anxieties, ECM sets out five key outcomes for children and young people including: being healthy, staying safe, enjoying and achieving, making a positive contribution to society and achieving economic well-being.

References

Armstrong, D. (1995). The rise of surveillance medicine. *Sociology of Health and Illness, 17*, 393–404.

Ball, K. (2005). Organization, surveillance and the body: Towards a politics of resistance. *Organization, 12*(1), 89–108.

Beckett, L. (2004). Editorial: Health, the body, and identity work in health and physical education. *Sport, Education and Society, 9*(2), 171–173.

Bullen, E., Kenway, J., & Hay, V. (2000). New labour, social exclusion and educational risk management: The case of 'gymslip mums'. *Educational Research Journal, 26*(4), 441–456.

Burrows, L., & Wright, J. (2004). The good life: New Zealand children's perspectives on health and self. *Sport, Education and Society, 9*(2), 193–207.

Burrows, L., & Wright, J. (2007). Prescribing practices: Shaping healthy children in schools. *International Journal of Children's Rights, 15*, 83–98.

Bury, M., & Gabe, J. (2004). *The sociology of health and illness. A reader.* London: Routledge.

Clough, P.T. (2003). Affect and control: Rethinking the body 'Beyond sex and gender'. *Feminist Theory, 4*(3), 359–364.

Clough, P.T., & Halley, J. (Eds.) (2007). *The affective turn: Theorizing the social.* Durham, NC: Duke University Press.

Conrad, P. (1992). Medicalization and social control. *Annual Review of Sociology, 18*, 209–232.

Conrad, P. (2007). *The medicalization of society: On the transformation of human conditions into treatable disorders.* Baltimore, MD: Johns Hopkins University Press.

Dawson, S. (2006). The impact of institutional surveillance technologies on student behaviour. *Surveillance and Society, 4*(1/2), 69–84.

Department for Education and Skills (DfES). (2003). *Every child matters* (Green Paper, Cm. 5860). London: The Stationery Office (TSO).

Department of Health (DoH). (2004). *Choosing health: Making healthier choices easier.* London: The stationary office.

Department of Health (DH). (2006). *Measuring childhood obesity: Guidance to primary care trusts.* Retrieved from http://www.dh.gov.uk/en/Publicationsandstatistics/Publications/PublicationsPolicyAndGuidance/DH_4126385

De Pian, L., Evans, J., & Rich, E. (2010, April). *Young people's decision making about health as an embodied social process: Reflections from the field.* Paper presented at 'Researching Young Lives: Power, Representation and the Research Process' conference, University of Limerick, Ireland.

Dowty, T. (2008). Pixie-dust and privacy: What's happening to children's rights in England. *Children and Society, 22*(5), 393–399.

Evans, B., & Colls, R. (2009). Measuring fatness, governing bodies: The spatialities of the body mass index (BMI) in anti-obesity politics. *Antipode, 41*, 1051–1083.

Evans, B., & Colls, R. (2010). 'Doing more good than harm'? The absent presence of children's bodies in (anti)obesity policy. In L. Monaghan, E. Rich & L. Aphramor (Eds.), *The Obesity Debate* (pp. 115–138). Basingstoke: Palgrave Macmillan.

Evans, J., & Davies, B. (2010). Family, class and embodiment: Why school physical education makes so little difference to post school participation patterns in physical activity. *International Journal of Qualitative Studies in Education, 23*(7), 765–784.

Evans, B., & Colls, R. (2011). Doing more good than harm? The absent presence of children's bodies in (anti-)obesity policy. In E. Rich, L.F. Monaghan & L. Aphramor (Eds.), *Debating obesity: Critical perspectives* (pp. 115–138). Basingstoke: Palgrave Macmillan.

Evans, J., Rich, E., Davies, B., & Allwood, R. (2008). *Education, disordered eating and obesity discourse: Fat fabrications.* London: Routledge.

Fairclough, N. (2000). *New labour, new language.* London: Routledge.

Fotel, T., & Thomsen, T.U. (2004). The surveillance of children's mobility. *Surveillance & Society, 1*(4), 535–554.

Fraser, S., Maher, J.M., & Wright, J. (2010). Between bodies and collectivities: Articulating the action of emotion in obesity epidemic discourse. *Social Theory and Health, 8*, 192–209.

Fullagar, S. (2009). Governing healthy family lifestyles through discourses of risk and responsibility. In J. Wright & V. Harwood (Eds.), *Biopolitics and the 'obesity epidemic': Governing bodies* (pp. 108–126). New York, NY: Routledge.

Gard, M., & Wright, J. (2005). *The obesity epidemic.* London: Routledge.

Gillies, V. (2005). Meeting parents' needs? Discourses of 'support' and 'inclusion' in family policy. *Critical Social Policy, 25*, 70.

Giroux, H.A. (1998). Public pedagogy and rodent politics: Cultural studies and the challenge of Disney. *Arizona Journal of Hispanic Cultural Studies, 2*, 253–266.

Giroux, H.A (2003). Racial injustice and disposable youth in the age of zero tolerance. *Qualitative Studies in Education, 16*(4), 553–565.

Green, S. (1999). A plague on the panoptican: Surveillance and power in the global information economy. *Information, Communication & Society, 2*(1), 26–44.

Griffith, A., & Smith, D. (2005). *Mothering for schooling.* Abingdon: Routledge Falmer.

Haggerty, K.D., & Ericson, R. (2000). The surveillant assemblage. *British Journal of Sociology, 51*(4), 605–622.

Halse, C., Honey, A., & Boughtwood, D. (2008). *Inside anorexia: The experience of girls and their families.* London: Jessica Lang.

Heir, S.P. (2003). Probing the surveillant assemblage: On the dialectics of surveillance practices as processes of social control. *Surveillance and Society, 1*(3), 399–411.

Henderson, A.C., Harmon, S.M., & Houser, J. (2010). A new state of surveillance? An application of Michel Foucault to modern motherhood. *Surveillance & Society, 7*(3/4), 231–247.

Horvat, E.M., Weininger, E.B., & Lareau, A. (2003). From social ties to social capital: Class differences in the relations between school and parent networks. *American Educational Research Journal, 40*(2), 319–351.

House of Commons Health Committee (HOC). (2004). *Obesity, third report of session 2003–04* (Vol. 1 report). Retrieved from http://www.parliament.the-stationery-office.co.uk/pa/cm200304/cmselect/cmhealth/23/2304htm#a6

Jutel, A. (2005). Weighing health: The moral burden of obesity. *Social Semiotics, 15*(2), 113–125.

Jutel, A. (2006). The emergence of overweight as a disease entity: Measuring up normality. *Social Science and Medicine, 63*(9), 2268–2276.

Katz, C. (2006). The state goes home: Local hypervigilance of children and the global retreat from social reproduction. In T. Monahan (Ed.), *Surveillance and security: Technological politics and power in everyday life* (pp. 27–36). New York, NY: Routledge.

Kellner, D., & Share, J. (2007). Critical media literacy: Crucial policy choices for a twenty-first-century democracy. *Policy Futures in Education, 5*, 59–69.

Kirk, D. (1993). *The body, schooling and culture.* Deakin: Deakin University Press.

Leahy, D. (2009). Disgusting pedagogies. In J. Wright & V. Harwood (Eds.), *Biopolitics and the 'obesity epidemic'* (pp. 172–182). New York, NY: Routledge.

Lyon, D. (2002). Editorial: surveillance studies – Understanding visibility, mobility and the phonetic fix. *Surveillance and Society, 1*(1), 1–7.

Lyon, D. (Ed.) (2006). *Theorizing surveillance: The panopticon and beyond.* Devon: Willan Publishing.

Lyon, D. (2007). *Surveillance studies: An overview.* Cambridge: Polity.

Marx, G., & Steeves, V. (2010). From the beginning: Children as subjects and agents of surveillance. *Surveillance and Society, 7*(3/4), 192–230.

McCahill, M., & Finn, R. (2010). The social impact of surveillance in three UK Schools: 'Angels', 'devils' and 'teen mums'. *Surveillance & Society, 7*(3/4), 273–289.

McIntosh, I., Punch, S., Dorrer, N., & Emond, R. (2010). 'You don't have to be watched to make your toast': Surveillance and food practices within residential care for young people. *Surveillance & Society, 7*(3/4), 290–303.

McPhail, D., Gwen, E., Chapman, G., & Beagan, B. (2011). 'Too much of that stuff can't be good': Canadian teens, morality, and fast food consumption. *Social Science and Medicine, 73*, 301–307.

Misra, K. (2006). Politico-moral transactions in Indian AIDS Service: Confidentiality, rights and new modalities of governance. *Anthropological Quarterly, 79*(1), 33–74.

Monahan, T., & Wall, T. (2007). Somatic surveillance: Corporeal control through information networks. *Surveillance & Society, 4*(3), 154–173.

Monahan, T., & Torres, R. (Eds.) (2009). *Schools under surveillance: Cultures of control in Public education.* New Brunswick, NJ: Rutgers University Press.

Nichols, N., & Griffith, A.I. (2009). Talk, text and educational action: An institutional ethnography of policy in practice. *Cambridge Journal of Education, 39*(2), 241–255.

Osmond, C. (2010). Anti-social behaviour and its surveillant inter-assemblage in New South Wales, Australia. *Surveillance & Society, 7*(3/4), 325–343.

Rail, G. (2009). Canadian youth's discursive constructions of health in the context of obesity discourse. In J. Wright & V. Harwood (Eds.), *Biopolitics and the 'obesity epidemic': Governing bodies* (pp. 141–156). London: Routledge.

Rich, E., & Perhamus, L. (2011). Editorial: Health surveillance, the body and surveillance. *International Qualitative Studies in Education, 23*(7), 759–776.

Rich, E., Evans, J., & De Pian, L. (2011). Children's bodies, surveillance and the obesity crisis. In E. Rich, L. Monaghan & L. Aphramor (Eds.), *Debating obesity: Critical perspectives.* Basingstoke: Palgrave Macmillan.

Rich, E., Monaghan, L., & Aphramor, L. (Eds.). (2011). *Debating obesity: Critical perspectives.* Basingstoke: Palgrave Macmillan.

Rose, N. (2000). Community, citizenship and the third way. *American Behaviour Scientist, 43*(9), 1395–1411.

Sandlin, J.A., O'Malley, P., & Burdick, J. (2011). Mapping the complexity of public pedagogy scholarship: 1894–2010. *Review of Educational Research, 81*(3), 338–375.

Savage, G.C. (2010). Problematizing 'Public Pedagogy' in Educational Research. In J.A. Sandlin, B.D. Schultz & J. Burdick (Eds.), *Public pedagogy: Education and learning beyond schooling* (pp. 103–115). New York: Routledge.

Schubert, W.H. (1981). Knowledge about out-of-school curriculum. *Educational Forum, 45*, 185–199.

Schubert, W.H. (2010). Outside curricula and public pedagogy. In J. Sandlin, B.D. Schultz & J. Burdick (Eds.), *Handbook of public pedagogy: Education and learning beyond schooling* (p. 10). New York, NY: Routledge.

Shilling, C. (2008). *Changing bodies: Habit, crisis and creativity.* London: Sage.

Steeves, V., & Jones, O. (2010). Editorial: Surveillance and children. *Surveillance & Society, 7*(3/4), 187–191.

Sylva, A., & Pugh, B. (2005). Transforming the early years in England. *Oxford Review of Education, 31*(1), 11–27.

Valentine, G., & Holloway, S.L. (2002). 'Cyberkids? Exploring children's identities and social networks in on-line and off-line worlds' Annals. *Association of American Geographers, 92*, 302–319.

Walkerdine, V. (2009). Biopedagogy and beyond. In J. Wright & V. Harwood (Eds.), *Biopolitics and the 'obesity epidemic'* (pp. 199–209). London: Routledge.

Williams, F. (2004). What matters is who works: Why every child matters to new labour. Commentary on the DfES green paper every child matters. *Critical Social Policy, 24,* 406–427.

World Health Organization (WHO). (1998). *'Obesity': Preventing and managing the global epidemic*. Geneva: Author.

Wright, J. (2009). Biopower, biopedagogies and the obesity epidemic. In J. Wright & V. Harwood (Eds.), *Biopolitics and the 'obesity epidemic'* (pp. 199–209). London: Routledge.

Wright, J., & Harwood, V. (2009). *Biopolitics and the 'obesity epidemic': Governing bodies*. New York, NY: Routledge.

Yar, M. (2003). Panoptic power and the pathologisation of vision: Critical reflections on the Foucauldian thesis. *Surveillance & Society, 1*(3), 254–271.

'Emboldened bodies': social class, school health policy and obesity discourse

Laura De Pian

Department of Education, University of Bath, Bath, UK

This paper examines the multiple ways in which health policy relating to obesity, diet and exercise is recontextualised and mediated by teachers and pupils in the context of social class in the UK. Drawing on a case study of a middle-class primary school in central England, the paper documents the complexity of the policy process, its uncertainty, its intended and unintended affects and effects on the lives and bodies of young people as they negotiate 'health' across a range of social contexts. Particular attention is paid to the voices of young people, whom by way of embodying imperatives found in health discourses become 'troubled bodies', 'emboldened bodies', or 'insouciant bodies', as such imperatives intersect with pupils' various subjectivities. It is argued that whilst all pupils appear to be affected by health policy, they are differently *effected* by it. The paper will outline how pupils were effected by health policy in emboldened and privileged ways and how the young people seem to not only remain unscathed by health imperatives but are also positively emboldened and privileged by them. This paper adds to understandings of social class and relationships between public health discourse and individual (e.g. pupil) subjectivity, and highlights both the complexity of the policy process itself as a product of the organisational and social relations of schooling, as well as the complex and idiosyncratic nature of young people's embodied subjectivities.

Introduction

In Australia and New Zealand, a far greater emphasis has been placed upon health education through school curricula than in the UK, where school Physical Education (PE), for example, has traditionally been dominated by competition and sport (Penney & Chandler, 2000). Until recently, health education in the UK has predominantly been taught outside of PE, for example in Personal, Social, Health and Economic (PSHE) education or as a marginal component of a PE curriculum. Increasingly, however, a 'whole school approach' is being adopted in the design and delivery of health education in UK schools. This approach has been heavily influenced by the rhetoric of the UK Government's National Healthy Schools Programme (NHSP), jointly funded by the Department of Health (DoH) and the Department for Education and Skills. The programme was first introduced in 1999 with revised standards published in 2005 stipulating that in order to achieve 'Healthy School Status', schools are required, through a whole-school approach, to provide evidence of specific health education criteria across four themes that comprise the 'healthy school': personal, social and health education; healthy eating; physical activity and emotional health and well-being (Department of Health [DoH], 2005). Furthermore, schools must evidence outcomes that have made an impact on pupils' learning, experiences and/or behaviour. The NHSP thus exemplifies the UK Government's drive to combat the 'obesity epidemic' by prescribing specific (desirable) health behaviours to young people, particularly around diet and exercise, through 'new health imperatives' in schools (Evans, Rich, Davies, & Allwood, 2008; Rich, Evans, & De Pian, 2009). In effect, schools in the UK are becoming totally pedagogised micro societies (TPMS) in which health education has become everyone's concern.

In recent years, a growing body of literature has been concerned with young people's experiences, interpretations and negotiations of these health imperatives in schools. Within this literature, some researchers (e.g. Evans et al., 2008; Halse, Honey, & Boughtwood, 2008, amongst others) have drawn attention to how young women experience and have been negatively affected by the imperatives of obesity discourse in that it had contributed to the development of disordered eating. Building on this and other research concerned with young people's interpretation and potential embodiment of obesity discourse (see Gard & Wright, 2005), this paper presents findings from the UK component of an international research collaboration, from which the other papers in this special issue derive. The UK research project, funded by the Economic and Social Research Council,[1] involved a larger and more diverse population of young people ($n = 1176$) compared with those used in previous research in this field (e.g. Evans et al., 2008). The methodology was designed and implemented in 2007/2008 to explore the relationships between demographic 'resources' (sociocultural capital) born of age, gender, class, ethnicity and (forms of) schooling; all sites and sources of influence on 'body knowledge' and individuals' relationships with their embodied selves. The sample of 1176 boys and girls is spread across eight schools (three primary, two middle and three secondary) and is representative of the ethnic and social class composition of the UK Midlands county in which this study took place. Questionnaires were completed by all 1176 young people aged between 9 and 16 years across these schools and semi-structured interviews were conducted with 90 of these participants, in pairs, where possible, but occasionally in groups of three where time and space were limited. Data from this research thus add nuance and complexity to understandings of relationships between public health discourse and individual (e.g. pupil) subjectivity, especially in its revelation of young people who seem to not only remain unscathed by health imperatives but who are also positively emboldened and privileged by them. The Deleuzian notion of the 'becoming subject' is applied throughout this paper, to illustrate the 'ongoing process of subject formation' (McLeod & Yates, 2006, p. 78). The term 'subjectivity' therefore takes precedence over 'identity' which has traditionally been used in the framing of 'adolescence' as something more fixed and rigid (McLeod & Yates, 2006).

The paper begins by focusing on questionnaire data provided by 1156 of the young people in the sample who responded to the prompt, 'I am happy with my current weight/size', by choosing from the options, 'never', 'sometimes' or 'all the time'. There are, of course, serious limitations to using questionnaire data alone to interrogate issues of subjectivity. It is drawn on here, using the responses to this one statement, to demonstrate the demographic trends in the young people's attitudes towards their bodies. Thus, the questionnaire data serve as a starting point for the analysis, with the intention to provide the most direct and straightforward illustration of how young people variously perceive and evaluate their body's weight/size (albeit at a particular moment in time). Figure 1 graphically displays the young people's responses to the prompt 'I am happy with my current weight/size'.

From these responses it is evident that there were young people in this study who, very worryingly, reported that they were 'never happy' about their weight/size (16%, $n = 183$). Elsewhere these young people have been referred to as 'troubled' bodies (De Pian, forthcoming; Evans, Davies, Rich, & De Pian, 2012). However, just under half of the young people in the sample (44%, $n = 507$) reported that they were happy with their weight/size 'all the time'. These have previously been defined as 'emboldened' bodies (De Pian, forthcoming; Evans et al., 2012). The 40% of the participants ($n = 466$) who indicated that they were 'sometimes' happy about their weight/size, are considered to have a more ambivalent, indifferent and/or transitory relationship with their body's weight/size. These have been described elsewhere as 'insouciant' bodies (De Pian, forthcoming; Evans et al., 2012).[2] Whilst this label perhaps implies that the participants in this group are somewhat nonchalant about their weight/size, it is also intended to capture those young people who had a less exact or fixed relationship with their weight/size. Of all three groups, it is this latter group of pupils, I would argue, which most clearly exemplifies the fluid nature of young people's relationships with their own bodies across time, place and space (De Pian, forthcoming).

If the number of those young people who are 'sometimes' happy is conflated with the number of young people who are happy 'all the time' (rather than with those who are 'never' happy) about their weight/size, these findings depict a relatively positive picture of young people's relationships with their body's weight/size (84%, $n = 973$) feeling 'moderately' to 'extremely' happy about their weight/size). Conflated with those who are 'never' happy with their weight/size, however, the figures illustrate a more ominous picture, revealing that just over half (56%, $n = 649$) of the sample are

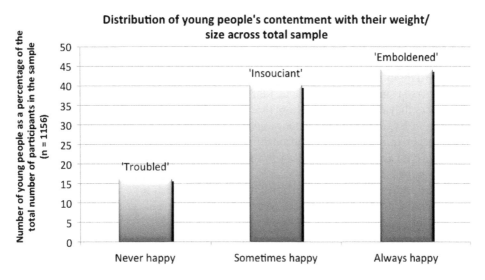

Figure 1.   I am happy with my current weight/size.

at worst 'not at all' happy and at best 'moderately' happy about their weight/size. Nevertheless, in either case, at least on the surface these data appear to offer some serious check on the perspective of previous research which has emphasised only the potentially determining, all consuming and destructive effects of obesity discourse for all young people's embodiment. On the basis of this evidence alone, the effect of obesity-related health imperatives on young people's subjectivity formation is likely far more complex and varied than may have been implied in previous work.

As mentioned earlier, the categories described above are somewhat problematic as they obscure both the complexity and fluidity of subjectivity in time, place and space. Over the course of this paper, detail and nuance are added to these data, and subsequently to the way in which one might begin to think about young people's subjectivities and their understandings of health and their bodies in particular. Rather than implying that the three body typologies referred to above and throughout this paper are fixed or exclusive categories, it is later argued that individuals' relationships with their weight/size, and indeed other aspects of their corporeality, exist on (and ebb and flow across) a continuum whereby all individuals have the capacity to demonstrate characteristics of each of these orientations at varying degrees across different contexts. In this respect, young people's subjectivities are ever in a state of flux and becoming (McLeod & Yates, 2006) and consequently, in some cases, may be thoroughly hybridised (Azzarito, 2010; Rich, 2011). Hence, the young people (as categories of subjectivity) presented here are merely to be thought of as idealisations – artefacts of the methodology – representing examples of those young people who displayed a higher tendency towards one body typology over another, first through their response to the questionnaire statement concerned with their relationship with their weight/size, and, second, when talking in interview about how they learned and felt about their bodies (i.e. at the time these data were collected).

Do schools matter?

There is no direct or linear relationship between obesity discourse, associated policies and individual (pupil) subjectivity (Evans, Rich, De Pian, & Davies, 2011; Evans et al., 2012). Rather, cultural messages are always and inevitably mediated and recontextualised through a complex set of relationships involving the individual (the young person in this case), their family, friends and peers and the pedagogic encounters they experience at school (see Braun, Maguire, & Ball, 2010; Evans et al., 2011). In order to explore the extent to which schools play a part in this 'assemblage' (Rich, 2011), influencing the relationships young people form with their weight/size, the above data are considered below in the context of each of the eight schools in this study (Figure 2).[3]

Figure 2 illustrates the proportions of pupils from each school who responded to the prompt, 'I am happy about my current weight/size'. This graph clearly indicates that whether young people are happy with their weight/size 'never', 'sometimes' or 'all the time', is far more complex and multifaceted a process than at first might appear. It is apparent that all eight schools accommodate, at varying levels, troubled, insouciant and emboldened bodies, regardless of the demographic composition of their intake and/or level of education (primary, middle or secondary in this case).

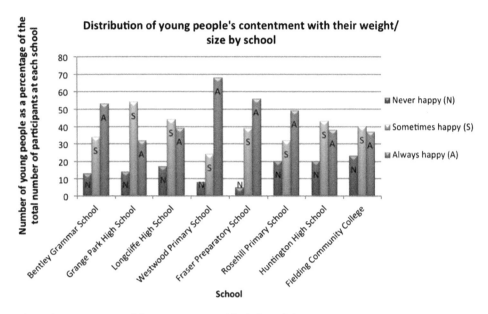

Figure 2.   Young people's contentment with their weight.

Looking across the schools presented in Figure 2, closer scrutiny of this data against the data for the sample as a whole in Figure 1 shows that with less than 15% of their participants reporting that they are 'never' happy about their current weight/ size, four schools (Bentley Grammar School, Grange Park High School, Westwood Primary School and Fraser Preparatory School) appear to house a below-average percentage of troubled bodies. Bentley and Grange Park are independent, suburban, single-sex secondary schools catering for pupils aged 10–18 years and 11–18 years, respectively (participants at both are aged 12–13 years and 15–16 years), from predominantly white, middle-class backgrounds. Westwood and Fraser reveal the lowest levels of troubled bodies within the whole sample (8% and 5%, respectively). Both are suburban/rural, mixed-sex primary schools (Westwood state-funded and Fraser independent), catering for pupils aged 4–11 years (participants at both are aged 9–11 years, also from predominantly white, middle-class backgrounds).

With over 16% of their pupils reporting that they are 'never' happy about their current weight/size, however, the other four schools in the study (Rosehill Primary School, Longcliffe High School, Fielding Community College and Huntington High School) reveal a higher than average percentage of troubled bodies. Rosehill, Longcliffe and Fielding are state-funded, inner-city, mixed-sex schools catering for pupils from ethnically diverse, predominantly working-class backgrounds: Rosehill, a primary school for pupils aged 3–11 years (participants are aged 9–11 years); Longcliffe, a middle school for pupils aged 11–14 years (participants are aged 12–13 years); and Fielding, a secondary school for pupils aged 11–16 years (participants are aged 13–15 years). The last in this group of four schools with an above-average percentage of troubled bodies, Huntington High School, is a state-funded, mixed-sex middle school for pupils aged 11–14 (participants spanned this age range) from predominantly white, lower-middle and working-class backgrounds in a rural village in the Midlands of England.

These findings suggest that lower than average percentages of troubled bodies are located among pupils attending schools largely populated by white, middle-class young people (Bentley, Grange Park, Westwood and Fraser) and higher than average percentages of troubled bodies are located at the schools housing ethnically diverse and/or lower-middle and working-class pupils (Rosehill, Longcliffe, Fielding and Huntington). The analyses in Wright, Burrows and Rich (this Special Issue) provide added insight as to why this might be so. Furthermore, with a mix of boys and girls from diverse class and cultural backgrounds across these eight schools reporting that they are 'never', 'sometimes' or 'always' happy about their weight/size, these findings appear to belie the literature, which suggests that troubled bodies are predominantly white, middle class and female (Evans et al., 2008). Further consideration of the statistics presented in Figure 2 reveals that two of the three primary schools (Westwood and Fraser) have a lower proportion of troubled bodies compared with the middle and secondary schools in this study (Longcliffe, Huntington, Fielding, Bentley, and Grange Park), suggesting (again against the rub of current evidence – see Hutchinson & Calland, 2011) that younger children perhaps reflect less frequently and/or less negatively on their weight/size. Alternatively, it could be argued that these younger children may reflect just as frequently and/or negatively on their weight/size as the older children in this research, but are better positioned than others (through an intersection of their age, gender, class, culture and/or school context) to nevertheless develop a positive relationship with their weight/size. This theorisation sheds some light on the alarming number of young troubled bodies at Rosehill Primary School and is corroborated later in this paper, with reference to the working class, culturally diverse context of Fielding Community College.

With more than half of their participants reporting that they are 'always' happy with their current weight/size, three of the four schools previously referred to as having a below-average percentage of troubled bodies (Bentley, Westwood and Fraser), reveal an above-average percentage of emboldened bodies. Of all the schools in this study, then, these three schools, all with lower than average percentages of troubled bodies and higher than average percentages of emboldened bodies appear to depict the most positive levels of young people's relationships with their weight/size. As mentioned earlier, these three schools cater for predominantly white, middle-class boys and/or girls aged 4–11 years (Westwood and Fraser) and 10–18 years (Bentley), therefore suggesting that young people from these backgrounds, independent of their age or gender, are more likely to form the most positive relationships with their weight/size.

With a proportion of troubled bodies comparable in size to those found at Bentley, Westwood and Fraser and a similar composition of white, middle-class pupils to those found at these schools, Grange Park High School is therefore expected to also demonstrate an above-average percentage of emboldened bodies. This does not appear to be the case, however. With a below-average percentage (32%) of emboldened bodies, and an above-average percentage (54%) of insouciant bodies (by far the highest proportion of insouciant bodies in the sample), Grange Park appears to add further complexity to the apparent association between the social class and ethnic composition of a school and the relationships the pupils therein form with their body's weight/size. Being an 'all girls' school, a below-average percentage of emboldened bodies at Grange Park was perhaps to be expected in light of previously mentioned literature concerned with the negative effects of obesity discourses on the relationships young females form with their body's weight/size (Evans et al., 2008; Halse et al., 2008). Rather than forming troubled relationships, however, many of the participants at Grange Park appear to be developing less exact (ambivalent or indifferent) relationships with their weight/size.

Unexpectedly again, given its high proportion of troubled bodies, Rosehill Primary School takes the place of Grange Park with an above-average percentage of emboldened bodies. With 49% of its participants reporting that they are happy with their weight/size 'all the time', Rosehill is the fourth and only other school in the sample to accommodate an above-average percentage of emboldened bodies. Thus, initial speculation that young people may reflect less frequently and/or less negatively on their weight/size is affirmed as all three of the primary schools in this research provide for an above-average number of emboldened bodies. This finding, however, further throws into relief the alarmingly high proportion (20%) of troubled bodies at Rosehill Primary School (the only primary school with an above-average percentage of troubled bodies), spurring exploration of the role of gender, cultural diversity, social class and health education curriculum in the relationships pupils form with their body's weight/size (see Wright, Burrows and Rich (2012) this Special Issue).

The remaining three schools in our study (Longcliffe, Huntington and Fielding), with above-average percentages of troubled bodies and below-average percentages numbers of emboldened bodies, provide some endorsement of earlier research claims regarding the destructive effects of obesity discourse in (some) schools.

Moreover, with 40% or more of their participants reporting that they are 'sometimes' happy with their weight/size, all four of the schools with a below-average percentage of emboldened bodies (Grange Park, Longcliffe, Huntington and Fielding) also accommodate an above-average percentage of insouciant bodies (54, 44, 43 and 40%, respectively), suggesting that the low proportion of emboldened bodies at these four schools could be explained by a relatively high proportion of insouciant bodies and in the case of three of these schools (Longcliffe, Huntington and Fielding), a high proportion of troubled bodies. So why are many young people such as those at Bentley, Westwood and Fraser forming an emboldened relationship with their weight/size when a large number of young people such as those at Grange Park, Longcliffe, Huntington and Fielding are forming less positive, insouciant, and sometimes troubled relationships with their weight/size?

The remainder of this paper will address this question and thus further explore the complexities of young people's learning about health and their bodies by focusing attention on one of these eight schools, Westwood Primary School, which in my view offers the clearest indication (e.g. especially when compared with Fielding) as to why some pupils appear to fare better than others in the relationships they develop with their own weight/size.

Westwood primary school: 'emboldened bodies'

With the second-lowest proportion (8%, $n = 2$) of troubled bodies and the highest proportion (68%, $n = 17$) of emboldened bodies (Figure 3), Westwood Primary School is one of three schools in this research to exhibit the most positive distribution of young people's relationships with their weight/size.

Why did pupils at Westwood feel particularly positive about their weight/size compared with pupils at some of the other schools in this study (Longcliffe,

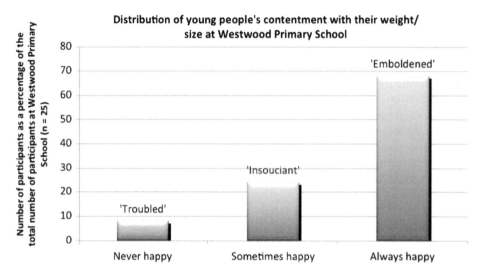

Figure 3. Young people's contentment with their weight (Westwood Primary School).

Huntington and Fielding, in particular)? Earlier, it was suggested that relatively low percentages of troubled bodies and high percentages of emboldened bodies reside in predominantly white middle-class schools (Bentley, Westwood and Fraser), and high proportions of troubled bodies and low proportions of emboldened bodies were generally found in the culturally diverse, lower-middle and working-class schools (Longcliffe, Huntington and Fielding). In addition, the pupil responses from all three of the primary schools in the study suggested high relative proportions of emboldened bodies and it was proposed earlier that this could be explained either by young boys and girls reflecting less frequently or indeed less negatively on their weight/size than older children, or through the theorisation that whilst these younger children perhaps reflect as frequently and/or negatively on their weight/size as older children, the intersection of their age, gender, class, culture, and school health curriculum contributes to the formation of subjectivities which are 'privileged' by obesity discourse. Qualitative data collected via semi-structured interviews with teachers and pupils at Westwood will be drawn upon throughout the remainder of this paper in order to explore these initial findings in more depth.

The school context

Westwood Primary School is a small, mixed-sex, state-funded Church of England primary school for pupils aged 4–11 years, located in a rural, middle-class village in the Midlands region of England. Westwood is described by Office for Standards in Education (Ofsted; UK Government schools inspectorate) (2008, p. 4) as 'a good school [which is] well led and managed by staff at all levels'. Being a smaller than average sized school, each member of staff takes on a number of roles, for example, Jess, Key Stage One Teacher for Reception Year One is PE Coordinator, Literacy Coordinator and International Schools Coordinator and Claire, Year 5/6 Classroom Teacher is Healthy Schools Coordinator and Numeracy Coordinator. In addition to their classroom teaching duties, Jess and Claire thus assume responsibility for the management and design of these specific areas of the curriculum, in consultation with other members of the teaching staff who are then responsible for the delivery of these areas. According to Ofsted (2008, p. 3):

> Almost all pupils [attending Westwood] come from White British backgrounds and no pupil is in the early stage of learning English as an additional language.

Children entering the Early Years Foundation Stage Reception Class are reported to have skill levels 'just above those expected for their age [and] [t]he proportion of pupils with learning difficulties is below average' (Ofsted, 2008, p. 3). Pupils at Westwood are said to:

> ...achieve well and reach above-average standards. [They] thoroughly enjoy school and this is reflected in their enthusiasm for all aspects of school life and above-average attendance. They enjoy the very wide range of activities offered and the way that teachers help them with their learning. They behave well [and] even remind themselves that they should be working when their attention wanders. (Ofsted, 2008, p. 4)

Ofsted describes the quality of care at the school, as 'particularly good' and based on:

> ...excellent [and] effective relationships with home [...] Teachers and Teaching Assistants have established effective procedures to ensure that care and welfare have a high priority and this is evident in the confidence with which children approach adults and the relationship between staff and parents.

Parents are reported to:

> ...think highly of the school and of, in particular, the welcoming environment of the school, the friendliness of staff and the wide range of activities provided. (Ofsted, 2008, p. 4)

In short, by Government-endorsed Ofsted definitions and criteria, Westwood is a 'good school' with good teachers providing 'care and welfare' to all its pupils, while enjoying positive relationships with parents and wider community. Ideational boundaries between school and family are weak; the formal and informal education/educations of the school and home synchronised to ensure the achievement of shared aims and ideals.

So what does health education at Westwood look like?

A recent shift in the way UK schools approach and deliver health education was documented at the beginning of this paper, highlighting an increase in the number of schools adopting a 'whole school approach' to health education, in line with the UK Government's NHSP. However, not all schools are sufficiently equipped (with financial resources, staff or time) to take on such an approach, nor does every school interpret and/or deliver associated health imperatives in a unitary fashion. Here Bernstein's (1990) notion of 'recontextualisation' is drawn upon to take account of the various versions of health education circulating within and across schools in the

UK (see Evans et al., 2008; Evans et al., 2011). This school case study thus provides an exploration of the design and delivery (recontextualisation) of health education at Westwood, highlighting the significance of context in young people's subjective learning about and engagement with health and their bodies.

The obesity crisis 'out there'

> I do think there is an obesity crisis out there. I don't think we have a problem personally, in this school or this village in particular, but nationally I think we are going down the American route as it were. (Jess, PE Coordinator)

Although the school had been awarded 'National Healthy School Status' by the UK Government for meeting specific health-related criteria outlined at the beginning of this paper and demonstrating a whole-school approach to health education, staff expressed a certain ambivalence towards obesity concerns. Jess, the PE Coordinator, like other staff in the school, voiced uncritical acceptance of the notion of an 'obesity crisis', as well as their own dislocation from this 'crisis' and its impending risks. The 'obesity epidemic' was clearly conceptualised in this context as a 'crisis', one step removed from the lives of all at Westwood – staff, pupils, parents – as well as the wider middle-class village community which the school served. Yet, 'knowledge' of the 'crisis out there' was readily available to and routinely accessed by staff through public health pedagogies concerned with the 'obesity epidemic': 'It's what you read in the paper [. . .] you hear it all on the news, don't you?' (Jess), again reinforcing their dislocated position in relation to the 'epidemic'. This 'knowledge', simultaneously drawn upon and affirmed when reading the bodies of 'others' in wider society, for example, 'seeing people in the streets' (Jess) shaped the way health education was then organised and delivered within the school:

> I mean it's a very affluent area and the parents are well educated so that has a knock-on effect I think with the children . . . I think these children generally are quite healthy. (Jess, PE Coordinator)

In this quote, staff, parents and pupils are simultaneously defined as privileged by virtue of their social class and as such positioned positively in relation to dominant health discourses. Considering pupils and their families to be 'wealthy' and 'healthy' with 'well educated' parents, staff at Westwood reported that they were 'not aware of anything standing out [or] any huge issues on [body] size' (Claire, Healthy Schools Coordinator). Clearly, then, 'health' was to be read through the embodiment of their pupils' (and parents') size, shape and appearance. The relatively privileged, embodied class position of those at Westwood in relation to obesity discourse thus begins to explain why pupils at this school felt particularly positive about their weight/size compared with other pupils in this research; they were emboldened by obesity discourse simply by virtue of their class position (affording them the resources to be able – or at least to appear to be able – to make the 'right choices' and therefore adhere to the health imperatives of obesity discourse), educated parents (reinforcing the above) and their extant embodiment (their physical presence as slim, 'healthy' bodies). Nevertheless, in line with dominant health and obesity discourses, the acceptance of a 'causal' relationship between a lack of education, poor lifestyle choices and obesity by staff at Westwood positions themselves and their pupils, regardless of their privileged subjectivities and extant embodiments, as perpetually 'at risk' of obesity. Intervention in the form of education by Government, schools and parents to encourage pupils to make the 'right choices' was therefore considered to be necessary 'from very young' (Claire) and all staff at Westwood appeared to fully embrace their role in this endeavour.

A totally pedagogised micro society

'Health', focusing on promoting physical activity and a 'healthy' diet, was a clear priority for staff at Westwood, both in their own lives outside of school (e.g. Claire says: 'I'm a fairly healthy person anyway and I believe you should try and eat healthily and be active, so things I do personally') and in the context of their role as educators within the school:

> I think it's a responsibility that we have to inform children and give them as much knowledge as possible so they can choose when they get older, we give them a curriculum and it's their choice what they do. (Claire, Healthy Schools Coordinator)

Commitment to health thus ideally had to be embodied (displayed and performed) by teachers as well as pupils in the school. Responsibility was therefore placed on the individual child to make the 'right' choice, informed by the knowledge they have been provided with. In effect they were expected to become good 'biocitizens' (Halse et al., 2008) taking responsibility for their own health, not only for their own good but also for that of their school and wider society. A 'whole school approach' to the delivery of health education at Westwood was thus operationalised to ensure that pupils were being equipped with 'as much knowledge as possible' (Claire) for their own and the school's sake. Claire explains:

> Health is not a subject on its own, it's the PSHE, it's the PE, it's everything [...] It's throughout the whole school, it's in everything that we do within the school, the ethos that we have [...] it's very difficult just to pin down and say 'we do this' because it's throughout the whole ethos of what we do and in everything we're teaching. (Claire, Healthy Schools Coordinator)

Westwood, therefore, in many respects, exemplified the kind of 'totally pedagogised micro society' discussed in Evans et al. (2008, p. 79) where pupils are inescapably located in a culture in which a plethora of imperatives throughout the school prescribes the 'choices' they *should* make (predominantly around diet and exercise) in order to avoid becoming like those 'out there' in the midst of the obesity 'crisis'. At Westwood, however, the potentially harmful and destructive nature of totally pedagogised approaches to the health of pupils reported in earlier work (Evans et al., 2008) does not seem to materialise. Westwood appears to be a TPMS comprised largely of emboldened bodies; why is this so? These data clearly highlight the significance of social class location and pupil intake to totally pedagogised schools in relation to the way teachers and pupils enact and embody obesity discourse. At Westwood, health education reinforces and indeed amplifies the school's and pupils' sense of separation, distinction and 'wellbeing' in relation to obesity imperatives, whilst also constantly reminding pupils of the 'need' for action to 'be healthy'. But why, then, are not all middle-class pupils in our research so emboldened? Grange Park High School was referred to earlier for its high proportion of insouciant bodies, and indeed there are pupils at Westwood, albeit in relatively small proportions, who reported insouciant and sometimes troubled relationships with their bodies. Evidently pupils, including those in the same school context, do not experience dominant discourse in a uniform way. The voices of teachers and pupils at Westwood are drawn upon later in this paper and further suggest reasons for the disproportionately large number of emboldened bodies found at this school.

A healthy curriculum?

It is evident that individual interpretations of 'health' by staff at Westwood are brought into the enactment of their health education. The uncritical acceptance of health imperatives concerned with diet and exercise in their personal lives, coupled with the UK Government's drive to prescribe specific behaviours around these two domains to young people (e.g. through the NHSP), shapes the design and delivery of health at Westwood. Thus, within this TPMS, an emphasis is placed on 'healthy eating' and PE, each of which will be briefly explored in the context of Westwood before examining the impact of these curricular on the pupils' understandings of health and their own bodies at the school.

Healthy eating

Of all the schools in our study, Westwood, through their whole school approach to health education appears to adopt the most integrated and prescriptive approach to 'healthy eating'. Health imperatives concerned with the pupils' diets dominate the TPMS at Westwood, particularly around snacks, because 'on the whole they were [previously eating only] crisps or cake' (Claire). In consultation with pupils, the school implemented a healthy snack scheme 18 months prior to our data collection. The scheme was described by Claire as 'a small guide to see that they eat healthily' and therefore involved the identification of unhealthy snacks which were to be avoided by pupils. Claire explains:

> We kept it very simple, and it was crisps, chocolate and cake that are the three things we consider not to be as healthy, so all other things are considered to be generally OK. (Claire, Healthy Schools Coordinator)

In practice, the scheme involved a daily snack register taken alongside the attendance register whereby each child was required to name the snack they had brought with them to school each day. Those who brought a 'healthy snack' to school 80% of the time (4 of the 5 days a week) or more were awarded certificates along with a 'healthy prize at the end of the year [...] last year they got a Frisbee' (Claire). The scheme was therefore designed to both survey and govern the actions of pupils towards their diet, ensuring that unhealthy 'risky' foods ('crisps, chocolate and cake') were avoided by rewarding pupils for bringing in 'healthy [safe] snacks'. The use of rewards in this way was clearly intended to have both emotional 'affect' and behavioural effect on the pupils; it aimed to 'condition' the pupils' behaviour in line with the health imperatives the school promoted around diet and although pupils at Westwood were said to 'enjoy' participating in this scheme, the reason given for this (by teachers) was, first and foremost, the rewards rather than the supposed health benefits. The scheme enforced a clear distinction between 'healthy', 'good', 'safe' foods and 'unhealthy', 'bad', 'risky' foods (see Welch, McMahon, & Wright, 2012) and this, perhaps unsurprisingly, was further refracted in pupils' judgement of their peers' behaviour and choices regarding diet:

> Jess: The children will notice if one of the others is eating too many crisps or [drinking too much] coke. We get the odd few that will come in with crisps in their bags and things like that, and I think especially in this school it is noticed.
>
> Int: Right, and it's noticed because you have a focus on healthy eating?
>
> Jess: Yeah.

The classification of food in this way meant that those 'odd few' in possession of 'unhealthy', risky foods were destined to stand out as deviant in the TPMS at Westwood, thus creating limited scope for the acceptance of alternative behaviours in this setting. Indeed, further research might reveal whether the 'troubled bodies' at this school were considered deviant or failing pupils.

Physical education

In addition to the promotion of healthy eating, staff at Westwood invested significantly more time and financial resources in PE (compared with other schools in our study). Again, this appeared to stem from the personal values of staff at Westwood:

> Personally, I come from a very sporty background; my family are quite sporty so personally I think it's important, that's why I've taken on the PE role [...] I'm very PE, I love PE. (Jess, PE Coordinator)

Jess' definition of health, in keeping with Government policy edict and wider discourse on obesity, is reduced to one primarily concerned with exercise, as means of 'tackling the obesity crisis out there'. She goes on to explain how her own investment in sport is not representative of the majority, however:

> People don't exercise as much anymore. People have got busy lives now with workload, family, and they may not fit it in [...] society in general I don't think is a sporty culture necessarily. (Jess, PE Coordinator)

Jess speaks of the ways Westwood's PE curriculum had benefited financially from the Government's investment in health education and the promotion of physical activity in particular had raised the profile and importance of PE and school sport in the school:

> I've got a lot of funding so I think the Government are putting a lot of money into providing high quality PE for schools. I mean we have a lot of PE, a range on offer right throughout the year [and] we've got all this money coming in and lots of people wanting

to come and offer us free clubs [...] We've got a lot outside of school so our children are getting what I think is high quality and a lot of sport that's there available to them [...] without the Government's interest in PE I wouldn't have had all this money really [...] We've even got the Sports Development people that come in for the little ones so it's open to them as well, and we've got a dance lady coming in now. Again, that's for Key Stage One as well. (Jess, PE Coordinator)

Jess reported that a wide range of extra-curricular sports clubs were available to all of their pupils and that 'the majority of them' do participate. Furthermore, additional money, collected through supermarket voucher schemes,[4] had allowed her to buy PE and playground equipment:

Now we're quite well resourced in the PE store for curriculum PE. So I spend usually half the money on the curriculum side of it and then half the money on our playground box so they get lots of games in there, they get skipping ropes, balls, all sorts of things that they can play with at play times and lunchtimes. They get a lot from it and we try and keep it topped up so they do use it. (Jess, PE Coordinator)

The value placed on physical activity by both the staff at Westwood and the UK Government had clearly privileged PE (and those who teach it) and as a result, '[pupils at Westwood] are getting a lot [of sport] compared to other schools' (Jess).

Emboldened bodies

Natured bodies

Given the strong emphasis placed on healthy eating and PE, both in dominant obesity discourse circulated through public pedagogies outside of the school, the UK Government's NHSP and the enactment of health education at Westwood, it is perhaps unsurprising that all of the pupils who participated in this study at Westwood ($n = 25$) defined health in terms of diet (commonly involving words such as 'healthy', 'balanced' and '5 A DAY') and exercise (with reference to specific types of exercise, e.g. 'going for a run' or 'playing football' as well as quantity of exercise, e.g. 'a lot' or 'daily'). Of particular interest, however, is the role such definitions played in the formation of different kinds of emboldened bodies at Westwood. Of the 17 pupils who reported in their questionnaires that they were happy with their weight/size 'all the time', 35%, ($n = 6$) continued with an explanation that this was simply by virtue of already being the 'right' weight:

I am not too heavy or not too light. (Daniel, aged 9)
I am not overweight. (Emily, aged 9)
I am always the right size for my age. (Jessica, aged 10)
There's nothing bad about it. (James, aged 10)
I am not overweight. (Joanne, aged 11)
It is average for my age. (Anna, aged 10)

These pupils considered themselves already 'naturally' 'privileged' in relation to obesity discourse (and were therefore emboldened by it) simply by virtue of their extant embodiment as slim 'healthy', 'right size' bodies. Whilst these pupils were not required (by virtue of their extant corporeal status) to comply with the imperatives of obesity discourse to reduce their weight; they were, none the less, not exempt from and could not escape its imperatives, which prescribed the choices they should be making around diet and exercise. All of the emboldened bodies at Westwood defined 'being healthy' in these terms, for example, when asked in the questionnaire 'what are the most important things someone can do to stay healthy?', Nicholas (aged 10 years) stated 'eat healthy food, play sport, start getting fit' and Emily (aged 9 years) wrote 'do some exercise and eat a balanced diet', and when asked what pupils learn about health in school, Chris responded: 'to eat healthy foods and get exercise'.

Thus, these pupils, like all others, were required to maintain their 'healthy' weight by eating the 'right' foods and doing 'regular' exercise; they did not escape the governing gaze of obesity discourse. In certain respects, then, these pupils emerged as the most 'privileged' of all the pupils in our research for not only 'naturally' conforming to the ideal weight/size promoted through dominant obesity discourse, but coming from privileged economic backgrounds, they also had access to the required resources ('healthy' foods and a wide variety of sports facilities and clubs) which allowed them to sustain their healthy lifestyle and profile. For example, Anna and Chris, 9-year-old pupils at Westwood, reported in their interviews that they ate a range of fruit and vegetables and attended a variety of clubs in and out of school including football, tap dancing, swimming and golf. This was in stark contrast to pupils such as Rory (aged 14 years) at Fielding Community College who reported:

> The Government says that we need to get healthier but if people like to want to eat more healthy it tends to cost more. I mean, apples are 50p and I think that's a rip off!

And whilst pupils at Fielding participated in the limited range of sports clubs their school had to offer, their disadvantaged class position restricted them from being able to participate in clubs outside of school such as those attended by Anna and Chris at Westwood:

> People round here they can't pay for enough like sports, yeah, you just go onto the field, but it's dangerous these days, so most parents don't want them going out on the streets and then so ... the only safe thing to do is to go to an actual place that's indoors or something and then play there, but children pretty much have to pay for themselves. If you get a paper round you can do it, it's just, you're just not rich enough to be able to do it these days. Everything's going up in price so you can't do it. (Rory, aged 14, Fielding Community College)

Exercised bodies

Another 3 (18%) of the 17 emboldened bodies at Westwood reported in their questionnaire that they were happy with their weight/size 'all the time', not because of a naturally privileged embodiment, as was the case with other 'emboldened' pupils discussed earlier, but because of their compliance with the imperatives of obesity discourse around diet and exercise. They were happy with their weight/size 'all the time' because:

> I do exercise all the time. (Nicholas, aged 10)
> I have lost a bit [of weight]. (Jack, aged 9)
> I play loads of sport. (Oliver, aged 10)

Thus, whilst these pupils did not necessarily conform to the ideal and privileged 'slim', 'healthy' weight/size, they were emboldened by obesity discourse through their actions, that is, by making the 'right' choices, doing the correct things. These young people were *seen* to be actively engaging with 'health' (performing risk avoidance) which itself provided them with a sense of achievement and indeed allegiance to their school. The imperatives of obesity discourse had, then, demonstrably entered into the thoughts, feelings and actions of all these young people, influencing the decisions they made around health. Again, coming from 'affluent' backgrounds with 'well educated parents', these decisions/achievements were enabled by their class position providing opportunities to participate in 'health', which other pupils in our research (e.g. at Fielding, in particular) simply did not have.

However, whilst many pupils at Westwood appear to have an emboldened relationship with their bodies, further critical exploration of their voices in this context reveals a yet more nuanced and less positive picture; one that leads us to question the degree to which emboldened bodies can be considered 'healthy' bodies. Just over half (53%, $n = 9$) of pupil participants at Westwood who reported that they were happy with their weight/size 'all the time', did not provide a reason for this in their questionnaires. There is, of course, any number of plausible reasons for this silence, amongst them, that these emboldened bodies were perhaps unaware of (or could not yet articulate) the reasons why. This data does, however, lend some support and add nuance to the earlier claim that children of this young age perhaps reflect less frequently and/or indeed less negatively on their weight/size than do older children.

However, this case also supports the earlier theorisation that age is not a solitary factor here; rather what influences the number of emboldened bodies at Westwood appears to derive from an intersection of a child's age with other aspects of their subjectivity: their gender, social class, ethnicity and school health education. Combined with these factors, then, it could be argued that the young age of participants at Westwood contributed significantly to the disproportionately large number of emboldened bodies in this school setting. Whilst a privileged class position may perhaps prevent the majority of these pupils developing negative relationships with their bodies as they mature and progress to secondary schooling, the fluid nature of young people's subjectivities means that this may not be the case for a small but significant number of these pupils, as the data from our middle-class secondary schools attest.

Conclusion

The above analyses has allowed exploration of the emplacement, enactment and embodiment of health imperatives, unveiling plausible reasons as to why some pupils appear to fare better than others in the relationships they are forming with their body's weight/size. If nothing more the data highlight the importance of acknowledging not only the intersections of age, gender, class and culture but also the 'mediating' health education practices of specific schools, if the corporeality of subjectivity is to be adequately understood. Clearly not all pupils are hurt or damaged by obesity discourse. To the contrary, a significant number are emboldened by it, at least initially so. However, even when this appears to be the case, such subjectivities cannot be taken at face value. That some of these emboldened relationships are determined by a young person's compliance with imperatives which prescribe the ways they should 'be' or behave in the name of 'achieving' health, calls to question the degree to which some of these emboldened bodies can be considered 'healthy' bodies. Furthermore, an ability to 'perform' 'health' in a particular setting and thus feel a sense of achievement, which, argued earlier, contributes to the development of an 'exercised' emboldened body is, of course, no guarantee that such behaviours, or indeed relationships with the body, will endure beyond or outside those settings. Nor is the desire to achieve or perform 'health' so narrowly defined, necessarily a good thing if it leads to obsessive attention to weight loss, excessive exercise and a pathological concern with the body as might be the case for the 'exercised' emboldened bodies. Again, we need be mindful that the body typologies discussed here are not fixed or exclusive categories; young people's relationships with their weight/size, and indeed other aspects of their corporeality, ebb and flow along a continuum whereby the emboldened and troubled bodies discussed throughout this paper represent two extreme positions. With this in mind, young people's relationships with their weight/size will be differently defined in other contexts. Emboldened bodies are not, then, necessarily healthy bodies, but merely privileged bodies in a culture that endorses slenderness, weight loss, 'healthy' diets and exercise as measures of good citizenship and health.

These young people are being inducted into (socially classed) self regulating modes of behaviour and attitudes of mind, encoded with reductive conceptions and principles of health, that will, perhaps inevitably, leave some deeply troubled and others 'merely' disaffected or dissatisfied with their bodies as they in later years experience the visceral demands of maturation and ageing, feeling and seeing their bodies change uncontrollably in size, shape and weight. Furthermore, that troubled, insouciant and emboldened bodies occur across a range of eight schools as culturally diverse as those included in this research, highlights both the complex and specific/idiosyncratic nature of young people's embodied subjectivities. Emerging patterns in the distribution of each of these body types across age, gender, social class and ethnicity thus warrant further exploration if we are to better understand the role schools play in the vastly different relationships young people appear to be forming with their bodies over time. These issues have only initially been addressed within the confines of this paper.

Notes

1. Led by Dr Emma Rich and Professor John Evans at Loughborough University.
2. The percentage figures for each of the body types illustrated in Figure 1 and referred to above are considered to be the average figures for the sample.
3. In the interest of ensuring anonymity, the name of each school has been replaced with a pseudonym.
4. Many supermarkets in the UK have been running voucher schemes in recent years (e.g. Sainsbury's 'Active Kids' scheme and Tesco's 'for Schools & Clubs' scheme) whereby members of the public, namely parents, can earn vouchers as they pay for their shopping which schools can exchange for teaching resources (e.g. PE and school sports equipment).

References

Azzarito, L. (2010). Future girls, transcendent femininities and new pedagogies: Towards girls' hybrid bodies? *Sport, Education and Society, 15*(3), 261–275.

Bernstein, B. (1990). *Class, codes and control: Vol. 4: The structuring of pedagogic discourse.* London: Routledge.

Braun, A., Maguire, M., & Ball, S.J. (2010). Policy enactments in the UK secondary school: Examining policy, practice and school positioning. *Journal of Education Policy, 25*(4), 547–560.

Department of Health (DoH). (2005). *National healthy school status: A guide for schools.* London: COI Communications, Department of Health Publications.

De Pian, L. (Forthcoming). *Embodying policy? Young people, education and obesity discourse* (Unpublished Doctoral dissertation). Loughborough University, Leicestershire, UK.

Evans, J., Davies, B., Rich, E., & De Pian, L. (2012). Understanding policy: Why health education policy is important and why it does not appear to work. *British Educational Research Journal.* DOI:10.1080/01411926.2011.647679.

Evans, J., Rich, E., Davies, B., & Allwood, R. (2008). *Education, disordered eating and obesity discourse: Fat fabrications.* London and New York: Routledge.

Evans, J., Rich, E., De Pian, L., & Davies, B. (2011). Health imperatives, policy and the corporeal device: Schools, subjectivity and children's health. *Policy Futures in Education, 9*(3), 328–340.

Gard, M., & Wright, J. (2005). *The obesity epidemic: Science, morality and ideology.* Oxon: Routledge.

Halse, C., Honey, A., & Boughtwood, D. (2008). *Inside anorexia: Bringing together the stories of people with anorexia and their families.* London: Jessica Kingsley.

Hutchinson, N., & Calland, C. (2011). *Body image in the primary school.* Oxon: Routledge.

McLeod, J., & Yates, L. (2006). *Making modern lives: Subjectivity, schooling and social change.* Albany, NY: State University of New York Press.

Office for Standards in Education (Ofsted). (2008). *Inspection report: 'Westwood'* [Anonymised reference]. UK: Crown Copyright.

Penney, D., & Chandler, T. (2000). Physical education: What futures? *Sport, Education and Society, 5*(1), 71–87.

Rich, E. (2011). 'I see her being obesed!' Public pedagogy, reality media and the obesity crisis. *'Health': An Interdisciplinary Journal for the Social Study of Health, Illness and Medicine, 15*(1), 3–21.

Rich, E., Evans, J., & De Pian, L. (2009, November). *Learning to be a healthy young woman: Body burdens and consumer culture.* ESRC Seminar Series: Young women in movement – Sexualities, vulnerabilities, needs and norms, Goldsmiths University, London.

Welch, R., McMahon, S., & Wright, J. (2012). The medicalisation of food pedagogies in primary schools and popular culture: A case for awakening subjugated knowledges [Special section]. *Discourse: Studies in the Cultural Politics of Education.*

Wright, J., Burrows, L., & Rich, E. (2012). Health imperatives in primary schools across three countries: Intersections of class, culture and subjectivity [Special section]. *Discourse: Studies in the Cultural Politics of Education.*

Health imperatives in primary schools across three countries: intersections of class, culture and subjectivity

Jan Wright[a], Lisette Burrows[b] and Emma Rich[c]

[a]Faculty of Education, University of Wollongong, Wollongong, NSW, Australia; [b]School of Physical Education, University of Otago, Dunedin, New Zealand; [c]Department of Education, University of Bath, Bath, UK

In this article, we want to focus on the impact of the new health imperatives on young children attending primary schools because the evidence from both our own and others work suggests that younger and younger children are talking in very negative and disturbing ways about themselves and their bodies. We see this in a context where in the name of getting in early, governments and authorities are targeting primary schools and primary school parents and children for messages about health and weight. Just as 'obesity' has become a global concern, we argue that globalisation of risk discourses and the individualisation of risk, the league table on which country is becoming the fattest have impacted on government policies, interventions, schools and children in ways which have much in common. In this article, then we argue first, that there *is* a problem (it is not one of children becoming fatter, but rather the way in which the ideas associated with the obesity crisis are being taken up by many children), and second, that the ways in which these ideas are taken up are not uniform across or within countries but depend on contexts: national contexts including, but not only, government policies and campaigns; and contexts within countries which vary with the social and cultural demographics of schools, in ways that are similar across countries.

Introduction

> I think there is a lot of pressure on yourself and thinking that your health and your future could all be depending on what you eat now. It is scary sort of, like ... (Maddie, Year 5, St Mark's Primary School).

It is not new that young people's relationships with their bodies are often troubled (see for example, Birbeck & Drummond, 2005; Burrows, Wright, & Jungersen-Smith, 2002; Evans, Rich, Davies, & Allwood, 2008; McSharry, 2009). This, however, is not the discourse that is taken up in government policies and health campaigns where there seems to be a singular lack of interest in how bodies are experienced and imagined from the point of young people themselves. Rather policy and campaigns are formulated in the context of a deficit idea of young people who are at risk to themselves and to the state because of their ungoverned/unruly behaviours and bodies (Evans, Evans, & Rich, 2002). An ubiquitous discourse that covers both children and young people is that of the 'obesity crisis' – that is, the idea that children and young people are at risk because of their increasing weight caused by sedentary behaviour and poor eating habits (Gard, 2008; Gard & Wright, 2001). In this article, we focus on the impact of this discourse, and what we call the health imperatives that flow from it, on young children attending primary schools in three countries – New Zealand, UK and Australia. The evidence from both our own and others' work suggests that younger and younger children are talking in very negative and disturbing ways about themselves and their bodies (Burrows, 2008; Burrows et al., 2002; Hutchinson & Calland, 2011).

Public concern over an 'obesity epidemic' has been manufactured and refracted in the media and politics of most western and increasingly non-western countries. Indeed, we argue that globalisation of risk discourses and the individualisation of risk, reflected, for example, in obesity league tables which claim to show which country is becoming the fattest (see Hope & Gardiner, 2010, as one example of many), have impacted on government policies, interventions, schools and children across many nation states and in ways which have much in common. In this article then, we argue, first, that there *is* a problem – and that it is not one of children becoming fatter, but rather the way in which the ideas associated with the obesity crisis are being manufactured and taken up by many children; and second, that the ways in which these ideas are interpreted and enacted is not uniform across countries, nor within countries, but rather depends on contexts. It depends on their 'emplacement' in the social and cultural contexts of schools and families as well as government policies and campaigns and on children's subjectivities, that is, the shape and appearance of their bodies and how they make sense of this.

Shilling (2010) suggests that in investigating the relevance of education to the ways ideas about bodies have been taken up in schools in the west there are two key issues to be addressed. The first is 'how we are to understand whether and how trends and processes external to the individual actually exert an influence on people's views, feelings, dispositions and actions' (p. 155). The second issue raises questions about 'how broad societal developments actually get *translated* into specific institutions via policies, messages and practices' (pp. 155–156). While we touch on the second issue in this article, it is the first with which we most engage: how have messages about health influenced views, feelings and dispositions of the children in the primary schools in our studies, and to a lesser extent their actions? This is not an easy task because dispositions cannot be simply understood as produced by school policies and programmes, or read from what teachers say and do with students (in their classrooms and elsewhere), or necessarily read from what students say and say they do. To be able to say something of substance about how social facts (including ideas) about health become part of someone's embodied experience requires a more extended engagement with children in different contexts. However, what we can do in this article is to examine how a large number of primary schoolchildren talk about health, and particularly the relationship between their talk and the meanings and practices associated with health in their specific school.

In addition, by looking more closely at two transcription texts produced from interviews with children from schools with very different social and cultural locations, we can say something about how the children's talk about health and their bodies is relational in a very personal way; how it is related to the intersection of the child's experience of their body with family relations, which in turn are shaped by the wider social and cultural context. This demonstrates both the predictability on some counts and the unpredictability on others of how children make sense of health messages and how they take these up. It demonstrates how their subjectivities, shaped by and through their many interactions with other people, texts and practices, influence the ways they make sense of their bodies and interpolate themselves into health and body discourses and practices.

Social class, health and the body

Our analysis suggests that social class as a concept does not travel easily across countries. As Ball (2006) writes: 'class is not the same everywhere . . . class meanings are inflected by culture and place' (p. 7). In the education literature in the UK and Australia, there has been a long tradition of explaining class inequalities in terms of disadvantage, influenced by neo-Marxist writing about the working and middle classes. More recently, those writing in the area of social class in education have drawn on Bourdieu and for some others, particularly in the UK, on Bernstein (for example, Evans & Davies, 2008). There has, however, been less attention to the intersection of race, ethnicity and social class. In New Zealand, in contrast, the starting point is often race in conjunction with the social and economic position of Maori and Pacifika peoples in New Zealand society (see, for example, Durie, 2005).

Although recent analyses have focused on 'income differentials' as precursors of 'health' (Germov, 2009; Pickett, Kelly, Brunner, Lobstein, & Wilkinson, 2005), in much of the mainstream health/health promotion research, social class often functions as the primary social determinant of health inequalities and healthcare disparities. However, this is often translated (rather reductively) into policy and popular consciousness through the media as the consequence of inappropriate (for example, single parent) family structures. Children's and families' choices are talked about primarily in terms of deficit; families purportedly do not know enough or do not care enough to educate children about appropriate food choices and exercise levels. Having nurtured the view that families/guardians do not take their responsibility seriously, schools and government agencies are then invoked as means of addressing the deficit through intervention. As Walkerdine writes, commenting on a chapter in the *Biopolitics of the Obesity Epidemic*:

> Poor people, [Murray] tells us, are thought not to make the right choices and so those have to be made for them. This presents us with the centrality of different modes of regulation for class and poverty, race and ethnicity, fat and thin. The already pathologized subject is not treated in the same way at all as a responsive and responsible subject (2009, p. 202).

Despite the many criticisms of social class analyses (Ball, 2006), we do not want to eschew a class analysis because it is difficult; rather, we want – following Compton (quoted in Ball, 2006, p. 6) – to explore 'a more flexible approach', one which takes into account demographics but which, like Evans and Davies (2008) sees social class (and we would add culture) as experienced in and by bodies often in very subtle but 'visceral' ways that cannot be simply correlated with, or explained by, demographics. The study described in this article was thus not so much interested in documenting health inequalities per se, but exploring the relationship between social class and culture and children's subjectivities. So while we ask whether the differences we see in how the children in the study talk about health and their bodies can in any way be explained in terms of social class and culture, we also ask what else beyond these categories. Following Butler (2004), we assume their subjectivities are not determined by, but are constituted *in relation to,* and also formed *in excess* of the categories of social class and culture; and not limited to singular positions in relation to health discourses.

Methodology

The data we draw on for this article come from a number of funded projects all investigating the impact of the policies and strategies associated with the obesity epidemic on schools and students. The study involved data collection in primary and secondary schools in New Zealand, UK and Australia. The schools in the study were selected first on the basis of social class demographics and second on the basis of ethnic diversity, with the intention of studying how social class and culture might have been implicated in the ways schools across the three countries re-contextualised popular, scientific and institutional meanings of health, and how social class might also be implicated in ways in which the children took up these ideas. In this article, only the data collected in the primary schools, specifically from children between 9 and 11 years of age, has been used. While the focus will be on the analysis of the interview data with the children in the schools, teacher interviews, field notes and documents collected from each school have also been used to provide context.

There were eight primary schools in total across the studies, three in the UK, two in New Zealand and three in Australia. In each school, between 10 and 12 boys and girls were interviewed in pairs ($n = 94$). The interviews in New Zealand and Australia used the same schedule of interview questions as their starting point; children's responses in the UK interviews were prompted by a set of cards with the words, 'obesity', 'body', 'school' and 'health'. All interviews were as conversational as possible with the interviewers working with the children's answers to help them elaborate on their meanings of health, the body and obesity. The interviews were all coded in QSR Nvivo. However, for this article while the various nodes have been used as a guide, all of the interviews from the three countries were read again closely by the first author to better understand responses in the context of the interview as a whole. This reading prompted the selection of two interview texts for a closer reading to answer the question: how were the children's subjectivities constituted in their talk and what could be made of the relational aspects of families, culture and social class?

The policy and syllabus context

In the past 10 years in the UK, New Zealand and Australia, the concern over what has been seen as increasing levels of childhood obesity have prompted government health campaigns and the funding of school-based initiatives in each country to avert the putative disaster. However, in New Zealand the election of a Conservative Government, and in the UK a Conservative/Liberal coalition motivated by more libertarian and individualist ideologies, has resulted in a shift away from what have been seen as 'nanny state' interventions, spending government funds on health promotion and social marketing programmes to a marketisation agenda where the expectation is that 'young people ... become more entrepreneurial and competitive'

(Roberts, 2003, p. 498). Some of the programmes which were in schools at the time of the data collection, for example, the six million dollar 'Mission-On' programme, regulatory requirements for schools to sell only 'healthy food' in canteens, youth websites set up to encourage more exercise and healthy eating have all been abandoned on the argument that the prior government was interfering in ordinary New Zealanders' lives. In the UK, there have been similar reallocations of funding with cutbacks in projects such as the Change4Life campaign. At the time of data collection, however, a health interventionist policy was still being promoted in both UK and New Zealand.

Australia and New Zealand have similar approaches to school health education through a health and physical education syllabus within the formal curriculum of the school. Both claim to make a contribution to the curriculum through a focus on the whole person and to be based on a broad notion of health 'that encompasses all aspects of an individual's well-being, inclusive of social, mental, physical and spiritual health' (New South Wales [NSW] Department of Education and Training, 2007, p. 5). Providing children with the knowledge to 'make informed decisions related to health and physical activity and to develop attitudes towards a healthy lifestyle' are central ideas in both syllabi. Further, both syllabi, at least on paper, endeavour to consider health-related issues 'in context', recognising the ways broader familial, community and cultural locations influence the choices and capacities young people can enact in relation to 'health'. Health-related fitness is a main credo of the both New Zealand and Australian syllabuses. Although it is emphasised that 'participation in regular physical activity is more important and more achievable for students than physical fitness' (NSW Board of Studies, 1999, p. 14), the purpose of physical activity both now and in the child's future is explicitly for health benefits. Children should be taught movement skills so that they develop the competencies to maintain a healthy active lifestyle in the future.

In the UK, while Physical Education is a statutory and examinable subject (except in independent schools), Personal Social and Health Education (PSHE) is only a 'suggested element of the curriculum'. Penney and Harris (2004) contrast the UK National PE Curriculum to that of New Zealand, particularly in relation to 'health'. They argue that an emphasis on motor skill acquisition and sporting performance, marginalises any exploration of health issues and that health in this context becomes a 'desirable inevitable outcome of involvement in organised sport' (p. 107). This 'narrow conceptualisation of health' is contrasted with the New Zealand Health and Physical Education (HPE) curriculum within which 'social, cultural, environmental and, most notably, critical discourses are visible rather than excluded or subordinated' (p. 102). For the purposes of this article, what the New Zealand and Australian HPE curricula include – and the UK does not – is a specific component of a key learning area which focuses on health. While PSHE looks like becoming a statutory subject in the UK schools in 2011, it is currently optional and can be and is taught by a variety of teachers and in a variety ways. At the same time, it should be acknowledged that the HPE in New Zealand and Australian primary schools is generally not taught by specialist teachers and the health component, in particular, is often assimilated across other areas or taught by outside school agencies such as Life Education. Life Education resources focus predominantly on assisting children and young people to make 'good' health choices, to avoid 'risky' behaviours and to understand how their 'bodies' work (Life Education Australia,

2010). While programmes like these share some of the intent of formal syllabi, the 'critical enquiry' emphasis of contemporary HPE syllabi is notably absent. What is common across many of the schools are intervention programmes specifically targeting healthy eating and exercise. The catholic primary schools in the UK were associated with the national 'Healthy Schools Project', and all of the Australian schools had at some point taken up 'Munch and Crunch', 'Munch and Sip' and 'Jump Rope for Heart', and the New Zealand schools, 'Push Play' and 'Jump Jam'.

The schools

The primary schools to be discussed in this article covered a range of demographics as indicated primarily by the populations of students on which they drew. In the UK, the two schools categorised as middle class were Fraser, a multi-cultural preparatory school and Westwood, a small catholic village school. The working-class school was Rosehill, a large multi-ethnic catholic school situated in an inner area of a major city with a large proportion of South East Asian immigrants. In Australia, population demographics and also indices of disadvantage (Australian Index of Relative Socio-Economic Disadvantage) were used in the selection of the schools. The middle-class school was St Mark's, a small catholic school with children from Anglo-Australian parents in largely professional and managerial occupations. Somewhere in between was Trimdon, a state primary school with children from families in professional and trade occupations, many from European (Italian and Macedonian) backgrounds. The school categorised as working class was St Claire's, a small catholic school with similar ethnic demographic to Trimdon, but also including children from Pacifika families. In New Zealand, the middle-class state school, Marivale, drew a student population primarily from Pakeha professional families. Toroa, in contrast, drew on a student population from Pacifika and Maori families, mostly in manual occupations. Labelling the schools in terms of social class was difficult, first because categorisation is in and of itself problematic, but also pragmatically in the use of terms with middle and working class common in the UK research, and low and high socio-economic status (SES) more common in Australian and New Zealand. We have chosen to use the terms working and middle class because these are more widely used in sociological and cultural analysis and because they, more so than SES, capture the notion of habitus or embodied dispositions that are 'constituted by a set of affectively loaded, social and economic relationships that are likely to strongly influence, if not determine and dominate, people's lives' (Evans & Davies, 2008, p. 200).

That schools are classed places is not disputed and was obvious in the ways the different schools approached the education of their children and the ways in which the teachers talked about the children. For example, Fraser, the primary preparatory school has particular children both in mind as its pupils and its graduates, and this is made quite explicit in school prospectuses and in the educational programme at the school. The same could be said of the teachers at Toroa who have the welfare of their Maori and Pacifika children high on their agenda and whose education programme reflects its high index of disadvantage in the New Zealand system.

Looking across all of the primary schools in the study, it has been much easier to demonstrate similarities in the middle-class primary schools and the ways children from these schools have talked about health, weight and their bodies. On the other hand, those schools which do not easily fall into the middle-class category were much more difficult to talk about in any general way. For the three schools that might be classified as 'working class' schools, the neat divide between working class and middle class just did not hold as a way of explaining how ideas about health were drawn upon by the students. It has been clear from the interviews that children's circumstances speak to family relations that do not fit neatly into predictions of a social class demographics, but rather are complicated by culture, parents' aspirations for their children, their children's health and the children's own experience of their bodies which are in turn socially and culturally mediated. The difficulty has also been to avoid the positioning of these schools as 'other' than middle class, because they do not fit into neat patterns of relations between school, home and student meanings of health.

The middle-class schools

At Fraser, the UK privately funded multi-cultural preparatory school, students were encouraged to work hard academically and take part in a range of extra-curricular activities. Health was strongly encouraged through a focus on sporting achievement, and health education was taught primarily through science, with some in PSHE. The teachers observed that overweight was not an issue at the school. From the perspective of the healthy schools coordinator, the role of the school was to guide and encourage the child, to prepare the child in ways which 'allow[s] them to have an active life, make sensible choices and be aware of things that they need to be aware of ... guidance on what you should eat, what you shouldn't eat, how much exercise you should do'.

Westwood, the small village school, took itself very seriously as a health-promoting school with a whole school approach to health education. Health education was delivered formally and informally across various aspects of the school, including science and PSHE, assemblies, and via the school involvement in the government sponsored 'Healthy School' Programme. The Physical Education (PE) coordinator reported that 'parents take the healthy schools seriously – provide healthy snacks all the time'. She said an aim of the School was to produce happy healthy 'all-round good people'. Again, overweight was not seen as an issue for the children at Westwood. Like Fraser, health promotion was closely associated with sport and physical activity, and government funding was used to bring in outside agencies to provide 'quality PE', which seemed to be mostly about bringing the teaching of sports such netball, hockey, tennis, badminton, as well as dancing into the school.

At the New Zealand school, Marivale, health and physical education were taught to meet National Administration Guidelines requirements around the development of movement skills and 'the promotion of healthy food and nutrition for all students' (New Zealand Education, 2010). Teaching about food in Year 5 was associated with a unit on what makes good learning, 'we spend a little bit of time talking about what foods help us learn better' (Year 5/6 teacher). The teachers did not see children's weight as an issue for children at their school, and there was no real concern about the school policing the school food environment. Indeed the principal thought this would be difficult with school fund-raising activities run by parents often taking the form of 'sausage sizzles' and chocolate sales.

The Australian school, St Mark's, was situated in an area well served by facilities, with a wide variety of community sports. The community was described by the principal as an 'active community' with the most of the children participating in sports and recreation activities outside the school. Although there seemed to be general agreement that there were few children who might be judged to be overweight or obese:

> I wouldn't have thought there'd be much of that (obesity) here, most of the kids seem pretty healthy and slim', the school had a very active healthy lifestyles agenda, promoted by one teacher, with health eating promoted through a 'Munch and Crunch' program, healthy canteen initiatives and 'Jump Rope for Heart.

The school also had a specialist physical education teacher shared with other schools including St Clare's.

Working-class schools

Rosehill, an inner city multi-ethnic primary school in the UK, was situated in an area lacking facilities and spaces for play, so exercise and diet were seen as the main health priorities of the school. Because of the perceived poor low levels of parental responsibility towards children's activity and health, this school saw its role very clearly in terms of modelling correct behaviour through its staff, thus made concerted efforts towards this by facilitating a 'staff fat club' with staff weigh-ins and many others were members of weight watchers. It also took a strong interventionist approach, adopting the view that the current health status of the students was assumed to have a future impact on their future lives and health. For example, children were no longer allowed to bring chocolate into school to celebrate a child's birthday, but instead were invited to 'bring a book for birthday rather than a box of sweets' (Healthy Schools coordinator). Children's diets were also monitored through lunch box inspections, and on occasions parents were contacted when lunch boxes were deemed to be 'just junk'. PE lessons involved heart rate measurements and students were encouraged to take part in a variety of sports despite not having their own sports field. External organisations were also brought into the school to deliver health education.

Children at Toroa primary school in New Zealand came typically from families where the adults had low-paid jobs and lived predominantly in government housing. Toroa was something of a poster-school for health promotion agencies, having achieved Gold status in the national healthy school awards delivered by New Zealand's Heart Foundation. It was inundated with policies and programmes focused on improving its children's health, its walls were graced with numerous posters promoting healthy food and physical activity, and pride of place was its Health-Promoting School trophy. The Education Review Office, an institution that examines the functioning of all schools in New Zealand, consistently reports Toroa as a school with a caring, whanau-style feeling and ethos (see also Burrow's paper in this Special Issue).

Like Toroa, St Claire's primary school in Australia celebrated diversity and placed a greater emphasis on social relations and community than on individual health behaviours. This is not to say that some of the teachers did not express a concern for the children's health in relation to their weight, nor that the school did not teach about 'healthy foods' and healthy behaviours, although this was mostly from the Life Education Unit. This, however, was not a prevailing theme in the school. The school had limited facilities for physical activity; it had a very small playground made smaller at the time of the study by its becoming a building site. The children were also being weighed for another health project.

Trimdon state primary school, sat somewhere between St Mark's and St Claire's in terms of demographics and Socio-Economic Indexes for Areas (SEIFA) and this is reflected in the students' responses. The school took seriously its commitment to multiculturalism and was also involved in an environmental initiative. The school was committed to encouraging children to participate in physical activity through offering a variety of sports. Teachers at the school did express a concern about the unhealthy food that came to school in lunch boxes, and saw overweight as an issue for a significant number of children at the school. The school used Life Education for health education and there were no obvious health intervention programmes at the school, beyond 'Munch and Crunch' for children in the early years.

What do the children have to say about health?

Across all countries and schools, the most likely first response, and the one most extensively elaborated, to questions of meanings about health was the connection between health and eating well and doing enough physical activity/exercise. Ideas promoted in the schools and in policy were 'well known' by the children – they made the appropriate and valued connections between physical activity, food intake and health. They separated food into good food (fruit and vegetables for the most part – rarely meat) and bad food/junk food (chocolate was high on the list and other foods that are regarded as high in sugar and fat). These simple associations were like a mantra. When asked about their own health, their evaluation generally mentioned their appearance, their level of fitness, or their behaviour – eating or not eating the right foods and getting enough exercise. Although the children at the two working-class schools in New Zealand and Australia came eventually to talk about health in these terms, their first responses were often less 'informed' and more personal. Reflecting some minor distinctions, New Zealand children also mentioned drinking lots of water and habits of hygiene that seems to have been part of the health messages to which they had been exposed. The following responses from Stacey and Jane (at Trimdon) have all of the elements common in so many of the answers:

Interviewer: What does health mean to you?
Jane: It means lots of healthy things to eat, exercise, all different things that other people think would be good, like apples, bananas and fruit and vegetables.
Interviewer: So is there anything that is not healthy then?
Jane: Well, there is lots of junk food like chocolate and ice cream.
Interviewer: What about you, S, what does health mean to you?

Stacey: Exercise, eat healthy fruit and do jogging and running and keep fit.

These shared understandings in Australian, New Zealand and UK schools reflect the similarities in government run campaigns, a similar syllabus, similar parental pre-occupations and the influence of the Life Education in New Zealand and Australia.

Talk about health often moved on to talk about weight or appearance. Many of the children understood health as a three-pronged relationship between eating, exercise and weight/shape. For many, this relationship was deterministic – what a person eats and how they exercise determines their weight/shape, which in turn determines their health. For most the problem was about overweight but other discourses have also had an impact with some children talking about the undesirability of being too thin.

Children at Fraser in the UK reported undertaking various regulative practices to monitor their own weight, for example, weighing themselves and using pedometers regularly. For example, in the following exchange Miele talks about personal behaviour in relation to managing her own weight:

Miele: Eat good food and exercise everyday 'cause it will burn off your carbs and make you fitter.

Interviewer: Why do you think you do those activities and try to eat healthily like you do? What are the main reasons?

Miele: Well, I don't want to be fat. I don't want to be thin either, I just want to be average size [...] I've lost quite a lot of weight since I've been eating my bananas and everything and doing my dancing.

Interviewer: How do you feel about that?

Miele: I feel really happy with myself because I've gone on a bit of a diet. This morning I didn't have any breakfast [...] I've got one on my bike. It tells me how many meters I've done in a day and when I clip it onto my belt it will tell me how many steps I've done in a day [...] I just want to know if I need to do more. I try to improve it, so say if I've done fifty in a day I'd do like seventy, and it also tells me how many carbs you've burnt off and how many stones you've lost.

And from Aisha at Marivale in New Zealand:

Interviewer: Yeah, how do you know these things, who's taught you about weight and shape, where have you heard about that sort of thing?

Aisha: My parents.

Interviewer: Ahh, your parents, OK.

Aisha: They worry about it all the time?

Interviewer: Do they?

Aisha: Yes.

Interviewer: What do they worry about?

Aisha: Like overweight and like looking big and yeah.

Interviewer: So they're worried that you might be, or they worry about just generally?

Aisha: Generally.

Interviewer: Yeah so they talk about it lots?

Aisha: Yeah.

The pre-occupation with weight, and particularly with being thin that was evident for some of the children at the middle-class schools (but less promoted by their schools) was also evident in how the children at Rosehill talked about weight. The strong health imperatives at this UK working-class school were evident in children's concerns about their changing weight and body shapes and all those interviewed reported engaging in practices of surveillance such as regularly checking their weight. Many of the students drew on emotive language when describing how *fearful* they were of becoming obese, for example, Dinesh said that he 'bad dreams about becoming obese', and Mark: 'Like a stage of growing and sometimes I'm scared what's gonna happen'. These fears drew on projected ideas about what life would be like in (a not so distant) future when, if they were to be put on weight, they would be bullied, unable to move, lazy and no longer able to play sport.

The fear of putting on weight in the future was particularly the case for the middle-class children for whom, healthy eating and exercise were not issues that they saw or their schools saw as affecting them now. The threat of being overweight in the future, however, could be a potent source of anxiety. For example, Marnie's (St Mark's) response in the following quote was to a question about her sources of information about *health*:

> I think that one of the biggest things that I get a big message I don't want to be overweight and stuff is when I go walking in the City and you see those people that are a bit overweight and I just don't want to end up being like that (St Mark's, female student).

And from Leon at Fraser in the UK in response to the question: 'Is there anything outside of school that makes you think about your body?':

> Well, sometimes when you're walking down the streets, you sometimes see quite big people. Then you think would I want to look like them and you think like that, and you think about where they might go to eat and stuff and then you think that could be me, so you eat more healthily (Fraser, Male student).

There was very little talk about weight at the two Australian working-class schools, St Claire's and Trimdon. At Toroa, weight was spoken about from immediate experience, either in relation to families and the risk of illnesses such as diabetes or the students' own personal experience of being teased about their weight. Being heavy or bigger than they would like to be was a personal experience for some of these children, the boys as well as the girls. At the same time being skinny was just as much a problem. The children at St Claire's and Toroa were also likely to speak with much less certainty about health knowledge and to be less dogmatic and prescriptive about health behaviours. For example, when Bo, from Toroa talked about his own health, he said that he was trying to get his 'health [weight] a little bit lower to try and make my size more um like skinnier yeah. Um so trying to eat like vegetables and healthy food that can help me . . . 'cause my weight is like whooa big'. He was, however, much less clear about how he was going to do anything about this although he said he thinks about food a lot and sometimes does exercise and stretches. He said he learns about what to eat from TV but he also talked about how his mum, dad and sister were 'kind of getting bigger' which he was worried about and how his dad sometimes exercised on the 'Ab King Pro' they have at home.

When it came to specific questions about 'obesity', the children from the middle-class schools were able to define it, linked the word with over-eating and insufficient exercise and in some cases with moral ideas such as laziness. We would suggest that for children in the middle-class schools, knowledge about 'obesity' formed part of the formal knowledge taught in science, PSHE, and at Marivale from its status as a health 'project' topic. Knowledge about obesity thus became part of their knowledge about the world – there is an 'obesity epidemic', and children are getting more and more obese. However, obesity is not something with which they are personally familiar – it is not evident amongst the people they know, rather it is associated with those others who are less regulated in the ways they eat, who eat 'takeaways' and whose parents care less than their own. As Meile says:

> They probably haven't raised their child healthy, 'cause some parents just let their children eat and eat and eat and if you eat and eat and eat you get a brain problem where your brain's just telling you to keep eating (Fraser, female student).

The children at Rosehill, Toroa and St Claire's were far less familiar with the technical term; most needed the term to be explained to them. This suggests that the schools did not directly use the ideas of the 'obesity epidemic' as a way of talking about children's health, but rather approached health in ways more associated with changing personal behaviour (see Burrows, in this Special Issue).

Subjectivity as mediated by social class and culture

This article thus far has provided a general sense of how the children talked about health and bodies across the schools and countries with some indications of differences between schools. In this last section of the article, we want to use a closer analysis of interviews with children from two schools, the middle-class school, St Mark's, and the working-class school, Toroa, to trouble some of these general-isations. While a more extended engagement with the girls whose interviews are used below would help us say more about the relationship between their biographies and the way they talked about health and weight in their interviews, what they had to say provides some ways of understanding their subjectivities at the time of the interviews. This in turn points to the ways people engage with health ideas are not simply predictable from class and social position, although the interviews also show the ways in which these play out in the children's subjectivities. All of the girls in this section describe themselves as overweight and their subjective experience of their bodies, formed itself in relation to class and culture, impacts on how they responded to the questions about health and bodies.

Mere

The first of the children is Mere, a female student at Toroa in Year 5/6. She was interviewed with a friend Ani, however, it is Mere who does most of the talking in the interview. When asked about how she feels about her health, Mere responds she feels 'OK'; asked why, says 'I don't really eat that much junk, like most of the time we eat like', cause I have this calendar thingy and it shows what to eat like cheese, fish and yeah'. In what follows it becomes evident that the calendar provides information about what to eat and that she records on the calendar what she eats on a daily basis. It is something she does with her dad who 'tests' her to see if she is 'still ok' and then decides whether she needs something more or less. It is something that just she and her dad rather than her other siblings do together. Dad can also be cajoled into buying her treats such as a pie, something not allowed when her stricter stepmother is around. Mere later speaks about her stepmother, with whom she seems to have a difficult relationship. The meaning of the calendar for Mere seems to go well beyond the recording of food; it seems to be as much about a special activity shared with her father as with a concern to monitor her food intake.

At the same time, Mere's weight is a problem for her. When she and Ani are asked if they think very much about their shape and weight, the two respond:

Ani:	Yes.
Mere:	Yeah. *[Laughing.]*
Interviewer:	What makes you think about it?
Mere:	Um, I think about it too many times because I'm sick and tired of being called names.
Mere:	Yeah, I hate it when people tease me.
Interviewer:	So does that happen at school?
Mere:	Yeah a lot.

Mere described being called names by children at school, her cousins and being belittled by her stepmother. She and her friend also described how they feel they are judged because of what they eat:

Interviewer:	Right, and what sorts of things is it that they're saying that make you annoyed?
Mere:	Ohh, stupid things, like I'd be like, ahh, you fat bastard, and like all that, ahh, look at you, shame, this person is much better than you. And then they will like list them. They say, see this is what you should eat, this is what you have got to eat this, and that.
Mere:	And when like we order stuff, they say that we're eating bad, and that.
Ani:	When we order.
Mere:	When we order pies, and they'd be like, see no wonder why you're fat. See, man, you should start eating what I'm eating, if they're eating an apple or that.
Interviewer:	So how does that make you feel then?
Ani:	I feel really sad.
Mere:	I feel really put down, like a put down.
Ani:	I don't feel like coming to school anymore when people do that.
Mere:	Yeah to me, I just want to go over there and you know start a fight.

She also described how she is judged by her stepmother:

Like she 'cause um like I'm saying like she doesn't know the inside of me like I can jog and you never know I might become thin. And on the outside she just judges us on the outside. She's like, ahh look, you fat thing. Man, if my daughters were here they'd show you what to do and then you could probably be like them. And she would tell me to go upstairs and bring her bag, and she brings a photo out of her daughter; she's very skinny like that, and I'm thinking, ohhhh.

After an exchange about how she copes with being teased about her weight, she says 'it hurts me inside' but then goes on to say: 'I don't care 'cause I'm happy with myself anyway...Yeah I am happy to be the person who I am'.

Mere talked about how she does try to lose weight: 'Once I tried [recording on the calendar] out I started to feel good about myself'. On one hand, it is clearly a constant struggle – knowing/wanting to eat 'healthy' – on the other hand, she loves the foods that she knows are likely to put on weight and derives considerable pleasure from eating these. When asked whether she and her friend eat anything that is unhealthy, they both laugh and say 'Yeah'. When prompted on what they like, Mere's answer is 'Pies, lollies, chocolate, fizzy drink'. When asked how she feels when she has it, she responds: 'I feel very good because like most of the time it's just healthy, healthy, healthy, that's all that's in my head, healthy, healthy, healthy. It's really good to get it out'.

In all of her talk about health, school barely gets a mention, despite the 'saturation of health messages' at Toroa. Her feelings about her weight seem to come more from the way other people make judgements about her and tease or bully her about it, than a visceral desire on her own part to be thin – indeed thinness is regarded as something you would want to avoid, it is not culturally desirable, it is to be like a 'broom stick'. Her information about healthy eating comes from the calendar, some from television and some from her stepmother, though messages from school should not be discounted. What features most frequently in her interview are her relations with family – with her father who helps her with her calendar and buys her treats, her stepmother who judges her but with whom she also goes walking, and cousins who tease her. School rarely features except as a place where she is judged. Mere cannot ignore her bigger body, but it is through her relations with others, whom she is in some ways able to dismiss, that she experiences her body as a 'problem'. These all get caught up in the relations of bodies, food and feelings about self. She does not interpolate herself into obesity discourses and seems generally able to resist being interpellated, although she recognises it when it happens – 'they judge me on what I buy from the canteen, what I eat'. She recognises the imperatives to eat 'healthy' food, but she also rejoices in treats and the food she likes; she is ready to take on those who would judge her; she does not accept their right to judge.

Lisa and Kate

The second mini-case is derived from an interview with Lisa and Kate, two Year 5 students (age 10) at St Mark's. Lisa's and Kate's interview was chosen because unlike the other children interviewed at their middle SES school, they describe themselves as 'big' and 'overweight'. Like the other boys and girls at their school, Lisa and Kate responded to the question about what health meant to them, with 'healthy eating, exercise' and 'keeping fit'. Kate's response to 'can you describe a healthy person' was with some giggling 'Well, someone who is not big', elaborating this with a gesture that described 'a big fat person'. When asked to add to their answer Kate says 'Well someone who is not big, someone who eats healthy. Lisa you have a go'. Lisa adds 'Like someone like that lady [*walking by*] who is walking and exercising and keeping fit'. When pushed a little further to elaborate 'are there other things that people might have or do in their life', Lisa responded 'Well maybe they are nice and bubbly and have a lot of energy and they have lots of self-esteem and like who they are'. When they were asked to rate their own health, Lisa say 'six or seven'. Her explanation for this is a good example of how many of the children at this and the other middle-class schools talked about their family in relation to managing their health:

Because mum always gives me heaps (of) healthy things to do, and sometimes we walk to school and we go for bike rides with my dad, and we always eat healthy meals during the day or we get little treats, and sometimes we choose little chocolate bars from the cupboard.

However, as the interview goes on, it becomes evident that Lisa and Kate regard themselves as 'big' girls, bigger than their 'tiny' peers. They have trouble fitting into dance costumes and they are teased about their size and feel 'out of place':

Lisa: Well last year I was getting really, really big and all my clothes weren't fitting and then I tried them on and I had to go and get all new ones because I got really, really big. So I've been trying to get smaller but it's really not working so much now; it's not working. I used to be small, but now I just got big since I've been here.

It seems it is not so much that these girls are overweight but that they feel big in comparison:

Interviewer: Don't you guys think that maybe you are just growing a bit sooner than some of the other kids in your Year, or something.
Kate: Yeah, but all the other kids in the Year are really small.
Lisa: They are all like skinny [runts] so you walk next to someone.
Kate: And they are quite short.
Lisa: Yeah they are all skinny.
Interviewer: And you feel quite big when you are around them because everybody else is really short.
Lisa: And you feel like you are out of place and you shouldn't really be there with them if you are too big.

While it is not clear whether Lisa is overweight from any measurable perspective, from her perspective she is, and she stands out as being different:

Yeah, like here you really don't feel like you fit in because there's like tiny people, like I don't know one person in Year Five who is overweight that is a girl, except for me.

Kate is also trying to get smaller; they both find it hard work but at the same time refuse any feelings of guilt. Lisa, for example, declares at the end of this first exchange, with what seems like some pride or perhaps a challenge: 'Eating is my hobby':

Kate: Yeah, like sometimes I try really hard, I go out for walks with my mum and then I try really hard at dancing.
Lisa: And then the next day you just go.
Kate: And then the next day I'm really tired and my shoulder blades hurt and I just couldn't be bothered to do anything else.
Lisa: So we sit in the lounge and eat.
Kate: Yeah, so you sit on the lounge.
Lisa: Eating is my hobby.

Later on in the interview when asked whether they get 'any information from TV about health?' Lisa responds, perhaps provocatively:

Yeah, I watch TV twenty-four hours seven days a week when I'm not playing sport or at school, or I go on the computer and watch videos on You Tube, but I don't watch healthy eating ones.

Kate also takes what seems to be an irreverent attitude to health knowledge and injunctions to be healthy:

Yeah, we had to make this food pyramid and we were always talking about healthy stuff and our health and sometimes it gets really annoying. You are trying and like everyone is telling you, like Miss N is saying to be healthy at home and then Miss N will say to you 'if you guys aren't healthy [. . .] I eat this today, I eat this today' it makes you feel like you are not doing enough.

Because from Kate's perspective what is the point?

Kate: Well, yeah because like, well no, not really, people, like we bring to school like all the big people like me, we bring to school really healthy things and then all the little people are bringing to school like chocolate mousse and [. . .]
Lisa: Like chips and . . .
Kate: And they are just eating it all around you and then they just stay as skinny as a little stick and if you ate that, whatever they ate, you would become . . . [left unsaid].

And later in the same interview:

Interviewer: It sounds like you guys take a fair bit of notice of what other people eat. Do you think people watch what other people eat in this school?
Lisa: Yeah, because you kind of feel like because one of my friends she eats healthy at school, because I went over to her house and she eats healthy at school and I think because she expected me to eat bad things because I'm big, she thought that I would normally eat chocolate freddo frogs and stuff but I don't. So at her house in the afternoon we have like, she asks if I want a chocolate freddo frog and she'll say 'yeah I want one' and then she asks again and I'm like no. But then she kind of expects me to.

On the one hand, there is considerable humour in the way Lisa and Kate talk about health messages, the strictures associated with being healthy – 'I watch TV 24/7', but at the same time they feel out of place and that they should eat less and exercise more in order to be 'smaller'. However, this seems an impossible task, because if you give in you could become 'like a ten tonne truck'. Lisa and Kate seem to have each other and a supportive family, they seem less troubled by this than some of the children that we cite above who may or may not be overweight but fear the risk. They refuse to be positioned as bad subjects, they refuse to feel guilty, at least in this interview. They recognise the discourse but refuse to be interpellated by it – 'I watch TV 24/7'; 'eating is my hobby'; they also recognise when others try to interpellate them – 'she [a friend] expected me to want to eat chocolate'. They reject the imperatives to monitor themselves, to stick to the kind of regimes that would lose weight, first, because they do not seem to work anyway, second, it is unfair (skinny people can eat what they like), and third, it is no fun.

In both these cases, the children's physical bodies, their size in particular, shape how they engage with the ideas about health and the body. There is, however, no neutral body – in both cases the way the children make sense of their bodies is mediated by class, culture and probably gender, although this is not pursued in this article. Bodies can only be talked about and we would argue interpreted by their owners through language. Bodily feelings and emotional responses once brought into language become socially constituted: the big body is not in itself a source of shame; it only becomes so when others see it as shameful, whether these are others close to the child (who themselves are drawing on discourses to make this judgement); or messages from the media (which provide the means to evaluate the body and instructions in how one should feel about it). Mere and Lisa and Kate come to understand their bodies in the context of these social messages but also through material circumstances. Lisa and Kate tower over their peers. How they interpret this, however, is social; if they were boys this would perhaps be a good thing; but for girls they are 'out of place'. Their largeness is further interpreted in terms of discourse of overweight and instructions of how to avoid it or to lose weight.

There does, however, seem to be a qualitative difference between the ways Lisa and Kate and Mere live with imperatives associated with health and the body which we argue are at least in part associated with social class and culture. Our readings of Lisa's and Kate's transcript prompted a chuckle, Mere's prompted feelings of sadness. Lisa and Kate seem able to directly take on what others have described as a neo-liberal discourse of self-management (Vander Schee, 2008); one that requires them to act in disciplined/self-disciplining ways in relation to food and activity. They make an object of the discourse and use humour to distance themselves and their own enjoyment of life from its injunctions. They do this from a position where they seem to be secure in a family environment that provides 'heaps of' healthy food and where physical activity is part of their family life. Mere, on the other hand, seems much more vulnerable. Her feelings about her body are inexorably intertwined with her family and peer relationships, most of which do not make her feel good about her bigger body. Although 'healthy, healthy is in her head', her everyday life makes it difficult to put this into practice. She does not have the ordered life which supports Lisa and Kate; rather, her relationships and material circumstances leave her vulnerable to feelings of shame and self-hate.

Conclusion

For all of the children in the study, across the three countries, the ways they engaged with health messages were always and inevitably mediated by body shape and size (that is, by the sense of their own corporeality in time, place and space) and importantly by class, culture and gender. They were also mediated by family relations and by the ways schools took up and transacted health imperatives, which were themselves mediated by class and culture. The extent to which many of these messages were congruent with each other, was evident in the certainty and the consistency with which the children talked about health as related to eating 'good' food (fruit and vegetables) and exercising. This also points to the ubiquity of the obesity discourse and its related translation into policy, media and school syllabuses and practices in the UK, Australia and New Zealand (and comparable countries).

On the other hand, the children's talk about weight and obesity we would argue was rather different for the children from the middle-class schools as compared to the working-class schools, particularly where schools had taken up the project of the health-promoting school. For the middle-class schools, the teachers and the children within those schools, obesity was associated with those 'others', the children who ate takeaway foods and whose parents did not care enough – a coding for children from home unlike their own, working-class children. While the children at the middle-class schools might learn about 'obesity', this was not directed at changing the children at these schools, where obesity was 'not a problem'. While these were often experts in healthy behaviours, their anxieties about eating were more likely to be about avoiding becoming like those abhorrent 'others'; this in turn required a close monitoring of their own behaviour. Some of these children were already engaging in self-regulating behaviours, monitoring their diets, in a context where they were assisted by parents, had ready access to 'healthy' foods and dispositions in part formed by a fear of becoming/looking like 'those others'.

In those working-class schools in which health promotion was taken to be part of the school's mission, the children were constituted as both the subject of obesity discourse and the target of behaviour change strategies. These children were understood to be directly at a risk of becoming overweight and intervention was required to prevent this. For some of these children, these messages created anxieties in contexts over which they did not always have control, over choices about food and access to physical activity, the constant message to be 'healthy healthy healthy' when their material and social circumstances made it difficult to comply. In this way, we argue schools and teachers re-contextualised obesity discourses in ways which maintained those hierarchies which are implicit in the discourse itself – hierarchies which link the material bases of children's lives to potential and imagined futures. For the children in these schools, health was clearly associated with weight, because this is what they have been taught, but for young people like Mere, while they feel bad about being fat, they also seem to feel that this is not within their control.

Our purpose in this article has been to suggest through examples some relationships between social class, culture, schooling and the ways children talk about and experience health, weight and their bodies. In doing so, we hope we have avoided pathologising those children and their parents who do not comply either through their behaviour or their embodiment with morally loaded health imperatives around food and weight. We also want to argue that there are 'risks' in the obesity discourse and its associated imperatives for how children feel about themselves and their bodies; risks we suggest that are different for children of different social class and cultural locations. These are risks that schools and governments could well reflect on in developing policy, curriculum and interventions for schools and children.

References

Ball, S.J. (2006). The necessity and violence of theory. *Discourse: Studies in the Cultural Politics of Education, 27*(1), 3–10.

Birbeck, D., & Drummond, M. (2005). Interviewing, and listening to the voices of, very young children on body image and perceptions of self. *Early Child Development and Care, 176,* 579–596.

Burrows, L. (2008). "Fit, Fast, and skinny": New Zealand school students 'talk' about health. *JPENZ, 41*(3), 26–36.

Burrows, L., Wright, J., & Jungersen-Smith, J. (2002). 'Measure your belly': New Zealand children's constructions of health and fitness. *Journal of Teaching in Physical Education, 22*(1), 29–38.

Butler, J. (2004). Changing the subject. In S. Salih & J. Butler (Eds.), *The Judith Butler reader* (pp. 325–356). Malden: Blackwell.

Durie, M. (2005). Race and ethnicity in public policy: Does it work? *Social Policy Journal of New Zealand*, (25), 1–11.

Evans, J., & Davies, B. (2008). The poverty of theory: Class configurations in the discourse of Physical Education and Health (PEH). *Physical Education and Sport Pedagogy, 13*(2), 199–213.

Evans, J., Evans, B., & Rich, E. (2002). Eating disorders and comprehensive ideals. *Forum for Promoting 3–19 Comprehensive Education, 44*(2), 59–65.

Evans, J., Rich, E., Davies, B., & Allwood, R. (2008). *Education, disordered eating and obesity discourse: Fat fabrications.* London: Routledge.

Gard, M. (2008). Producing little decision makers and goal setters in the age of the obesity crisis. *Quest, 60*(4), 488–502.

Gard, M., & Wright, J. (2001). Managing uncertainty: Obesity discourses and physical education in a risk society. *Studies in Philosophy and Education, 20*(6), 535–549.

Germov, J. (2009). The class origins of health inequality. In J. Germov (Ed.), *Second opinion: An introduction to health sociology* (4th ed) (pp. 85–110). Melbourne: Oxford University Press.

Hope, J., & Gardner, D. (2010). Now Britain is the fattest country in Europe (and the fifth most overweight in the world). *Daily Mail.* Retrieved from http://www.dailymail.co.uk/news/article-1314807/How-Britain-fattest-country-Europe-fifth-overweight-world.html#ixzz1LFOOkGPp

Hutchinson, N., & Calland, C. (2011). *Body image in the primary school.* London: Routledge.

Life Education Australia. (2010). *Primary school program.* Retrieved from http://www.lifeeducation.org.au/what-we-do/our-program/13-primary-school-program

McSharry, M. (2009). *Schooled bodies? Negotiating adolescent validation through press, peers and parents.* Stoke on Trent: Trentham Books.

New South Wales Board of Studies. (1999). *PDHPE syllabus: Principal's package.* Retrieved from http://k6.boardofstudies.nsw.edu.au/files/pdhpe/pdhpek6_principal.pdf

New South Wales Department of Education and Training. (2007). *Personal development health and physical education K-6 syllabus.* Retrieved from http://k6.boardofstudies.nsw.edu.au/files/pdhpe/k6_pdhpe_syl.pdf

New Zealand Education. (2010). *National administration guidelines.* Retrieved from http://www.minedu.govt.nz/NZEducation/EducationPolicies/Schools/PolicyAndStrategy/PlanningReportingRelevantLegislationNEGSAndNAGS/TheNationalAdministrationGuidelinesNAGs.aspx

Penney, D., & Harris, J. (2004). The body and health in policy: Representations and recontextualisation. In J. Evans, B. Davies & J. Wright (Eds.), *Body, knowledge and control* (pp. 96–111). London: Routledge.

Pickett, K., Kelly, S., Brunner, E., Lobstein, T., & Wilkinson, R.G. (2005). Wider income gaps, wider waistbands? An ecological study of obesity and income equality. *Journal of Epidemiological Community Health, 59*, 670–674.

Roberts, P. (2003). Contemporary curriculum research in New Zealand. In W.F. Pinar (Ed.), *International handbook of curriculum research* (pp. 495–516). Mahwah, NJ: Lawrence Erlbaum Associates.

Shilling, C. (2010). Exploring the society-body-school nexus: Theoretical and methodological issues in the study of body pedagogics. *Sport Education & Society, 15*(2), 151–168.

Vander Schee, C. (2008). The politics of health as a school-sponsored ethic: Foucault, neoliberalism, and the unhealthy employee. *Educational Policy, 22*(6), 854–874.

Walkerdine, V. (2009). Biopedagogy and beyond. In J. Wright & V. Harwood (Eds.), *Biopolitics and the 'obesity epidemic'* (pp. 199–209). London: Routledge.

Neither good nor useful: looking ad vivum in children's assessments of fat and healthy bodies

Valerie Harwood

Faculty of Education, University of Wollongong, Wollongong, Australia

Fat bodies are not, fait accompli, bad. Yet in our international research, we found overwhelmingly that fat functioned as a marker to indicate health or lack of health. A body with fat was simply and conclusively unhealthy. This article reports on how this unbalanced view of fat was tied to assessments of healthy bodies that were achieved by *the act of looking*. Despite the efforts of health education in each of the three countries in our study, children and young people cited the act of looking at bodies to assess health and when did they arrived at the conclusion that fat on bodies is unmistakably bad. The article uses a Foucauldian analysis of medical perception together with material from Conrad Gessner's sixteenth century *Historia Animalium* to outline how the children in our study placed great reliance on information about fat to make almost exclusively visual assessments of health. The article makes the case that, despite a great deal of health education in schools, these judgments reveal a tendency for children to make incorrect assessments of health.

Introduction

Interviewer: How do you know what a healthy body is?
Student: For me a healthy body is someone who doesn't have much weight on them, say maybe an extra five kilograms on them of actual fat. I'm not really quite sure of the rest. (Interview with male student, aged 16 years, Australia)[1]

In the interview extract above, fat is considered a possibility in a healthy body. As I will go on to outline, this comment on fat and health was one of the rare statements that emerged from our research with children and young people in Australia, New Zealand and England. Overwhelmingly the data revealed how fat functioned as a marker that served to indicate health or lack of health: absence of fat on bodies meant health and its presence almost always meant lack of health. In sum, a body with fat was simply and conclusively unhealthy. By contrast, our interview participants granted greater leeway to fat that is consumed. Consumed fat could be permissible and was not pejoratively bad; that depended on quantities and type, with eating too much fat by people perceived to be fat the fundamental issue. This unbalanced view of fat was tied to assessments of healthy bodies that were achieved by *the act of looking*. Despite the efforts of health education in each of the three countries in our study, children and young people cited the act of looking at bodies to assess health, and when they did they arrived at the conclusion that fat on bodies is unmistakably bad.

Fat on bodies is not, fait accompli, bad. There are anomalies with fat such as the problem of lean people being at greater risk of atherothrombotic diseases (Andreotti, Rio, & Lavorgna, 2009). Such instances point to the inaccuracy of typecasting fat as always bad and question painting it as of no use or value. Recent research on brown adipose tissue (BAT) adds strength to the argument for a balanced view of fat on bodies. BAT is referred to as the 'good fat', with white adipose tissue the bad fat (Rutkowski, Davis, & Schere, 2009; Tan, Manchester, Fuentes-Broto, Parades, & Reiter, 2010). This good fat has qualities that include burning energy:

> Cells in brown fat, considered a 'good fat' for its energy-burning qualities, contain many little droplets of lipid, each with its own power source, which enables heat generation. Babies have ample stores of brown fat at birth as a defense against the cold, but it mostly disappears, as adults have very little of this calorie-burning tissue. (Johns Hopkins Medical Institutions, 2011)

This is a useful counter to the bad and non-useful claims, even taking into account the issue that dichotomy between the good and the bad may prompt further health moralising (Gracia-Arnaiz, 2010; Le Besco, 2010). This is suggestive of the need for a nuanced understanding of fat and how fat is connected with health, but is far from how children and young people understand and recognise fat on bodies.

In our study, the children's and young people's reliance on looking for fat on bodies to assess health pointed to two important problems in their understandings of health. The first is the considerable lack of knowledge about healthy bodies. Our participants seldom described what might occur inside bodies that could contribute to a healthy body. Comments that drew on physiological change within a body were atypical, 'if you exercise more your blood vessels keep their shape and if you eat too much junk food they can get clogged up ... and you get heart attacks and that' (Male, 10 years, New Zealand). Repeatedly, fat was discussed as neither good nor useful and the way this was determined was via looking. This overriding reliance on looking as a means to assess health is the second problem, in so far as this is the predominant way that they produced their understandings of healthy bodies.

The purpose of this article is to consider these two problems in order better understand how the children and young people made health assessments. Drawing on Foucault's (1994) analysis of medical perception, my contention is that the children in our study used a particular form of looking to make their assessments and that this form of looking was treated with special emphasis that achieved authority. Interestingly – and by way of building a useful analytic juxtaposition – the person who was the first to discover BAT is also famous for introducing to Natural History extensive use of naturalistic pictorial representations of animals (Ashworth, 1996). In the sixteenth century, the famous natural historian Conrad Gessner marked out the authenticity of his pictures by including the descriptor 'ad vivum' (from life) (Panese, 2005).[2] This descriptor served to convey how representations were achieved and simultaneously assert their veracity. In this article, I draw on this work from the Renaissance to examine the children and young people's assessments of health. This comparison creates an opportunity to examine how children and young people could employ looking to definitively assess health. I thus use Gessner's work in the Foucauldian sense to shed light on contemporary practices of looking and how these portray truths about fat and healthy bodies. My intention is to draw on a style from Foucault's (1994, 2006) investigations of medicine and psychiatry as well as to take account of Gilman's (2011) cogent point concerning the study of images in the history of medicine. As Gilman observes, it is important for historical work on images to 'come much closer to their underlying epistemic value in any given system' (p. 73). A Foucauldian approach with its attention to historical sources can highlight particularities of truths, and in so doing, bring attention to the epistemic values present in children's decisions about health (Harwood, 2011).

The article begins with discussion of how the children and young people used 'looking' to assess health and what it was that they looked at to make these assessments. This leads to my discussion of Conrad Gessner's use of 'ad vivum'. In this section, I refer to historical images from Gessner's sixteenth century compendium *Historia Animalium* as well as his discovery of BAT to build my analysis of the children's mode of looking. Lastly, working with the juxtaposition of Gessner's ad vivum, I discuss the children's understandings of health and their idiosyncratic looking ad vivum. The ad vivum methods Gessner used to gather information to represent creatures provides a point from which to stretch back to consider a different way of looking, employed more than four centuries ago. As I hope to convey, considering this Renaissance work alongside findings from our study – as well as accepted contemporary scientific practices – can point to the problematic knowledge produced via children's and young people's contemporary way of looking ad vivum at fat.

Assessing health by looking at fat

One of the notable findings from our recent international study was the large degree to which children and young people reported that they 'assessed by looking'. The fieldwork reported in this article is from an international project funded by the Australian Research Council (ARC) and the UK Economic and Social Research Council (ESRC). This project investigated how prevailing attitudes and practices relating to 'obesity', food, physical activity and health are embedded in school policy and in the curriculum, actions and attitudes of teachers and how this affects teachers and students in the ways they understood health, their bodies and theirselves.[3] Fieldwork for the project was conducted with nine primary schools and six secondary schools across Australia, England and New Zealand, and included State schools and Independent Schools from a mix of geographic and socio-economic areas.[4] Data collected totalled 2636 surveys (Australia: 900; England: 1176; New Zealand: 560), 212 interviews (Australia: 82; England: 90; New Zealand: 40) and detailed field observations.[5]

To make assessments of health, the children and young people relied on looking at bodies. The Australian and New Zealand surveys asked the question, 'How do you know if a person is healthy?' with the responses conveying that children and young people were confident in assessing health, and could achieve this via looking at how others looked. In the cohort of 15–16 year olds at one Australian secondary school only one student stated that you need to 'ask them' and only one said, 'I don't know'. The children simply had the conviction that there was no need to ask questions in order to test for health. In the English surveys a minority of 15 out of 1176 responses described assessing health as difficult or not possible. This prominence of looking is surprising given the availability in schools of devices such as scales as well as the function of these in providing scientifically authorised assessments (Cambrosio, Keating, Schlich, & Weisz, 2009; Rabinow, 1992). The surveys in England revealed '38% of students had been weighed at school' (Rich and Evans, 2009, p. 16), a figure that suggests the children might possibly more often select weighing for gauging health. This, however, was not the case with their health assessments being based on how a person looked.

Assessments based on looking used three key categories: shape, movement and intake, an identification process that is explicit in the interview excerpt below:

Interviewer: We're looking at these four categories – health, body, school and obesity. Could you tell us what immediately comes to mind when you see those four categories?

M: Exercise, shape, food. (Male, 12 years, England)

Across the different sites, we repeatedly found participant responses that relied on looking to assess health, with patterns consistently based on categories of shape, movement and intake. The most frequent responses that defined health in each of these categories is summarised in Table 1. When such responses linked health and obesity, they relied assessment of fat, and, as I go on to outline, these were based on shape, movement and intake.

Shape

Shape was an important means for assessing health. In the English interviews, children were shown different pictures of people and asked whom they may or may not like to look like. The responses connected shape with health, such as 'her dress doesn't fit her; she's big and that's so tight for her' (Female, 11 years, England). When shown a picture of a man measuring his (large) waist, children commented that 'he don't look that healthy' and explained this was because 'the measure fits around his whole belly' (Female, 11 years, England). The New Zealand and Australian surveys included the question, 'Do you think a person's shape or size has anything to do with their health?' Of the 148 primary students who responded, 68% of students described 'shape' as related to health. The children demarcated shapes in terms of two options: fatness or thinness, with fatness connected to health far more than thinness or skinniness. Height counted little as a shape, with few mentioning tall or short. While there were comments about the size of stomachs or evidence of muscles as indicators of health, large shapes were the predominant indicator of fatness. Health could thus be determined if fatness were absent (and to a much lesser degree, thinness). In one of the Australian secondary schools, 51% of the

Table 1. Assessing health by looking: categories and criteria.

	Shape	Movement	Intake
Healthy	Non-fatness	Exercise, physical activity	Does not affect shape
Non-healthy	Fatness	Lack of movement	Affects shape

male students aged 13–14 described health in terms of 'the way they look', with this appearance being judged in terms of body shape, as well as weight and fat.

Attention to shape as an indicator was likewise evident in responses to the Australian and New Zealand survey question, 'have you ever thought you needed to get thinner?' Responses to this question were influenced by gender and by age, with 'yes' responses varying between older and younger boys. In the primary/inter-mediate Australian and New Zealand schools, 46% of girls answered 'yes', compared to 20% of boys (153 responses). For the older students this percentage increased, with 58% of the female secondary school students and 34% of the male students responding 'yes'. When asked 'how health is assessed', the younger students tended to focus on body shape, weight, fatness and skinniness, and older students included indicators such as body image and appearance. Older secondary students' responses suggested that they were concerned to be thin and at the same time aware of their appearance to those around them. In this regard, it is not the case that shape decreased as a measure of health; rather other indicators were added to and consequently extended on an existing repertoire of shapes for gauging health. Indicators such as body image could thus be linked to a barometer of shapes that had been established at an earlier age.

'Tone' was another shape that was held to be important. As with other shapes, tone equalled health and could be assessed easily by visual inspection. Two female students discussed this in one of the interviews, explaining that:

> Being toned is quite good, it looks quite good and it looks like you eat healthily and it looks like you are happy but it just look like they feel more comfortable with who you are. I associate being thin with not being comfortable with who you are and really insecure. (Female, 16 years, England)

Students related fatness and obesity to putting individuals at risk of illness, as well as using the terms alongside one another. One Australian secondary school student remarked, 'Health can be anything as long as you are not actually sick or unhealthy like obese or anything' (Male, 13 years, Australia). These perceptions of shape were not necessarily used in isolation and would often be linked with important evidence amassed from observation of movement and intake. In practice this meant that children could look for health by detecting the relationship that they perceived between the presence or absence of fat and movement.

Movement

Health was also assessed through movement, which, like shape, was tied to fatness or obesity. Results from three of the questions in the English survey reveal the importance placed on movement for gauging health.[6] In these surveys, respondents had the opportunity to select or record more than one option. The frequency of responses provides a means to compare across the choices, such as between diet, well-being or exercise. In the question about 'what being healthy means' students were asked to write their response (they could provide more than one). Movement (exercise or physical ability) was the most frequent choice, with a frequency of 988 responses and intake rated second, with a frequency of 886 responses. Shape (the body) and well-being both rated third with 356 responses. Other interpretations scored significantly lower: positive self-perception, 44 responses; social, 27 responses; mental ability, 45 responses; and lifestyle, 70 responses. In the survey question that asked about 'the most important things that someone can do to stay healthy', diet rated higher than exercise, with diet receiving 1279[7] responses and exercise 981 responses. One of the survey questions specifically asked students about how they gauge health: 'I can tell a person is healthy because ...'. For this question, the body had the highest frequency with 880 responses compared to movement, which had 591 responses. Intake had 255 responses, which was almost equalled by well-being that had 253 responses. In the English survey only 15 responses indicated that it was *not* possible to tell if a person is healthy, and a lack of bullying (no one makes fun of you) had only one response. These survey results suggest the extent to which children and young people rely on movement as well as body shape and intake as indicators of health.

Lack of movement meant lack of health, and was again linked to fat and obesity. One method of assessing health, therefore, was to look for movement. As one child explained, 'You look at them kind of they might be kind of big, like you can tell cause they might not be able to run far' (Female, 11 years, New Zealand). These children also described how such unhealthy individuals become:

> Puffed and everything, and that sometimes their face and like their eyes are kind of all droopy if they've been smoking their teeth can be and their legs are fat. *[Laughs]* (Female, 10 years, New Zealand)

Another young person explicitly connected movement with weight, stating health could be gauged by 'the person's weight, reaction, if they're tired in class or if they are failing school or fitness' (Student, 14 years, Australia).

The relationship between fatness and movement meant that children could quickly assess health in terms of fatness and conclude the remedy is to exercise. This line of thought is exemplified in the following quote, where a young person describes her reason for avoiding the television show *The Biggest Loser*:

> Well, I don't really watch *The Biggest Loser* or anything because I know if you see the people and then you compare yourself to them and you're like I'm as fat as them or something then you go out and even if you're not that fat you might exercise more even if you don't need to. (Female, 13 years, Australia)

This description provides a good example of the way sources from contemporary visual culture are used by children and young people to gauge not only health, but to assess themselves.

Intake – the end of epicureanism?

Enjoyment of food was seldom mentioned by the children and young people. Rather, food was discussed in terms of its capacity for outcomes such as affecting shape or determining energy or in relation to types and quantities of food consumed. The results described above show how in the English survey intake was rated second to movement for defining 'what healthy means'. As a key site for food, the school canteen was frequently mentioned with discussion focusing on selling the correct types of food. This reflects the emphasis schools place on the canteen controlling the types of foods consumed. Student comments picked up on this emphasis with students using words such as 'force' to explain how eating is moderated in their school, 'they do try and force eating right with the canteen and stuff' (Male, 16 years, Australia).

Children also described how they or others would watch the content and quantity of intake. Observation and vigilance could be acute, as evidenced in this description of a child's endeavours to avoid surveillance:

Interviewer:	So what sort of stuff do you guys bring for school lunch?
M:	Sometimes I don't bring it because I am too shy to bring it.
Interviewer:	OK so you don't bring anything at all? What makes you feel shy?
M:	Um, eating too much.
Interviewer:	Right, yeah the other kids watching or just yourself?
M:	Um, myself. (Male students, 10 years, New Zealand)

Children and young people rarely described how they ate, whether they shared food or described tasty or delicious food. This focus echoes Klein's (2010) observation about the American relationship to food, where a focus on science is at odds with Epicurean ideals. Klein explains that 'health for the Epicurean is more a matter of art than of science, more an aesthetic than a biological question' (p. 20). The children's and young people's views were far removed from concerns with food as art or aesthetics. Food was almost always linked with an understanding of the science of food concerned with health, fat and obesity.

Attentiveness to shape, as well as movement and intake patterns could also be used to detect mental problems. An Australian Year 11 student applies this connective logic to explain how he assessed a person's mental state:

You think you are healthy, physical appearance I guess. Usually it depends on attributes as to how healthy a person could be. A healthy body is you can talk about their mental state. If they don't look too stable then you would question that a little. Ask questions mainly, just ask, like just have a look, sit back and watch them to see what they are like ... you look for physical, see how they cope, just walking around and how active they are through the day. (Male students, 16 years, Australia)

With fatness, thinness and tone so intricately tied to gauging health, it is not surprising that obesity was wielded as a measure of pathology or sickness. This again points to how health (even mental health) is considered to be assessable via the procedure of 'looking'. To explain how this process of looking can be understood I begin by turning to consider the ad vivum of Conrad Gessner, the Renaissance natural historian who discovered BAT.

Ad vivum

... nec pinguitudo, nec caro ... [neither fat nor flesh]. (Gessner, 1551, p. 842)

Brown adipose tissue, 'the good fat' was discovered by Conrad Gessner, who noted it was *nec pinguitudo, nec caro* [neither fat nor flesh] (Gessner, 1551, p. 842). This discovery was made in a somewhat similar way to present day scientific procedures, via dissection and direct observation of the alpine marmot (*Marmota marmota*).[8]

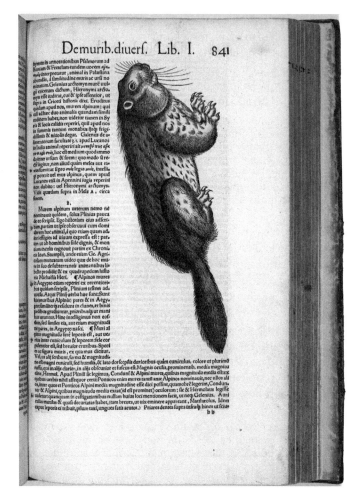

Figure 1.   Marmot, Gessner (1551) *Historia animalium,* p. 841. Source: Cambridge University Library, N.1.19. Reproduced by kind permission of the Syndics of Cambridge University Library.[9]

The illustration of the marmot and the surrounding text (Figure 1) is taken from Gessner's *Historia Animalium*. Similar to all of the entries, this contains a picture and extensive textual references that span numerous pages. These entries include details ranging the names of the animals, regions inhabited, appearances, sounds, diets as well as 'fables and folklore' (Ashworth, 1996, p. 19).

Given that dissection and direct observation were used to discover the substance that Conrad described as 'neither fat nor flesh' (later known as BAT), it would appear logical to assume that this was the mainstay of Gessner's method. This assumption, however, overlooks the varied procedures Gessner employed to gather information ad vivum (Kusukawa, 2010). 'Ad vivum' translates as 'from life' (Speake, 1999), which for Gessner did not stipulate recording from direct contact with the creature itself.[10] From this perspective ad vivum meant 'either having them drawn himself or accepting from trustworthy friends pictures similarly drawn' (Kusukawa,

2010, p. 307), with information that supplied these illustrations coming from sources that included 'artists, broadsides, books, and manuscripts' (p. 307). This marks a substantial difference between the methods used to collect and represent information in the *Historia Animalium* and those used in twenty-first century life science.

At first glance, *Historia Animalium* is startlingly unusual. Illustrations of mythic, domesticated and exotic creatures are placed next to one another in an impressively large and detailed catalogue (see Figures 2–4). The wide variety of sources used to produce depictions of animals in the *Historia*, sources that, while cited as ad vivum, did not depend on the manner of observation integral to contemporary life sciences. Two apposite examples are the unicorn and sea monster (Figures 3 and 4), both of which were derived from reliable sources and based on Gessner's extensive research into the knowledge of the animals of his day.

The *Historia Animalium* has five-volumes[11] and contains over 4500 pages and is regarded one of the first compendiums of its kind.[12] While the books are extraordinary in size and content, it is arguably the beauty of the illustrations that has made them especially famous. In this compendium, Gessner endeavoured to compile every creature known at the time, seeking to 'report every little thing said about any animal' (Pinon, 2005, p. 249). Each of these volumes was designed as a 'dictionarium' where 'such a presentation is easily followed and renders it possible for the reader to learn all that he requires of an animal with minimum of trouble' (Gessner, cited in Fischer, 1966, p. 278). To accomplish this monumental task, Gessner drew on reports made from his own experience of animals and the reports of others (Pinon, 2005) and '[r]arely was direct experience or observation the sole criterion for including an animal, while the existence of a textual description was' (Kusukawa, 2010, p. 306). The ad vivum of Gessner could be characterised as one

Figure 2.   Rabbit, Gessner, *Historia Animalium*, I, p. 394. Source: Courtesy of the US National Library of Medicine.

Figure 3.   Unicorn, Gessner, *Historia Animalium*, I, p. 781. Source: Courtesy of the US National Library of Medicine.

where the assertion of authority of direct observation was predicated on the author's direct experience, with direct experience being inclusive of processes such as textual description as well as seeing the animal itself. In this sense, the ad vivum has a

Figure 4.   Sea Monster, Gessner, *Historia Animalium*, IV, p. 175. Source: Courtesy of the US National Library of Medicine.

particular meaning for the time of Gessner; one that is achieved through a process of observation from life that can include his own experience (such as with the marmot and the discovery of BAT), as well as the direct experience of textual references of creatures such as the unicorn. For this reason, the unicorn, the sea monster and the satyr can be true for Gessner – without his ever having to have directly observed them.

The illustrations in the *Historia Animalium* are accessible and striking but the text is not, being only available to readers of Latin. While no exact translation of the original work exists,[13] accounts of specific entries offer a glimpse of the textual content. Ashworth (1996), for example, draws on a translation of the entry on the fox to outline the many details provided. As indicated earlier, these range from physical descriptions to the inclusion of 'folktales and myths'. Reference to the latter could be interpreted by contemporary standards as a sign of the unreliability of the *Historia Animalium*. On this premise:

> ...one might choose to believe, as many commentators have, that Gessner was simply a lousy natural historian; that for all his humanistic fervour he patently lacked the common sense to discriminate between fact and fiction. (Ashworth, 1996, p. 20)

Against this appraisal, Ashworth (1996) suggests that 'Gessner used every available thread because he was trying to weave the richest tapestry possible' (p. 20).

While the unusual collections of animal representations distinguish the *Historia Animalium* from contemporary scientific works, I suggest that the difference is instructive for analysing how the children and young people in our study made truthful assessments of fat and health. To ask, for example, how it was possible for representations of unicorns, sea monsters and rabbits to be considered truthful, light can be shed on both the way in which knowledge was construed at that moment and in that culture. This question also requires consideration of how Gessner secured descriptions of these creatures, and why, at this time, these descriptions were acceptable.

This is not to put forward the claim that the young participants in our study replicated the methods used by Gessner. Rather, it is to consider Gessner's work and approach as a means to gain a better understanding of the way in which the participants in our study looked at bodies to assert a kind of ad vivum authority which they employed to make conclusions about fat and health.

Our respondents did not just provide detailed accounts that wove, as Gessner did and to paraphrase Ashworth (1996, p. 20), 'the richest tapestry possible'. Their tapestries were meager by comparison. While this may be so, the tapestries that were described reveal a good deal about the ways our participants told truths about health and fat and the means by which this truth was arrived at, namely 'looking'. This I contend is useful for understanding how children and young people use looking to make their truths about fat, health and healthy bodies.

Looking ad vivum to assess health

Looking ad vivum at information on shape, movement and intake was the way students assessed health. Many of their responses include the word 'look', with reports that they know if a person is healthy by 'looking at them' by 'how they look', 'the way they look' or that they could assess health 'by looking at their figure and seeing what they eat' (Year 10 student, Australia). When juxtaposed with Gessner's ad vivum it can be argued that the labels 'looked' or 'looking' provided substantial authority for the children's and young people's assessments. The phrase 'I looked at them' functioned as a statement of authority (what I am calling looking ad vivum).

Taking this juxtaposition further it is evident that Gessner searched out many sources to produce accounts of many animals. Here the children differ significantly, for what cannot be found in their accounts is a breadth of perspective. There are simply glaring omissions in their summaries of what makes a healthy body and how fat is not good and not useful. For instance, while they may express moderation in relation to consumption, their accounts vary greatly between what can go into their mouths and that permissible on a healthy body. Unlike Gessner, their assessments of health are brief and formulated on limited information. Compared to Gessner's numerous canvassing of sources, sparseness is the most notable feature of the accounts that we collected.

The children and young people's accounts and ways of looking at health and fat also differ from a contemporary scientific gaze. Most noteworthy, they concentrate on only on exteriors. This is not the case in the twenty-first century representation of BAT (Figure 5).

The illustration 'hBAT in Adults and Infants' (Figure 5) portrays a gaze that reaches to interiors and pinpoints the anatomical location of hBAT. Describing the capacity of the clinical gaze to penetrate its object, Foucault's point is not that it saw

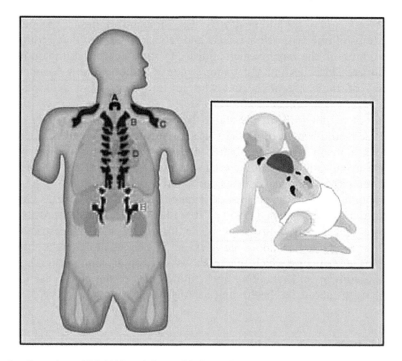

Figure 5.   Location of hBAT in adults and infants. Source: Enerbäck (2010). Reprinted from Cell Metabolism, 11/4, Enerbäck Human brown adipose tissue 248–252, Copyright (2010), with permission from Elsevier.

its object with more precision, but rather it was the effect the gaze had on what it saw. The clinical gaze in this sense is 'bringing them nothing more than its own light' (Foucault, 1994, p. xiii). This meant that 'the residence of truth in the dark centre of things is linked, paradoxically, to this sovereign power of the empirical gaze that turns their darkness into light' (Foucault, 1994, p. xiii). The hBAT illustration bears the hallmarks of such a scientific clinical gaze and also functions to deliver the message of accuracy. This is because diagrams such as these emphasise the precision secured via visual inspection and as such, add to an already powerful visual culture of the science of health (Gilman, 2011).

This depiction differs quite markedly from both the exterior gaze produced by the children and young people's looking ad vivum. It is also quite different from the report of the marmot in *Historia Animalium*, where illustrations were integral for chronicling creatures but the location of BAT (neither fat nor flesh) within the marmot remained unseen.[14] These differences underscore the degree to which looking ad vivum by the children and young people is out of step with contemporary health knowledge practices. Unlike the scientific drawings commonly made available in education or in the media (Bender & Marinnan, 2010), rarely did looking encompass description of what might lie below the surface – or suggest that healthy bodies are connected to what is happening inside. In other words, ad vivum looking of children and young people occurs so strongly in a culture replete with diagrams that probe below surfaces of things to reveal hidden structures that it points to significant issues with the perception of bodies. This I suggest is a finding that raises questions concerning the outcome of health initiatives that target obesity. The reliance on looking ad vivum thus reveals a good deal about the emphasis that imperatives of health and obesity have on the cultural worlds of students.

Although taking from life to assess health meant accessing the range of sources that offer information about health and obesity, it is important to take a cautionary approach to assuming that students devour such messages uncritically. As Burrows (2010) argues in her discussion of eating and exercise programs in New Zealand, it is not necessarily the case that children will follow messages as they are conveyed or intended. Indeed, they can at times disrupt health imperatives and ask questions, actions which 'elucidate children's capacity to modify the "truths" to which they are exposed and to disrupt taken for-granted assumptions about what constitutes good or healthy food' (Burrows, 2010, p. 246).

If children make modifications and disruptions to health messages about food, the question needs to be asked, what about how they assess health and the notion of the healthy body? Unlike the above, the assessments by the children in our study modified truths in so far as they were inaccurate, interpreting health messages to an extreme. To offer an assessment where fat could be useful and not all bad would demand a different engagement with health messages that would require momentous shifts in looking ad vivum at shape, movement and intake. It may even be the case that this particular emphasis on looking is the product of health messages.

Capacity for disruption might also need to take into account the effect of lay epidemiology. Following Frankel, Davison, and Smith's (1991) line of argument, the emphasis on shape, movement and intake could be linked to perceptions of candidacy for fatness and obesity.[15] This observation lends insight into the difficulties of conceiving of health differently, especially the degree of influence that the visual has in the meaning-making of health (Gilman, 2011).

The conclusion that fat is neither good nor useful, together with the reliance on looking as prima facie method, means that we need to pay attention to the influence of visual interpretations in children's and young people's assessments of health. In the interview excerpt below, visual interpretations of shape, movement and intake are brought together by students to make assessments:

S   We're the fattest nation.
C   That is the first thing that comes to my mind when I think of it. You hear Australia is now the fattest nation in the world.
S   I think it's definitely from the media like we hear about it. So obviously that is how we heard about it. I guess you see it, like you see overweight people and stuff and you think it is getting more of an issue like with little kids. (Female student, 14 years, Australia)

In this explanation, the information came from both the media and 'seeing it' for themselves. The young women then provide a detailed example:

S   You see a little kid at the beach with their parents and they are feeding them hot chips and they are already overweight and you are like what is this doing for this child, like their self-esteem is going to be low when they're older and they are going to learn these unhealthy habits. So you obviously see it and you hear about it and like I think it is just all around us all the time. (Female student, 14 years, Australia)

This description does not stop at providing an assessment of intake and shape in a child, but also speculates about the child's unhealthy future. Using lay epidemiology (Davison, Smith, & Frankel, 1991), this 'little kid' could be viewed as a prime candidate for ill-health as opposed to a child who is assessed as non-fat and who does eat 'hot chips'. The latter child would not be seen as a having the same candidacy for ill health. In this way, health perceptions premised on the visual inspection for fatness produce inaccurate health assessments.

The concept of ad vivum can be used to capture these idiosyncratic ways that children and young people use specific visual cues to authoritatively assess healthy bodies. Over and over what stands out is the veracity achieved by looking at the source, which are shapes, movements, intakes. This reference to the process of looking can be considered a contemporary action of an ad vivum practice in the sense that it conveys a connection between the child selecting the source from life and using this as the basis of their authority. The practice is reminiscent of Panese's (2005) account of changes in Renaissance scientific drawings where Gessner inserted additions on pictures such as 'ad vivum expressus' (expressed from life). In this period, such additions became a 'label of distinction and quality' (Panese, 2005, p. 71) serving to distinguish works via the acknowledgement of source. On reflection, it could also be the case that citing 'I looked at him/her' or 'I can tell be looking' function as a label of authority for assessing health. This observation points to the need for interpreting children's claims of looking as wielding an authority, perhaps far more than may have been previously acknowledged.

It is interesting that in many ways the children and young people in our study drew on a modern medical rationality described by Foucault (1994, p. xiii); one that 'plunges into the marvelous density of perception, offering the grain of things as the first face of truth, with their colours, their spots, their hardness, their adherence'.

What is confounding is that while they deploy a clinical gaze, they do not produce clinically informed reports (for example, the conclusion that health is absence of fatness is inaccurate). They do not draw on clinical tools and devices, such as scales, nor do they delve below surfaces to the extent we might have expected. We are more likely to discover contemporary clinic-inspired depictions when they evaluate fat and food. When they speak of body fat, we are uncannily taken to an image of exteriors that are oddly more similar to those of Gessner's Renaissance marmot circa 1551 (and not of hBAT, circa 2010).

This focus on looking, and more specifically looking from life, is dominated by visual and discursive assemblages (Deleuze & Guattari, 1987) of health-obesity that include scientific discourses on obesity amongst a plethora of sources that give meaning to shapes, to movement to intake. These include schools, media, public health policies, peers and family (Burrows, Wright, & McCormack, 2009; Wright, Burrows, & Rich, 2012) as well as images of obesity that have a rich history (Gilman, 2010). Intake, for example, is subject to heightened censorship by schools (Welch, McMahon, & Wright, 2012) that not only exerts controls on what children consume but influences what they *take from life* to mean health. The assemblage is one means for describing the culture from which the children and young people source their information about health. One of these influences on perceptions, the media, was evident in many of the responses, in both surveys and interviews. In the English interviews, for instance, participants were shown three media health headlines and asked which one stood out. In one interview two children chose 'Child Obesity has Doubled in Ten Years' and explained 'this was the more serious' (Female, 10 years, England). In another interview conducted in England, two students discussed a children's show that featured 'obesity':

R: On Blue Peter one of the presenters was obesity for a day and he described that it was really hard to be on the streets when people were looking at you and maybe when you go into shops it feels embarrassing to buy-
G: Clothes-
R: Big clothes and other people, some other people are maybe looking at you thinking...(Female students, 8 years, England)

Reliance on media were at times troubling, with young people drawing on media representations for their knowledge even when they were engaging in a level of critique:

I don't think it's real fair to say that they're not real. Obviously in magazines, with all the air-brushing and stuff we perceive them to be pretty amazing, but as people, they're probably you know, quite healthy and good looking as such. (Female, 16 years, England)

Even with this critique of techniques such as 'airbrushing', the status of the non-obese who are viewed as thin, 'healthy and good looking' are the means to assess health.

Teachers in our study commented on the influence of the media and children's perceptions of health. This is evident in the quote below where a teacher describes one of her colleague's classroom activities:

Well J did a really interesting thing with her class; she got them to cut out things in magazines that they thought were healthy. And all of the kids cut out thin people; if you're not thin you're not healthy. (Female primary school teacher, New Zealand)

This description indicates the teacher's sensitivity to media representations as well as revealing how these aspects of contemporary visual culture are integrated into the classroom. Media representations were also influential on teachers, as one of the teacher respondents explained:

...the media certainly influences me a lot, there's no doubt about that. What I'm hearing on television and reading in the newspaper, you know, I certainly base a lot of what my feelings are on obesity on that. (Male primary school teacher, Australia)

Reminiscent of the children and young people, teachers were also influenced by shape, making observations about children's shapes in a variety of ways. One comment by a primary schoolteacher stands out. This teacher made a comparison between current students and her former school. The former students were described as 'fine physical specimens' (Female primary schoolteacher, New Zealand), a choice of language and objectification that places young bodies squarely in the particular kind of gaze that is at once clinical but not the type of 'below surface clinic' that we might expect.

These examples of teachers' perceptions point to the ways visual and discursive assemblages of health-obesity are integrated in schools. Children and young people draw on these when they look from life to assess health. It is useful here to pause to consider how Gessner's ad vivum is interpreted. Kusukawa (2010, p. 322) maintains that understanding Gessner's ad vivum demands appreciation of the visual culture of that period:

The lesson for us here is that images from the *Historia animalium* were part of a larger visual culture encompassing live, dried or partial specimens, drawings, prints and illustrated books, in which direct observation of the original was not yet a strict requirement for its images to be 'ad vivum'.

Looking, for Gessner, entailed surveying and collecting a variety of information on a range of creatures, a catalogue of truthful representations documenting descriptions of sea monsters, rabbits and marmots. This, however, is not the case with the findings from our study. Looking ad vivum by the children and young people supported the creation of impoverished tapestries to explain healthy bodies. It would be a mistake to grant these the status of truth in the same way that historians of science have assessed Gessner (Ashworth, 1996; Kusukawa, 2010). Rather, what might be more useful is to appreciate how the new health imperatives impact on children's and young people's assessments of healthy bodies. It is, therefore, crucial to recognise that reliance on looking ad vivum needs to be accounted for as an issue to recognise if health understandings are to be improved.

Conclusion

Children and young people report their truthful representations of visual and discursive culture when they look ad vivum. They take up certain information about fat and this enables them to *look* at health. When they do this they are reporting on understandings of health that pick up on what Gilman (2011) points out is a momentous visual attention to obesity. This is an important insight for grasping how a generation of children are now interpreting health in terms of looking ad vivum at the surfaces of fatness. These findings underscore the importance of recognising that when children and young people assess health they are producing understandings heavily orientated by ad vivum looking. Equating fat with health, together with the authority of looking, provides the rationality from which it is possible to look at shapes, at movement and at intake and be completely confident this will reveal health. This is also the means by which children and young people can include or exclude themselves and others as candidates of ill health. This in itself has significant implications for education initiatives that seek to prevent ill health. If we are not satisfied with these misunderstandings, the point is not to turn to correct the children, but rather, to dutifully consider how and from where they are assessing health, to critically examine how they are being taught to rely on looking and to act to rectify the misunderstandings that are created in the manner that this looking ad vivum is applied.

Notes

1. All names and identifying information have been removed and replaced where necessary with pseudonyms or initials.
2. Therefore, important was Gessner's identification of this structure that contemporary scientific discussions of BAT reference the discovery (Cannon & Nedergaard, 2008; Enerbäck, 2010; Tews & Wabitsch, 2011). Now termed as 'the good fat', BAT it is reported as a preventive for obesity in scientific journals (Chao, Yang, Aja, Moran, & Bi, 2011), with international newsprint media reporting it as a scientific breakthrough in the battle with obesity (Gray, 2009; Paddock, 2011; Wang, 2010). BAT even has its own Facebook page.
3. Funded by ARC and ESRC Grants. ARC Linkage International Social Science Collaboration 2007–2010 The impact of attitudes and policies relating to obesity and related health issues on school policy and practices: J. Wright, V. Harwood, UOW, Australia; L. Burrows, University of Otago, New Zealand; E. Rich, & J. Evans, Loughborough University, England.
4. For reasons of space, social class, gender and ethnicity are not treated separately in this paper. In depth analysis of these subjectivities in terms of the ad vivum of students is the focus of a forthcoming essay. See Wright et al. (2012) in this special issue for discussion of class. For detail on fieldwork in England see Rich (2011).
5. Surveys were with primary and secondary school students. Interviews were with teachers (including deputy principals, principals) and with primary and secondary school students. Number of interviews – Australia: 22 teacher interviews, 62 student interviews; England; New Zealand: 10 teacher interviews, 30 student interviews.
6. These were questions 21, 22, 23 on the survey instrument developed for the English cohort. A different format of the survey instrument was used in Australia and New Zealand.
7. This number is higher than the number of participants (1176) because subcategories allowed respondents to select more than one answer within each category. Numbers are indicative of frequency of response and allow comparison of the numbers of responses across possible answers.
8. This creature inhabits alpine areas in Europe, including the mountainous areas in Switzerland in proximity to where Gessner lived and worked (Fischer, 1966).
9. While reference to Gessner's discovery can be found in contemporary publications discussing BAT the marmot illustration in *Historia Animalium* has to my knowledge remained unpublished.
10. One hundred years later the famous *Histoire des animaux* (Perrault, 1671) was based solely on direct observation and dissection (Guerrini, 2006). This book can be accessed online at http://www.archive.org/details/mmoirespourserv00bzgoog.

11. The fifth was published posthumously, with the volumes.
12. Volume V was published posthumously.
13. An edited translation with additions was made into English by Edward Topsell in 1658, titled *The history of four-footed beasts and serpents: describing at large their true and lively figure, their several names, conditions, kinds, virtues... countries of their breed, their love and hatred to mankind, and the wonderful work,* London: Printed by E. Cotes for G. Sawbridge, T. Williams, and T. Johnson.
14. It is the case that illustrations were made of interior of humans and creatures prior to the eighteenth century, however, these differ in many ways from latter scientific drawings, including style, naturalism and representation of object and subject (Hall, 1996).
15. My thanks to the anonymous reviewer who pointed to the connections with lay epidemiology.

References

Andreotti, F., Rio, T., & Lavorgna, A. (2009). Body fat and cardiovascular risk: Understanding the obesity paradox. *European Heart Journal, 30*(7), 752–754.

Ashworth, W.B. (1996). Emblematic natural history of the renaissance. In N. Jardine, J.A. Secord & E.C. Spary (Eds.), *The cultures of natural history* (pp. 17–37). Cambridge: Cambridge University Press.

Bender, J., & Marrinan, M. (2010). *The culture of the diagram.* Stanford: Stanford University Press.

Burrows, L. (2010). 'Kiwi kids are Weet-Bix™ kids' – Body matters in childhood. Sport. *Education and Society, 15*(2), 235–251.

Burrows, L., Wright, J., & McCormack, J. (2009). Dosing up on food and physical activity: New Zealand children's ideas about 'health'. *Health Education Journal, 68*(3), 157–169.

Cambrosio, A., Keating, P., Schlich, T., & Weisz, G. (2009). Biomedical conventions and regulatory objectivity: A few introductory remarks. *Social Studies of Science, 39*(5), 651–664.

Cannon, B., & Nedergaard, J. (2008). Developmental biology: Neither fat nor flesh. *Nature, 454*, 947–948.

Chao, P.-T., Yang, L., Aja, S., Moran, T.H., & Bi, S. (2011). Knockdown of NPY expression in the dorsomedial hypothalamus promotes development of brown adipocytes and prevents diet induced obesity. *Cell Metabolism, 13*(5), 573–583.

Davison, C., Smith, G.D., & Frankel, S. (1991). Lay epidemiology and the prevention paradox: The implications of coronary candidacy for health education. *Sociology of Health and Illness, 13*(1), 1–19.

Deleuze, G., & Guattari, F. (1987). *A thousand plateaus: Capitalism and schizophrenia* (B. Massumi, Trans.). London: University of Minnesota Press.

Enerbäck, S. (2010). Human brown adipose tissue. *Cell Metabolism, 11*(4), 248–252.

Fischer, H. (1966). Conrad Gessner (1516–1565) as bibliographer and encyclopedist. *The library, XXI*(4), 269–281.

Foucault, M. (1994). *The birth of the clinic: An archaeology of medical perception.* New York: Vintage.

Foucault, M. (2006). *History of madness* (J. Murphy & J. Khalfa, Trans.). Abingdon, Oxon: Routledge.

Frankel, S., Davison, C., & Smith, G.D. (1991). Lay epidemiology and the rationality of responses to health education. *The British Journal of General Practice, 41*(351), 428–430.

Gessner, C. (1551). *Historiæ animalium lib. I* [studies on Animals]. Tiguri: Apvd Christ. Froschovervm.

Gilman, S.L. (2010). *Obesity, the biography.* Oxford: Oxford University Press.

Gilman, S.L. (2011). Representing health and illness: Thoughts for the 21st century. *Journal of Medical Humanities, 32*(2), 69–75.

Gracia-Arnaiz, M. (2010). Fat bodies and thin bodies. Cultural, biomedical and market discourses on obesity. *Appetite, 55*(2), 219–225.

Gray, R. (2009). Obesity: Why fat itself may be the answer: Reprograming body fat is the key to weight loss, not working out says Richard Gray. *The Daily Telegraph.* Retrieved from http://www.telegraph.co.uk/science/6083234/Health-warning-exercise-makes-you-fat.html

Guerrini, A. (2006). The 'virtual menagerie': The histoire des animaux project. *Configurations, 14*(12), 29–41.

Hall, B.S. (1996). The didactic and the elegant: Some thoughts on scientific and technological illustrations in the middle ages and renaissance. In B.S. Baigre (Ed.), *Picturing knowledge. Historical and philosophical problems concerning the use of art in science* (pp. 3–39). Toronto: University of Toronto.

Harwood, V. (2011). Connecting the dots: Threat assessment, depression and the troubled student. *Curriculum Inquiry, 41*(5), 586–609.

Johns Hopkins Medical Institutions. (2011). Turning 'bad' fat into 'good': A future treatment for obesity? *Science Daily*. Retrieved from http://www.sciencedaily.com/releases/2011/05/110503132704.htm

Klein, R. (2010). What is health and how do you get it? In J. Metzl, M. & A. Kirkland (Eds.), *Against health: How health became the new morality* (pp. 15–25). New York, NY: New York University Press.

Kusukawa, S. (2010). The sources of Gessner's pictures for Historia animalium. *Annals of Science, 67*(3), 303–328.

Le Besco, K. (2010). Fat panic and the new morality. In J.M. Metzl & A. Kirkland (Eds.), *Against health: How health became the new morality* (pp. 77–82). New York, NY: New York University Press.

Paddock, C. (2011). How to burn calories instead of storing them: Turn bad fat into good fat? *Medical News Today*. Retrieved from http://www.medicalnewstoday.com/articles/224183.php

Panese, F. (2005). The accursed part of scientific iconography (D. Thomas, Trans.). In L. Pauwels (Ed.), *Visual cultures of science: Rethinking representational practices in knowledge building and science communication* (pp. 63–89). Hanover: Dartmouth College Press.

Perrault, C. (Ed.). (1671). *Mémoires pour servir à l'histoire naturelle des animaux* [Memoirs for a natural history of animals] (2 vols). Paris: Imprimerie royale.

Pinon, L. (2005). Conrad Gessner and the historical depth of Renaisance natural history. In G. Pomata & N.G. Siraisi (Eds.), *Historia: Empiricism and erudition in early modern Europe* (pp. 241–268). Cambridge, MA: MIT Press.

Rabinow, P. (1992). Studies in the anthropology of reason. *Anthropology Today, 8*(5), 7–10.

Rich, E. (2011). Exploring the relationship between pedagogy and physical cultural studies: The case of new health imperatives in schools. *Sociology of Sport Journal, 28*(1), 64–84.

Rich, E., & Evans, J. (2009). *The impact of the new health imperatives in schools: Full research report ESRC End of Award Report* (RES-000–22–2003). Swindon: ESRC.

Rutkowski, J., Davis, K.E., & Schere, P.E. (2009). Mechanisms of obesity and related pathologies: The macro- and microcirculation of adipose tissue. *FEBS Journal, 276*(20), 5738–5746.

Speake, J. (Ed.). (1999). *The Oxford essential dictionary of foreign terms in English*. Oxford: Oxford University Press.

Tan, D.X., Manchester, L.C., Fuentes-Broto, L., Parades, S.D., & Reiter, R.J. (2010). Significance and application of melatonin in the regulation of brown adipose tissue metabolism: Relation to human obesity. *Obesity Reviews, 12*(3), 167–188.

Tews, D., & Wabitsch, M. (2011). Renaissance of brown adipose tissue. *Hormone Research in Paediatrics, 75*, 231–239.

Wang, S.S. (2010). A new way to lose weight? Scientists see the potential in the calorie-burning value of 'good' fat in adults. *The Wall Street Journal Online*. Retrieved from http://online.wsj.com/article/SB10001424052702304506904575180053884870776.html

Welch, R., McMahon, S., & Wright, J. (2012). The medicalisation of food pedagogies in primary schools and popular culture: A case for awakening subjugated knowledges. *Discourse: Studies in the Cultural Politics of Education, 33*(5).

Wright, J., Burrows, L., & Rich, E. (2012). Health imperatives in primary schools across three countries: Intersections of class, culture and subjectivity. *Discourse: Studies in the Cultural Politics of Education.*

The medicalisation of food pedagogies in primary schools and popular culture: a case for awakening subjugated knowledges

Rosie Welch, Samantha McMahon and Jan Wright

Faculty of Education, University of Wollongong, Wollongong, NSW, Australia

In this study we interrogate the ways nutrition and health have become increasingly influential to children's everyday life practices and conceptualisations of food. We challenge the orthodoxy of meanings afforded to food that draw a distinct binary between 'good'/'bad' or 'healthy'/'unhealthy'; ideas widely promulgated in health texts, popular culture and pedagogical practice. Whilst these dominant medico-scientific discourses are pervasive in accounts of food, they are not the only meanings that permeate the popular cultural and pedagogical landscape; for instance, there has been a burgeoning interest in culinary cooking programmes and food sustainability in recent years. In this study, we use Foucault's notion of biopower to trace the various ways food is governed through interventions; pedagogised by popular culture; and, taken up in school policies and practices. We draw on interviews with 32 Year five students from Australian public and private primary schools. Not surprisingly, the analysis demonstrates how students reiterated food as a practice of 'temptation' and 'risk', similar to nutrition-based knowledge of food circulated in popular culture and health programmes. This suggests that other meanings of food are often socially and pedagogically marginalised. We argue that because of the perceived risk attached to food practices, these young people see food as an object of guilt and a reason for self-surveillance. After discussing the results we consider some of the consequences for young peoples' sense of self and their relationships with food in every day life, particularly in light of the perilous effects of deeming food as 'good'/'bad' from such a young age. As a point of departure we explore some of the subjugated knowledges that can be brought to the table of food pedagogies in schools in order to bring about a broader assemblage of food 'truths'.

Introduction

What do you like when you roll out of bed?
A nice warm slice of homemade bread?
Dip it in egg,
Slop it in cream,
Fry it in butter,
or Whipped mar-jar-een (sic).
Pour on a syrup
You like the most
Love that breakfast with warm French toast! (*Mudlicious*, 1986)

It is hard to imagine the above excerpt from the song 'What do you like to start the day?' (Irving & Currie, 1987, p. 28), disseminated as a teaching resource in the *Early Childhood Education Journal,* over two decades ago, making it into primary school teachers' choice of food-based activities in the current schooling epoch of 'healthy food choices' and healthified canteen menus. The food options suggested in the song would now be considered extremely 'unhealthy' because of their association with a multitude of health risks, with heart disease, diabetes and obesity heading the list. The sentiment inherent in this song – choosing foods because of the pleasure associated with their consumption – is at odds with that of contemporary primary school initiatives, canteens and curriculum enactments. Rather, discourses of risk and nutrition, often associated with health and weight, are entwined in and through both school pedagogies and children's popular culture. Other scholars have provided detailed critiques of the 'obesity epidemic' as one of the most influential discourses informing our thinking and pedagogies of health and the body (Evans, Davies, & Rich, 2008; Kirk, 2006; Leahy, 2009; Wright & Dean, 2007). It is not our intention to take up these debates, but, rather, to submit that obesity discourse, along with other health 'risks' such as cardiovascular disease and diabetes, has given rise to nutritional-based pedagogies of food in schools, popular culture and widespread government campaigns such as *Go for 2 & 5* (Australian Government Department of Health and Ageing, 2008; NSW Department of Health, 2003).

Methodology

Like the other studies in this Special Issue collection, we are drawing on the large data-set from an international study, funded by the ARC and ESRC, that investigated schools' uptake of overweight and obesity-related school policies and practices. The analysis in this study is informed by one component of the data: the interviews with children from three primary schools in Australia. All 32 Australian children interviewed were in Year 5 or Year 6 and were typically 10 or 11 years old. The children were interviewed in pairs at their school, during school hours. The interviews were designed to engage with young peoples' meanings of health, their sources of health knowledge and how they perceived school health practices. All interviews were audio-recorded and then later transcribed. Transcriptions were uploaded to NVivo™ data analysis software and then thematically coded against research nodes pre-identified by the research team and according to emerging themes in the data-set. Through this process, we were concerned with comparing, contrasting and contextualising participants' interview texts with broader discourses on the topic. Together, these analytic processes raised questions as to why such unexpectedly 'grown up' notions of food knowledge and practice featured so prominently in the schoolchildren's talk.

We utilise the notion of biopower as derived from Foucault (1978) to understand not only the ways the children in this study considered food, but also the pedagogical, pop-cultural and government interventions that promulgate discourses that constitute particular understandings of food and health. Specifically, we adopt the analytical tools of biopower as explicated by Rabinow and Rose (2006, p. 197) to examine how particular 'truths' influenced the ways the children came to understand food, health and the body. Rabinow and Rose (2006) outline three minimum elements of biopower as a historical 'plane of actuality' that imparts knowledge and make meaning:

1. One or more truth discourses about the 'vital' character of living human beings and an array of authorities considered competent to tell the truth;
2. Strategies for intervention upon collective existence in the name of life and health that may be addressed to the population or collectivities (in this, case children, and to a lesser extent, parents); and
3. Modes of subjectification, through which individuals are brought to work on themselves . . . by means of practices of the self in the name of their own life and health. (Rabinow & Rose, 2006, p. 197)

Adopting Rabinow and Rose's three elements facilitates analysis of biopower's pedagogies of 'life' as applied to children, specifically the 'truths', strategies for intervention and modes of subjectification pertaining to the current framing of the relationship food and health. In adopting Rabinow and Rose's framework, this study will point towards the consistency with which 'biopedagogies', that is, 'the art and practice of teaching of "life"' (Harwood, 2009, p. 21), related to food as a nutritional practice, are entangled across young people's everyday experience, at school and in popular culture. Further, we will explore how pedagogical practices work to govern bodies in everyday life and practices around food.

Lastly, in this study, we offer considerations of the subjugated knowledge of food in both popular culture and children's everyday experiences. In doing so, we present the case for a broader discussion of food practices in the primary school, and the need to reconsider the use of medicalised and 'healthified' pedagogies in the ways we talk about food with young people.

'Truth' discourses about food: medico-scientific discourses of food and health

Over time, the roles and responsibilities of the state, family and child have been differently emphasised in relation to children's health. Albon and Mukherji (2008, p. 1) describe five historical periods of food policy development since 1906, each illustrating different ways in which food has been valued within primary schools: a philanthropic concern (pre-1906); a residual service (1906-Second World War); a universal service (1944–1979); a return to the market (1980–1996) and safeguarding futures (1997 onwards). Among the concerns raised over these periods are cleanliness and manners, malnourishment and food quantity over quality. Various processes of industrialisation, the processing of foods and the marketisation of food have also contributed to changes in food availability and function; and these have filtered into school food practices (Chamberlain, 2004). Albon and Mukherji (2008) suggest that, since 1997 there has been a concern with the nutritional value of food and its role in ill-health and disease prevention, that is, food has increasingly been regarded as instrumental in safeguarding children's futures.

The development of nutrition as a science over the last century as a means to prevent illness has been rapidly taken up in everyday life (Apple, 1996; Chamberlain, 2004). By scientifically attributing certain health and risk values to food, discourses associated with food have become increasingly medicalised; that is, food has become valued for its contribution to preventing disease, or vilified for its contribution to ill-health. Medicalisation (Illich, 1975) is defined as a process whereby 'non medical problems become defined and treated as medical problems usually in terms of illness or disorders' (Conrad, 1992, p. 209) by laity, the media, educational and medical institutions (Jutel, 2006; Zwier, 2009). Scrinis (2008) associates the medicalisation of food with a wider trend within nutrition science; one that reduces the value of food to its nutrients and their health-giving properties. He describes this trend as 'the ideology of nutritionism' and links its dominance to the food industry's marketing strategies.

The conflation of food with medicine and science is a powerful alliance and one that constitutes 'truths' in public discourse that are difficult to contest. Representations of food in the different sites of advertising (Zwier, 2009), the home and popular culture (Chamberlain, 2004) increasingly feature food for its 'health giving' nutritional contents (e.g. protein and antioxidants; Scrinis, 2008). Fruit and vegetables are valued for vitamins and minerals or fibre and their generally low energy value; on the other side are foods judged to be low in vitamins and minerals and high energy value (high 'empty calories'). All this becomes translated into the shorthand of 'junk' and 'fast' food. As Lupton (1996, p. 27) states 'one powerful binary opposition which is often invoked in popular and medical discourses relating to food is that between "good" and "bad" food'. Chamberlain (2004, p. 469) describes how 'fruits and vegetables changed their status from inessential delicacies to essential foods for good health' and how nutritional science 'opened the way for the state to intervene in the regulation and surveillance of food'. This is apparent in the ways the Australian Government, for instance, disseminates nutritional guidelines and food promotion campaigns to citizens. The early years are seen as a key stage of health development and prevention of ill-health and disease, and food is valued for its medicinal role in safeguarding futures. Medico-scientific food truths, then, are intimately connected with children's everyday life practices and work to constitute and regulate understandings of 'morality' and 'risk'. For instance, fast foods are characterised as bad because of assumed low nutritional and high energy value, but also because they carry associations of food prepared outside the home, demonstrating a lack of a caring relationship between parents (particularly mothers) and children (Lupton, 1996).

Healthy eating is largely seen as a public health concern, however, those who are privileged, and those who are marginalised by constructions of food are rarely considered in such accounts and the research that fuels them (Chamberlain, 2004). A common undertaking in these accounts of health promotion and education is to 'educate' for behaviour change. This is a key tenet of what Crawford (1980) describes as 'healthism', a notion well established as a feature of modern society and the rise of neo-liberalism, where health is promoted as the individual's responsibility invoking a shift towards considering individuals as health consumers. Yet, concluding that particular social groups and individuals need education in order to change their behaviour fosters a practice of blaming individuals, and fails to consider socio-cultural worlds that contribute to individuals' practices of the self (Lupton, 1996). These renderings of food and the body fail to take into account the complex relationships that make up health and the structural causes underpinning food disadvantage (Coveney, 2000). All of these truths re-present food as a means of corporeality and health utility before pleasure. These truths of food, then, produce a dominant permutation of what it means to be 'healthy' by drawing on medicalised classifications and food binaries, separating those who 'can/do' from those who 'can't/don't' eat well.

Interventions: bio-pedagogies of food in the primary school

Food knowledge is taken up in strategies for intervention and (re)produced through the pedagogical practices of parents, teachers, marketers and media. According to the elements of biopower, these varied and collective sites of knowledge production tacitly govern children's food knowledge, beliefs and behaviour in relation to life and health in both subtle and overt ways. Schools are particularly central to the enactment of public health food agendas, as they are seen as convenient sites to access children in order to foster their 'development' of food habits for health and longevity. Wright and Dean (2007), for example, point to the ways school health texts (websites and text books) commonly draw on medicalised knowledge and contribute to normative positions that value food and exercise for their role in controlling health and weight.

The overhaul of 'healthy' canteen legislation in schools is another way food is pedagogised in the battle over children's health. The NSW *Fresh Tastes @ School Strategy* (NSW Department of Education and Training, 2004) largely arose from concerns about childhood overweight and obesity and has had a direct effect on the ways food is provided in schools in New South Wales. The *Fresh Tastes* 'Healthy Canteen Menu Planning Guide' legitimates its implementation across NSW primary school canteens via a 12 page commentary on the 'issue' and 'risk' of overweight and obesity which includes: statistics of the 'prevalence of overweight and obesity'; the case to dispel 'the myth of puppy fat'; images of young people playing computer games; and, health risks of overweight and obesity. Other Australian states have similar versions of the *Fresh Tastes @ School* initiative similarly motivated by the concern about 'childhood obesity': *Smart Choices* (Queensland), *Go For Your Life* (Victoria), *Healthy Food and Drink* (Western Australia) and *Right Bite* (South Australia). These moves to 'healthify' school canteens have been accorded further status through a range of canteen awards distributed by organisations such as the *Parents Jury*, and *Fresh Tastes*, all of which contribute to the canteen as a space of school 'performativity' (see Ball, 2003). The health promotion intervention *Crunch and Sip* is another popular school-based programme in Western Australia. It advocates the consumption of fruit and water in class time at the exclusion of all other foods; and promotes water and fruit as a means to physical and mental performance in the classroom (Government of Western Australia, 2005).

Collectively, these initiatives discursively subject young people to the requirement to be attentive to their health and bodies through monitoring the food and drink they consume. These accounts of food and health place children constantly at risk of the consequences of 'unhealthy' eating and moralise 'good' eating. Such campaigns prompt children and their parents to monitor and regulate children's eating behaviours, in order to avoid health risks, in particular overweight and obesity. Other writers have urged that such practices serve to normalise and regulate children's relationships to food and their bodies (Cliff & Wright, 2010; Gard, 2006; Gard & Wright, 2001; Leahy & Harrison, 2004). Paradoxically then, the modes of food disciplinary power tend to be framed as either: serving an 'educational' role where children are prompted to make healthy decisions; or, by governing children's exposure to, and removing choice of, un/healthy food through legislation and codes of conduct.

Popular media as a biopedagogical site

Narratives of food in children's popular media texts appear to be discursively similar to the healthism rhetoric and binaries of un/healthy food cited in schools. What follows are examples of public pedagogical interventions directly aimed at children (and their parents) that promote via the popular media, medico-scientifically derived notions of food – that is, a simple relationship between food and health. Several of these are commercially produced television and video programmes, and one is a national government campaign. In this section we also draw on some of the data from the interviews with children to highlight direct links in their talk to the popular cultural resources being documented.

Beginning in 2005, the multi-million dollar *Go for 2 & 5* campaign was first disseminated throughout Australian media (magazines, television, billboards, online) by the Australian Government in an attempt to make fruit and vegetables a central part of adult's and children's food thoughts and practices. The campaign targets children, parents and carers of children and is prescriptive in tenor, encouraging individuals, both children and parents, to increase the amount of fruit and vegetables that they consume (Australian Government Department of Health and Ageing, 2008). The campaign continues to provide information about overweight and obesity risks and the relationship between diet and disease on its website. The promotional material is made readily available and distributed to childhood educational sites and interested health educators. The success of this campaign is evident in that half of children in our study mentioned the campaign directly when talking about health. For instance: 'I listen to the commercial to eat two fruit and five veg' (Jorge, Trimdon Primary School); 'the past year and stuff they have had a lot of ads about eat two and five' (Amir, St Mark's PS); 'it's [a pop up on the computer] like five vegetables or five servings of fruit and two vegetables' (Jordy, St Clarie's PS); 'every year (at school) for a few months we would all do two and five' (Johnny, St Mark's PS); or 'I remember going up in front of the school and presenting this poster of why you should be eating two to five vegs…we also read through this little booklet for the two and five thing' (Liz, St Mark's PS). The success of the campaign can also be inferred from the prominence given to fruit and vegetables in all of the children's responses to questions about health. Responses that exemplify this prominence will be detailed later in this study.

In August 2006, *Hi5*, a successful children's entertainment group, became engaged with the issue of combating childhood 'overweight and obesity'. Charlie Delany, one of the band members, stated that whilst she was 'not a mum', *Hi-5* were helping out in fighting the epidemic by getting the kids singing, dancing, keeping them active and writing songs about eating vegetables (Huntley, 2008). Another popular children's group, *The Wiggles*, released a DVD titled 'The Wiggles Hot Poppin' Popcorn' in 2009. In a scene from this DVD, Murray (one of the four characters that make up The Wiggles and depicted wearing the authoritative cover of a white lab coat) states, 'yes everyone, popcorn is a lovely treat to eat at the circus or at the movies and some foods are just for eating on special occasions'. Pointing to a plate of food containing chocolate, lollies, croissants and cupcakes, he says, 'these seem to be special occasion foods and sweet treats'. He then indicates the plate of fruit and vegetables and says, 'while these are delicious healthy treats you can eat quite often'. In response, Anthony, the idiosyncratically, ever-hungry Wiggle says, 'Wow, professor Murray! You know, I think I can eat all the food, all the time. And, even if I can't I'll try to eat it all!' To this, Murray looks worried and replies 'Anthony! Eat the healthy food, mate. The occasional foods can give you a tummy ache if you eat too much of them'. The other Wiggles members nod emphatically in agreement as Murray warns, '[a]nd if you have a tummy ache, you might have to call Food Man to help you'. Food Man, another character in the Wiggles' armory derives his superpowers from his profound knowledge of healthy foods and a self-confessed and much-sung-of compulsion to 'fly away from cream pies'. Throughout this particular Wiggles DVD, Food Man helps the constantly tempted and apparently weak-willed Anthony to make 'good' food choices. These exchanges of food knowledge consistently characterise Anthony as misguided in his knowledge about how much food and what kinds of food he should eat and as lacking in self-control – the opposite of what any good child should aspire to.

Designed for older children and their parents, celebrity chef, Jamie Oliver's televised projects, 'Jamie's food revolution' and 'Jamie's school dinners', present another example of the ways food is both medicalised and imbued with particular moral values. These projects, although tailored differently for UK, USA and Australian contexts, have as their central rationale the combating of obesity through food 'education'. In an invited Television Entertainment Design 'award speech' where he was awarded $100,000 prize money, Jamie talks about the aforementioned projects' role in health:

> . . . fast food – it's sloppy joes, it's burgers, it's wieners, it's pizzas, it's all of that stuff. Ten percent of money we spend on health care as I said earlier is on obesity and it's going to double. We're not teaching our kids, there is no statutory right to teach kids about food. (TED Conferences, 2010)

This is a particularly explicit enunciation of food as a risk to health and to the national good of the economy. Jamie Oliver's programmes, instruct children about cooking food as an important skill for health and avoiding the risk of overweight and obesity. He considers teaching people to cook (children and caregivers) as the answer to the 'obesity epidemic' (Australian Broadcasting Corporation [ABC], 2010). To do this, he has implemented a healthy eating programme in a range of UK and US schools, and a cooking centre in Ipswich, Australia, all of which have received a great deal of media and television coverage in the Australian context (ABC, 2010).

The Biggest Loser, a popular 'reality' television programme provides a further example of a site of 'medicalised' food knowledge accessible to children. The show was referred to by many of the children in their interviews when asked about health information. For example:

> Int: So the next question is how do you decide what health information to believe?
> R: Some TV shows are about fitness like the Biggest Loser, I watch that and they tell you like they have temptations to see what has got the most vitamins, and what is good, but has got lots of fat. (Renee, St Claire's PS)

The messages of temptation and guilt are likely to resonate with those children who watch it as they make connections between weight and foods with 'lots of fat'.

Collectively, these popular cultural interventions deploy forms of biopower by taking a singular, authoritative approach to food. Explicitly for Hi5 and Jamie Oliver and the Wiggles, they assume straightforwardly that there are foods children should eat and foods that they should not eat. For the Wiggles there is an acknowledgement that the foods children should not eat are those from which children might derive the most pleasure and therefore are the most tempting. Together, these texts act as popular pedagogical sites and 'strategies for intervention upon [the] collective existence' of children (Rabinow & Rose, 2006, p. 197). Thus, initiatives such as those mentioned above, and others that are founded on helping children to make healthy choices based on their development of values and beliefs in the younger years, work to discursively constitute food knowledge that takes as its focus the relationship between health and weight.

Having identified some of the medicalised truth discourses of food circulating in schools and popular culture and the ways these operate as biopedagogies to incite children to think about food in particular kinds of ways, we now consider children's meanings of food and health via the lens of the third operational tool of biopower: technologies of the self. What is central to this notion, and useful to our analysis, is how individuals invest in self-forming practices or 'ethical work' in order to transform themselves into ethical or desired subjects through constant self-monitoring and self-surveillance.

A moral project: children's conceptions of un/healthy foods

One of the earliest questions in the interview schedule was designed to probe the primary schoolchildren's meanings of health. Students' responses to the question, 'what does health mean to you?' indicated that much consideration was afforded to food, particularly through the classification of food in binary forms as either healthy/unhealthy or good /bad. Interestingly, however, when the children's descriptions of what constitutes 'healthy foods' were probed further, the term 'healthy foods' was not found to include all foods falling outside the category of its binary opposite, 'unhealthy'. Instead, 'healthy foods' were conflated predominantly with 'fruit and vegetables'. Whilst, at face value, this seemed consistent with previous studies (e.g. McKinley et al., 2005; Persson Osowski, Göranzon, & Fjellström, 2012), in all of the interviews with the Australian primary schoolchildren, 'fruit and vegetables' were offered as *the* examples of 'healthy' foods when asked 'what does health mean to you?' There was one exception, Lior, who also spoke of 'meat' and 'protein' when describing healthy foods. This seemingly exclusive conflation of concepts (i.e. healthy food = fruit and vegetables) has the effect of creating a tacitly known category for food beyond the un/healthy classification binary. The children appeared to deploy a triple-taxonomy for food: 'unhealthy foods'; 'healthy foods' = 'fruit and vegetables'; and, by inference, 'other foods'. This notion of 'other foods' was an unexpected and underdeveloped one that warrants future investigation. With a large data-set at hand, it was surprising to see such recurrent homogeneity across the children's definitions of 'healthy' food. The data also showed that primary students seemed to use the words 'healthy' and 'good' interchangeably, thus overtly placing a positive moral value on making healthy food choices. In this sense, eating healthy food (or, for these children, 'fruit and vegetables') was portrayed as tantamount to virtuousness.

What was forfeited in the children's knowledge were more diverse knowledges of health and the relationship between food and health. This was unanticipated, particularly when considering the NSW PDHPE syllabus (Board of Studies New South Wales, 1999) that encourages children to recognise a *variety* of foods as contributing to good health. For instance one of the 'Personal Health Choices Outcomes and Indicators' listed in the syllabus suggests that a child at PHES1.12 level (Early Stage 1) 'identifies a range of foodstuffs and groups them according to their sources, e.g. vegetable, meat, dairy, fruit that keep them healthy'. In addition, 'The Food Plate', assembled by The Australian Government Department of Health and Ageing, which has commonly replaced what was known as the Food Pyramid, is a common teaching resource for knowledge about food and health in the primary school (Wright & Dean, 2007). However, its catchphrase, 'enjoy a variety of foods every day' along with its descriptions of food groups that extend beyond fruit and vegetables did not feature in the children's descriptions of what constitutes healthy or 'good' food.

Moral judgments about food were also evident in the primary children's discussion of unhealthy foods as 'bad'. For the children in the study unhealthy/ bad food was equated with foods that were high in sugar or fat, 'fast' or 'junk' foods. Mention of 'fatty foods' and foods high in sugar in the data was unsurprising, considering the extent to which these permeate the message of the health promotion campaigns and interventions mentioned earlier. The following quotes illustrate the kinds of associations the children made between 'bad' food and specific risks of ill-health:

Int: So the first questions are just about health. So the first one, D___, could you have
       a go at this one, what does health mean to you?
D: Safe food, like if you don't eat properly you'll get sick or you'll get diabetes or
       something like that, if you eat too much sugar. (Damien, Saint Claire's PS)
Int: What does health mean to you?
D: Like keeping in shape like don't eat too much of the wrong foods, like eat healthy
       stuff. (Derren, Trimdon PS)

The second quote here demonstrates the way a simple relationship between fast food (food eaten outside the home, as well as food containing 'bad' ingredients) and the risk of overweight was so often made:

Int: What kind of health stuff do you learn?
J: Not to eat really fast food because then if you try to lose weight it will just come
       back to you. (Jordy, Saint Claire's PS)

In the interviews the consumption of the 'wrong' or 'junk/fast food' was always regarded as dangerous and transgressive, signifying 'bad' and 'sinful' practices. The interview texts below exemplify the ways the children are incited to work on themselves in relation to 'truths' or discourses of healthy food through technologies of the self. Designating some food as bad, and thus forbidden, generated the possibility of being tempted by and/or feeling guilty for eating, and/or being addicted to, certain types of foods. Amongst the children's talk of how they rated their health and kept themselves healthy were expressions of temptation, addiction and guilt.

J: . . . lollies, like if you try a lolly you want more and more and more because it tastes nice. (Joe, Year 5, Trimdon PS)

M: Well I know that once I tried this breakfast cereal, I won't say the name of it. But I know that it was really, really nice and then we didn't always have it with the milk and we just took it out of the box and then we said 'oh yum' and then take another one and another one. (Mae, Year 5, St. Mark's PS)

Int: Okay what do you reckon John what would you have to do to be a ten [out of ten health rating]?

J: I'd have to stop eating a lot of chips; I really like chips like barbecue, those ones. I really like them and I eat them so much like Jacob said I have to have some limits and start eating some healthy food. (Jorge, Year 5 Trimdon PS)

Int: So do you guys think that there are things that get in the way of people being healthy like are there things that sort of stop them or slow them down?

A: Yeah, birthday parties, temptations.

Int: What kind of temptations?

A: Lollies, chocolates, like some people in the whole world they might be fat but that is not their fault, like that might have been through their family.

And later

Int: Anything else that you reckon gets in the way of people being healthy?

A: Yeah.

Int: What about people your age, do you reckon there is anything?

A: Yeah, at school when you see someone with a lot of food at recess or lunch you just feel I should have some more or something and sometimes you get tempted to buy it off them or something.

V: Like you want to trade or something.

A: Yeah you trade some chips for five lollies or something. (Amir and Vance, St Mark's PS)

Taken together these examples from the children, particularly the comments about the need to 'set some limits' and resist addictions, temptations and eating too much, are further indications that the Australian primary schoolchildren conferred a certain (im)moral value on particular types of foods; particularly, 'bad' foods. Food temptation is not a new concept, particularly in the context of western cultural food practices and binaries of food as 'good' or 'bad'. However, the notion of food temptation amongst primary schoolchildren hinging on the desire for foods deemed 'risky' to health or for weight gain is a relatively new finding.

Discussion

From what we have found in this study, children are particularly aware of consuming food as an un/healthy practice and the health risks associated with eating particular kinds of foods. This contrasts to Lupton's (2005) finding that young people and children had little interest or knowledge of the healthy or unhealthy aspects of their diets and were the least concerned, in comparison to their adult counterparts, when it came to maintaining a healthy diet.

The relations of food knowledge across the varied sites of government initiatives, policy, popular culture, school canteen menus and curriculum initiatives, draw on knowledge from the fields of epidemiology, medicine and nutrition to reproduce a relatively consistent and reductionist message to young people about what is considered 'healthy' (i.e. fruit and vegetables) and that which is unhealthy (i.e. fast food, sweets and fat). The consistency and intensity of this message, we argue, constructs children as in need of saving themselves from 'unhealthy' food behaviour and in turn limits children's 'healthy' food knowledge. Our concern here, lies with how these truths about food and nutrition shape the thoughts of individuals in ways that can conjure up feelings of shame and disgust (Burrows, 2010). The sensation of conflict between an imagined or immediate desire of something and the conscious thought of the associated risks in acting upon such a desire creates feelings of temptation, self-surveillance and guilt. These feelings appear counterproductive to the project of 'health' itself (Burrows, 2010; Burrows & Wright, 2007; O'Dea, 2005; Wright & Dean, 2007).

We do not wish to suggest that the food knowledge and practices we have described above act as governing pedagogies in a totalising sense or that they are not hybridised with other ways of knowing; however, we do argue that they contribute as 'slow, subtle, and often invisible dispositions and maneuvers that have occurred in the domain of knowledge in society over time' (Cooter & Stein, 2010, p. 110). Ivinson and Duveen (2006, p. 10) point out that '[w]hile teaching involves fostering skills, practices and knowledge, at the same time pedagogic discourse inducts children into becoming particular kinds of moral agents'. The prevalent conceptions of food and its role in governing life and the somatic experiences of bodies is one, we argue, that needs to be critiqued in schools, teachers', parents' and media's production of healthy food knowledge. It is here where the ethical issue of food in schools, public health agendas, popular culture and parenting resides as well-intentioned interventions and teaching methods reinstate destructive truths about food and the body. We suggest O'Dea's (2005) article, 'Prevention of childhood obesity: "First do no Harm"' has ongoing value in response to governments, educators', academics' and practitioners' concern with childhood obesity prevention. Taking as its premise what she calls 'one of the most important principles of modern medicine and health prevention science, first do no harm' (p. 259), O'Dea stresses that those involved with health education need to pay attention to how, what may be well-intentioned prevention efforts, are tied up in generating undesirable effects. Rather than simply critiquing the unintended effects of health prevention, however, in the next section we endeavour to offer some alternative meanings of food – meanings that may expand rather than narrow the range of practices, thoughts and dispositions children link to food in their everyday lives.

Pedagogical 'counterpoints': bringing subjugated knowledges of food to the surface

Austin contends that 'nutritional public health should be viewed first and foremost as an ideological project, driven far more forcefully by the logics of materialism and deviance than by its own empirical method' (Austin, 1999. p. 245). We consider this an important starting point for bringing 'subjugated' knowledges to the surface. By 'subjugated knowledges' we mean knowledges that have been disqualified as inadequate in the hierarchy of knowledge 'beneath the required level of cognition or scientificity' (Foucault,1980, pp. 81–82). We support calls to recognise food as a political issue, and urge a more critical examination of food as it is related to health in pedagogical settings. As Chamberlain (2004) asserts:

> Food can be differently valenced, providing us with pleasure and fulfilment but simultaneously offering anxieties and fears; food can offer health and life but it can also bring illness and death. Hence food is not a simple entity, but something that is constructed, negotiated, socialized and contextualized (p. 468).

In this sense, subjugated knowledges, or the contradictions and variances in meanings about food are important to consider in order to diversify the scope of children's food knowledge and thus what they are able to do with this.

There has been a burgeoning popular interest in food-based television shows that represent food for its culinary, sensory, cultural and geographical virtues rather than for its nutritional value and contribution to physical 'health'. Indeed, a pluralism of food products and gastronomic experiences have infiltrated the market as globalisation, cosmopolitanism and reflexive modernity have shaped the foodscapes of western, developed cities (Germov & Williams, 2008). Since the late 1990s, food in popular culture, particularly directed to adults has gained a great deal of traction. *Iron Chef*, first televised in 1993, followed by *Two Fat Ladies* in 1996, *Jamie Oliver's Naked Chef* launched in the UK in 1999, *Nigella Lawson* (2000–2010 under various names), *Mave O'Mara's Food Safaris, Kitchen Chemistry, and Heston's Mission Impossible* with Heston Blumenthal, Gordan Ramsay's various programmes and most recently *MasterChef (Junior)* are but a few of the more popular television cooking programmes. Whilst it is apparent that 'food as a visceral and culinary pleasure' and 'the virtues of home cooking mastery' (Huntley, 2008, p. 130) have had considerable air play, these meanings afforded to food are often at odds with health interventions and discourses that emphasise the role of food as a means to health and the prevention of illness and disease.

MasterChef Junior is one example of the ways food is valued, particularly by children, for its inherent nature as palatably pleasing or indulgent. The programme tends to intentionally omit notions of 'unhealthy' or 'immoral' food based on nutritional components. Rather, foods that are often less common to everyday eating, expensive and arguably inaccessible to many, such as lobster and truffles are commonly featured. The premise of this programme is concerned with a kind of 'haute cuisine' similar to that served in European restaurants and the show's evaluation of dishes portrays its uptake of discourses of food that emphasise the 'indulgent', 'creative', 'distinguished' and historical production and consumption of food. Whilst this temperament of the show has been met with much controversy for not incorporating a 'healthy' agenda (Mediawatch, 2010; Saxelby, 2011; VicHealth. State Government of Victoria, 2010), the show has maintained its identity without paying concessions to health rhetoric.

Further to these discursive resources, we have seen a 'wholesome', 'back to basics', sustainable approach to food make an emergence, similar to that espoused by the Stephanie Alexander Kitchen Garden Project (SAKGP). Many schools are already adopting 'alternative' approaches to food through the SAKGP (Stephanie Alexander Kitchen Garden Foundation, 2008) and other similar initiatives such as *Kids in the Kitchen*. Despite popular purchase in contemporary social spaces and media, such messages about food did not seem to appear in the knowledge expressed by schoolchildren in this study. The *SAKGP*, whilst funded under the banner of government obesity prevention (Virtual Medical Centre, 2008), omits references to food related to the medicalised terms of 'overweight and obesity' in its online resources and objectives (Stephanie Alexander Kitchen Garden Foundation, 2008). Rather, the project appears to be aligned with sustainable and ecological practices of food together with promulgating an appreciation of where food comes from, how to cultivate, and cook it. Such movements can be seen, beyond school contexts, in the growing interest in farmers markets and specialty food cooperatives as individuals seek out sustainable, local and fresh produce (Huntley, 2008).

McAuliffe and Lane (2005, cited in Albon & Mukherji, 2008) suggest that pedagogical practitioners need to ensure that they give equal value and respect to familiar and unfamiliar foods, including where and how the foods are produced, who produces them, and how they are eaten. There is also a case for emphasizing that the pleasure we derive from food is also one of the main sources of anxiety around eating (Coveney, 2000). To support pedagogues wishing to diversify the types of food knowledges presented in their classrooms, drawing on Buddhist conceptions of 'mindful eating', observing Kosher or Halal religions and philosophies, embracing traditional indigenous Australian bush foods and its associated socio-ecological approaches to food and the land, emphasising Fair Trade and vegetarianism may offer some alternatives. Whilst we do not suggest that schools should, or should not, adopt such ideologies, it is worth noting the myriad ways food can be thought of and deployed in educational pursuits in both implicit and explicit ways. This is a task beyond the scope if this study; however, it is one that warrants attention.

Conclusion

In this study we have argued that discourses of childhood obesity, 'health', weight and longevity, as disseminated by public health agendas, constitute a form of biopower that dominates the contemporary landscape of children's 'healthy' food pedagogic practices. Whilst we do not disregard the agentic capabilities of children, teachers and other practitioners to resist such dominant discourses of food, we do suggest that the dominant ways food is pedagogised around health and weight need to be reconsidered. The last thing needed for children is more education around simplistic, shorthand, notions of healthy or good versus bad food. We contend that re-envisioning discourses of food may result in a variety of other ways of thinking about food which are currently compromised, unimaginable and marginalised in children's food knowledge. Whilst health policies and programmes that set out to provide young people with skills to make better choices and resist partaking in 'risky' and 'unhealthy' eating may seem harmless, from our analysis, they also limit what young people can feel by negating any pleasurable, alternative knowledges or the social and cultural benefits of foods.

Whilst there are examples of exceptions to the dominant healthification of food in stories of food in popular culture, stressing its culinary and fresh produce merits, for the most part, the children in this study almost universally referred to food as either bad/good or un/healthy. In this sense, then, we contend that technologies of biopower have converged. This convergence we have evidenced through: medicalised 'truths' about food and the body being circulated; healthy food interventions that govern school food practices; and, the ways children govern their food beliefs and practices through technologies of the self. Children, then are compelled to regulate their practices of food in everyday life by the exigencies of medicalised or 'healthy' food practices. As a final point of departure, we urge pedagogues to consider new ways of thinking about food and nutrition with young people. We also point to the importance of more research that explores alternative food knowledges and pedagogies to those of the medicalisation of food and the everyday classification of food within this framework.

References

Albon, D., & Mukherji, P. (2008). *Food and health in early childhood*. London: Sage Publications Ltd.

Apple, R. (1996). *Vitamania: Vitamins in American culture*. New Brunswick, NJ: Rutgers University Press.

Austin, S.B. (1999). Fat, loathing and public health: The complicity of science in a culture of disordered eating. *Culture, Medicine and Psychiatry, 23*(2), 245–268.

Australian Broadcasting Corporation (ABC). (2010). Jamie Oliver cooking school in Ipswich. *Life Matters*. Retrieved from http://www.abc.net.au/rn/lifematters/stories/2010/3075489.htm

Australian Government Department of Health and Ageing. (2008). *Go for 2 & 5*. Retrieved from http://www.health.gov.au/internet/healthyactive/publishing.nsf/Content/about

Ball, S. (2003). The teacher's soul and the terrors of performativity. *Journal of Education Policy, 18*(2), 215–228.

Board of Studies New South Wales. (1999). *Personal development, health and physical education K-6*. Sydney: Author.

Burrows, L. (2010). 'Kiwi kids are Weet-Bix kids' – Body matters in childhood. *Sport, Education and Society, 15*(2), 235–251.

Burrows, L., & Wright, J. (2007). Prescribing practices: Shaping healthy children in schools. *International Journal of Children's Rights, 15*(1), 83–98.

Chamberlain, K. (2004). Food and health: Expanding the agenda for health psychology. *Journal of Health Psychology, 9*(4), 467–481.

Cliff, K., & Wright, J. (2010). Confusing and contradictory: Considering obesity discourse and eating disorders as they shape body pedagogies in HPE. *Sport Education and Society, 15*(2), 221–233.

Conrad, P. (1992). Medicalization and social control. *Annual Review of Sociology, 18*(1), 209–232.

Cooter, R., & Stein, C. (2010). Cracking biopower. *History of Human Sciences, 23*(2), 109–128.

Coveney, J. (2000). *Food, morals and meaning: The pleasure and anxiety of eating*. London: Routledge.

Crawford, R. (1980). Healthism and the medicalization of everyday life. *International Journal of Health Services, 10*(3), 365–388.

Evans, J., Davies, B., & Rich, E. (2008). The class and cultural functions of obesity discourse: Our latter day child saving movement. *International Studies in Sociology of Education, 18*(2), 117–132.

Foucault, M. (1978). *The history of sexuality, Vol. 1: The will to knowledge*. London: Penguin.

Foucault, M. (1980). Two lectures. In C. Gordon (Ed.), *Power/knowledge. Selected interviews and other writings, 1972–1977* (pp. 78–108). Suffolk: Harvester Press.

Gard, M. (2006). HPE and the 'obesity epidemic'. In R. Tinning, L. McCuaig & L. Hunter (Eds.), *Teaching health and physical education in Australian schools* (pp. 78–87). Frenchs Forest: Pearson Education.

Gard, M., & Wright, J. (2001). Managing uncertainty: Obesity discourses and physical education in a risk society. *Studies in Philosophy and Education, 20*(6), 535–549.

Germov, J., & Williams, L. (2008). *A sociology of food & nutrition* (3rd ed.). South Melbourne: Oxford University Press.

Government of Western Australia. (2005). *Crunch and sip.* Retrieved from http://www. crunchandsip.com.au/default.aspx

Harwood, V. (2009). Theorizing biopedagogies. In J. Wright & V. Harwood (Eds.), *Biopedagogies and the 'Obesity Epidemic'* (pp. 15–30). New York, NY: Routledge.

Huntley, R. (2008). Eating between the lines: Food and equality in Australia. Melbourne: Black Inc.

Illich, I. (1975). *Medical nemesis.* London: Calder and Boyars.

Irving, J., & Currie, R. (1987). Breakfast starts the day. *Early Childhood Education Journal, 15*(1), 28–33.

Ivinson, G., & Duveen, G. (2006). Children's recontextualizations of pedagogy. In R. Moore, M. Arnot, J. Beck & H. Daniels (Eds.), *Knowledge, power and educational reform: Applying the sociology of Basil Bernstein* (pp. 109–126). New York, NY: Routledge.

Jutel, A. (2006). The emergence of overweight as a disease entity: Measuring up normality. *Social Science and Medicine, 63*(9), 2268–2276.

Kirk, D. (2006). The 'obesity crisis' and school physical education. *Sport, Education and Society, 11*(2), 121–133.

Leahy, D. (2009). Disgusting pedagogies. In J. Wright & V. Harwood (Eds.), *Biopolitics and the 'obesity epidemic'* (pp. 172–182). New York, NY: Routledge.

Leahy, D., & Harrison, L. (2004). Health and physical education and the production of the 'At Risk Self'. In J. Evans, B. Davies & J. Wright (Eds.), *Body knowledge and control: Studies in the sociology of physical education* (pp. 130–139). London: Routledge.

Lupton, D. (1996). *Food, the body and the self.* London: SAGE.

Lupton, D. (2005). Lay discourses and beliefs related to food risks: An Australian perspective. *Sociology of Health and Illness, 27*(4), 448–467.

McAuliffe, A., & Lane, J. (2005). *Listening and responding to young children's views on food.* London: National Children's Bureau.

McKinley, M., Lowis, C., Wallace, J., Morrissey, M., Moran, A., & Livingstone, M. (2005). It's good to talk: Children's views on food and nutrition. *European Journal of Clinical Nutrition, 59*(1), 542–551.

Mediawatch. (2010). *Junk food and Junior MasterChef* [Episode 35, 4 October]. Retrieved from http://www.abc.net.au/mediawatch/transcripts/s3029145.htm

NSW Department of Education and Training. (2004). *Fresh Tastes @ School: NSW Healthy School Canteen Strategy: Canteen menu planning guide.* Retrieved from http://www.schools. nsw.edu.au/media/downloads/schoolsweb/studentsupport/studentwellbeing/schoolcanteen/pr esentation.pdf

NSW Department of Health. (2003). *Prevention of obesity in children and young people: NSW Government Action Plan, 2003–2007.* Sydney: Author

O'Dea, J. (2005). Prevention of childhood obesity: 'First, do no harm'. *Health Education Research, 20*(2), 259–265.

Persson Osowski, C., Göranzon, H., & Fjellström, C. (2012). Children's understanding of food and meals in the foodscape at school. *International Journal of Consumer Studies, 36*(1), 54–60.

Rabinow, P., & Rose, N. (2006). Biopower today. *London School of Economics and Political Sciences, 1,* 195–217.

Saxelby, C. (2011). *Junior MasterChef: What does it teach kids?* Retrieved from http://foodwatch. com.au/hot-issues-in-the-news/junior-masterchef-what-does-it-teach-our-kids.html

Scrinis, G. (2008). On the ideology of nutritionism. *Gastronimica: The Journal of Food and Culture, 8*(1), 39–48.

Stephanie Alexander Kitchen Garden Foundation. (2008). *About the program.* Retrieved from http://www.kitchengardenfoundation.org.au/abouttheprogram.shtml

TED Conferences. (2010). *Jamie Oliver's TED prize wish: Teach every child about food.* Retrieved from http://www.ted.com/talks/jamie_oliver.html

VicHealth. State Government of Victoria. (2010). *Fast food outlets plate up junk during Junior MasterChef.* Retrieved from http://www.vichealth.vic.gov.au/en/Media-Centre/Partner-media-releases/Fast-food-outlets-plate-up-junk-during-Junior-Masterchef.aspx

NEW HEALTH IMPERATIVES ON EDUCATIONAL POLICY AND SCHOOLING

Virtual Medical Centre. (2008). *Schoolkids to fight obesity.* Retrieved from http://www. virtualmedicalcentre.com/news.asp?artid=12357

Wright, J., & Dean, R. (2007). A balancing act: Problematising prescriptions about food and weight in school health texts. *Journal of Didactics and Educational Policy, 16*(2), 75–94.

Zwier, S. (2009). Medicalisation of food advertising. Nutrition and health claims in magazine food advertisements 1990–2008. *Appetite, 53*(1), 109–113.

Teachers' talk about health, self and the student 'body'

Lisette Burrows and Jaleh McCormack

School of Physical Education, University of Otago, Dunedin, New Zealand

Adrienne Rich's phrase 'the personal is the political' is well-worn in feminist literature. In a context where health imperatives are deeply embedded in school cultures and programming, we suggest the phrase has renewed purchase. Drawing on the testimonies of three New Zealand teachers, we explore the ways in which personal health dispositions and practices contour what and how physical and health education is envisaged in diverse school contexts and who is regarded as particularly 'at risk' of poor health outcomes. Teachers' perceptions of their students' health needs, their understanding of the role of schools in ameliorating children's health problems and the pedagogical choices made are each, we suggest, intimately linked to their lived histories of 'health', their understandings of their own and others' bodies and their personal convictions about what, for them, constitutes a 'good' and/or 'healthy' life. While the ubiquitous nature of health discourses, particularly those linked to obesity reduction, might at first blush, invoke notions of a shared agenda and a uniform commitment to improving children and young people's health, our analysis points to the *diverse* ways in which teachers constitute their role as health and physical educators, 'care' about students and teach health and physical education curricula.

Introduction

'How many vegetables should I eat? What's the right way to exercise? What causes disease? What are STDs? What helps me feel well?' Health Education is a mandatory part of New Zealand's state school curriculum (Ministry of Education, 2007), yet which (if any) of these questions are foregrounded in schooling is anybody's guess. The gazetting of a new curriculum in February 2010 has ushered in a newfound flexibility around what is taught and how it is taught. Assuredly a raft of achievement objectives (Burrows, 2009a; Robertson, 2005; Ross, 2004) afford some guidance, yet teachers are urged to prioritise content that meets the specific needs/ interests of their student body rather than slavishly follow a monolithic recipe for health teaching. This is ostensibly good news for teachers and for socially critical scholars, who have argued for a less prescriptive health curriculum (Burrows, 2009a; Quennerstedt, 2010; Sinkinson, 2009). It is also good news for children who presumably have diverse health needs and interests (Alton-Lee, 2003; Mayall, 2000), yet what and who do teachers draw on to make decisions about how to teach health? In a climate where health messages pervade public spaces (Evans, Rich, Davies, & Allwood, 2008; Gard & Wright, 2005), what values, beliefs and dispositions do teachers bring to the health education arena? What shapes a teacher's capacity to be 'ready, willing and able' (Carr, 2001, p. 9) to teach about and/or for health in specific ways?

Researchers across the UK, Australia, Canada and New Zealand have recently been assembling a fairly compelling cadre of data around the way young people are taking up health imperatives in and around schools. Much of this work points to the range of ways well-intentioned health policies and programmes can shape the subjectivities of young people, their dispositions towards their own and others' bodies, and their capacity to experience themselves as healthy (e.g. Burrows, 2008, 2010; Burrows & Wright, 2004; Evans et al., 2008; Lee & Macdonald, 2010; Rail, 2009; Rich & Evans, 2005). To date, however, there has been little research specifically addressing how teachers, rather than students, are making sense of the raft of health imperatives reaching into their school gates – the multifarious outside agencies pedalling health programmes that proclaim an alliance with curriculum mandates, and the popular yet pricey initiatives, like Life Education, Zumba and Jump-Jam, that are regarding schools as ready markets for their merchandise (Macdonald, Hay, & Williams, 2008).

Research investigating Physical Education teachers' life histories (e.g. Rich, 2004; Sparkes, 1999; Sparkes & Templin, 1992), their occupational socialisation (e.g. Curtner-Smith, 2001; Stroot & Williamson, 1993; Templin & Schempp, 1989), their response to curriculum change (e.g. Curtner-Smith, 1995; Ha, Wong, Sum, & Chan, 2008; Kirk & Macdonald, 2001; Sparkes, 1990) and their value orientations (e.g. Ennis & Chen, 1995; Green, 2003; Martino & Beckett, 2004; Rovegno, 2003) has yielded considerable insight about what and who shapes teachers' professional learning and dispositions in relation to physical education. Gender, ethnicity, ability, prior experience, habitus, and as Green, Smith, & Thurston (2009) suggest, 'the impact of emotion as well as reason' (p. 418) have all been implicated in the production of particular professional knowledge and orientations towards both subject matter and students in physical education settings. Rather less has been said about primary school teachers' perceptions, although Petrie, Jones, & McKim (2007) and Petrie (2009) have usefully extended our understanding of what primary teachers might need in terms of professional development in New Zealand physical education, and Garrett and Wrench (2008) have illustrated how personal experiences can shape the proclivities of generalist primary student teachers in Australia.

While cognisant of the aforementioned contributions, there remains relatively little that specifically addresses teachers' perceptions about what constitutes health, and the role of schooling in children's health. Leahy's work is one exception. Her ethnographic work within school health classrooms in Australia (see Leahy & Harrison, 2004, and Leahy, 2009) compellingly points to the ways teachers and their pedagogies are implicated in the production of an 'at-risk' self. We suggest that the ubiquitous nature of health messages – the fact that most people have a perspective on what health means and what should be done about it – makes it potentially more likely that personal concerns may overlap with professional ones. It is this intersection between the personal and the professional, the biopedagogical devices (Leahy, 2009) and rationales that teachers advance that are of central interest in this paper. As Leahy suggests, 'school based health education [can] be understood as a governmental assemblage in and of itself with complex linkages and connections to other assemblages' (p. 173). It is how and why teachers, as key players in this governmental assemblage, envisage the students they work with, where their ideas about what children might need or should do come from, the ways in which their pedagogical priorities do or do not gel with 'common knowledge', and what effects their governmental 'work' yields for young people in schools that concerns us.

We ground our analysis of primary school teachers' testimonies in post-structural commitments to an understanding of practice as discursively constituted (Davies, 1994; Gavey, 1989; Wright, 2004). We wish to examine how personal histories and public health narratives contour teachers' interpolation of health, their expression of health knowledge within school contexts and the pedagogies they deploy with students. While of course there is no simple translation of the personal to the political, of individual experience to public pedagogy, we are nevertheless interested in examining the ways teacher values and knowledge mediate the enactment of school-based health education pedagogy. We are particularly interested in what Evans, Rich, Davies, and De Pian (2010) refer to as the 'capriciousness and instabilities of policies as they flow through specific school contexts and intersect with "local" institutional cultures and expectations and interests' (p. 1). In other words, the way teachers make sense of health initiatives prevailing in popular and governmental apparatuses is of interest, but so too is the way that the 'local' contours (not determines) how teachers think and act.

We begin by mapping the methodological and theoretical resources drawn on to conduct this study before briefly describing the school context. We then draw on the teachers' testimony in an effort to understand how their own investments and experiences in relation to health shape their perceptions of what children need and their beliefs about the role of schooling in children's health. We conclude by reflecting on the shared and dissonant dispositions displayed within this school and what these might mean for how children experience health and/or physical education.

What we did

As part of an international collaboration with colleagues in the UK and Australia during 2007–2009, we engaged in an ethnographic project with students, teachers and administrative staff in two primary and two secondary schools located in lower North Island cities in New Zealand. The schools were distinctly different from each other, with socio-economic index ratings at either end of the scale, ethnically diverse students and a range of health policies and practices enacted in each.

The main thrust of the study was to explore children's understandings of health and fitness in the context of the 'obesity epidemic'. In order to contextualise children's understandings and to consider the role of their schools in imparting health knowledge, we interviewed their teachers. Thirteen teachers shared their views about children's health needs, the role of schools in children's health and the obesity epidemic, and information about the health policies, programmes and teaching practices within their schools. These interviews (between 40 and 60 minutes), together with observations, collation of school policies and classroom teaching resources, provided a detailed and nuanced dataset that we have re-read in light of a realisation that teachers' personal health values, experiences and understandings appeared to be influencing their practice, and that this may account for some of the variation in children's health understandings.

In this article, we draw specifically on the testimonies of just three teachers who work at Toroa (Helen, Pete and Wendy). We do so in an effort to point to the shared and dissonant meanings and practices enacted within a single school context. Throughout, we consider how these teachers' dispositions, beliefs and practices are connected to their own health values, experiences and understandings. We also endeavour to consider the potential and evidenced effects and affects of teacher practices on students' understandings and experiences of school-based health and/or physical education. While not wishing to imply any one-to-one causal relation between teacher disposition and student experience, we maintain that throughout this study there is sufficient evidence to suggest that the personal and political aspirations of teachers inevitably impact what is taught in the name of health and/or physical education and how it is taught. Despite the ubiquity of health messages (Burrows, 2010), these are read, re-read and enacted differently by teachers. Indeed, we start from a presumption that it would be surprising if they were not.

As signalled above, post-structural theoretical resources guided our enquiry in this study. We were interested in what discourses teachers drew on to articulate and render intelligible to themselves and others, their priorities for health and/or physical education teaching in their respective schools. Underpinned by an understanding that what is thinkable, doable in any context is always already linked to the available discursive repertoires (Weatherall, 1992), we wanted to know where teachers get their notions about what constitutes health, what guided their intentions with the particular cohort of students they work with, and how their own values, dispositions and beliefs about health influenced (or not) their teaching of this subject in primary schools.

We also drew on understandings derived from the sociology of childhood where scholars have long attested that what adults do to and for children is premised on an understanding that children are particular kinds of beings (Hendrick, 1997; Jenks, 2005; Stainton Rogers & Stainton Rogers, 1992). Some regard children as adults in the making, some view them as agentic beings with rights to participate in decisions about their own lives (including schooling), while others conceive of children as innocent and potentially vulnerable and therefore in need of protection. In analysing teacher testimonies, we were attuned to how teachers expressed what children need, their conceptualisations of who children are, and how they expected them to behave. To begin, we provide a brief description of the Toroa school context together with a portrait of each of the teachers whose testimony we draw on.

Toroa

Toroa is a public primary school near a major North Island city and serves a predominantly Maori and Pasifika population. Children at Toroa come from families typically parented by adults who have low-paid jobs and live predominantly in government housing. Toroa is something of a poster-school for health promotion agencies, having achieved Gold status in the national healthy school awards delivered by New Zealand's Heart Foundation. It is inundated with policies and programmes focused on improving its children's health, its walls are graced with numerous posters promoting healthy food and physical activity, and pride of place is its Health Promoting School trophy. The Education Review Office, an institution that examines the functioning of all schools in New Zealand, consistently reports Toroa as a school with a caring, whanau-style feeling and ethos.

Helen is a 40-plus-year-old woman, a parent and a teacher well regarded for her innovative pedagogies in physical education. Helen's role on advisory bodies for national agencies, and professional commitment to remaining abreast of relevant research in the health and physical education field, informs her conceptualisation of children's health needs. So, too, does her nuanced understanding of the unique school and community context of Toroa. Helen is what Smyth (2001) would refer to as a critical pedagogue, consistently evaluating her own and others actions in relation to what she perceives her students need, and broader structural and ideological matters.

Wendy, as a parent of two children, a self-confessed physical education 'clutz' and a teacher of Year 5 students at Toroa, expressed deeply held convictions about the key issues her students are facing. Drawing variously on her experiences as a parent, informal observations and conversations with health professionals (e.g. school dental nurses), she advances a range of, at times, contradictory, yet strongly expressed views about what Toroa children need and the role of schooling in their health.

Pete is a teacher who, like Helen, thinks deeply about the specific needs of his school's predominantly low socio-index cohort. His testimony points to a keen awareness of the structural and social barriers his students face in relation to health incomes, something that influences his assessment of the raft of health policies and interventions his school currently deals with. All of Pete's responses were infused with a genuine care for and commitment to the children he worked with.

What do children need? What (if anything) is the problem?

In 1994, Australian scholar Richard Tinning asked, 'If physical education is the answer, then what is the question?' (Tinning, 1994, p. 1) and a similar question could be asked of school-based health education. That is, what is it that health education should/could be addressing? Teachers in our study advanced clear perceptions about what children's health needs are, drawing on discourses circulating in public health, lay media and their teacherly understandings of children in their schools. While some teachers were adamant that schools should be implicated in addressing these health needs, for others the role of schooling in ameliorating the health problems children faced was a fraught and complex conundrum. In what follows we highlight teacher commentary that points to the diversity of perspectives these teachers display together with their varied positioning in relation to discourses of health and childhood.

Understanding health in situ

Given that both Pasifika and Maori populations are currently portrayed as two of the groups most 'at risk' of poor health outcomes related to obesity (Burrows, 2009b), and in light of the inundation of schools like Toroa with health programmes, initiatives and interventions, it would not have been surprising to find that Toroa's teachers were concerned about their students' weight. However, while cognisant of the obesity issue, Helen and Pete displayed more concern about how obesity knowledge was being disseminated to and taken up by their students, than they did about the state of their students' waistlines. That is, it was how children understood health rather than their physical health per se that preoccupied these two teachers:

> Um, there's probably a lot of mixed messages I would think about just what is healthy. I think a lot of the kids are bringing the message that you know slim is fit, and that has implications of course, because a lot of the kids suspect that they're not healthy, they're not fit... because they're not slim, but I think a lot of them are... (Interview, Pete)

Pete is acutely aware of the slim = fit = healthy triplex that has pervaded popular health consciousness for some time (Colquhoun, 1990) and is concerned that Toroa students may be drawing on this message to evaluate their own health and/or ill health. Like Pete, Helen felt that the media's focus on obesity was less than helpful for youngsters in her school. She expressed her own confusion about the 'lose weight' message when confronted with prominent sportspeople who are technically obese yet fit and displaying what she calls 'healthy' body-shapes and pondered on the negativity embedded in much of the health rhetoric her students seemed to be drawing on. While her children 'can spout a lot of ideas... about their own health and the health of others and the health of the people in their family and in the community', according to Helen, 'they don't always have the big picture'. For Helen, many of the messages her students receive and regurgitate are both negative (such as, 'an awful lot of don't do this, don't do that') and 'segmented', focusing almost exclusively on corporeal matters.

Like Helen and Pete, Wendy does not rate obesity highly on her list of serious health issues for children at Toroa. Rather, she tops her list with 'tooth decay' adding that lack of sleep, nits, ear problems, infections and school sores are key priorities for Toroa children. While Helen and Pete display a keen awareness of the ways socio-economic, geographic and cultural matters contour Toroa children's capacity to engage in 'healthy' behaviours, Wendy suggests that unaware and potentially 'neglectful' parents are largely responsible for the volume and nature of health issues Toroa children face. As her testimony below illustrates, she regards the Toroa cohort, in a similar way to many health agencies, as a special case:

> We see the extremes of things here that we wouldn't really encounter at my children's school – a lack of care of them after when they get them. I do think it's an awareness thing. We certainly have difficulty sometimes convincing parents to take their children to the doctor. I mean, how many schools have a health nurse that comes in once a week? (Interview, Wendy)

For Wendy, health is predominantly a corporeal matter. Reigning in infection rates, turning around tooth decay, fixing school sores, getting enough sleep, are things schools can and should help with. As she suggests:

> Um, well, certainly at a teacher level I'm very aware that probably we're the first point of noticing. We had one child who was new to New Zealand and was really unhappy, and I couldn't work out what was wrong. He didn't speak any English, and he went out. I asked the reading language teacher who had him to see if she could find out what was wrong. And she found out that he had a really sore ear. So you know we got him, and finally the only way that the school could solve the problem was – we had a temporary, we took a temporary, I think it was temporary guardianship or something. (Interview, Wendy)

The above, albeit briefly expressed testimonies of Pete, Helen and Wendy suggest three very different orientations towards what matters for children's health. They illustrate that it is not only 'local' cultures that shape the ways health messages are received, but also that personal/political understandings of individual teachers are very much implicated in any answer to the question 'what is the problem?' In the following section, we examine more closely the resources that each of these teachers draw on to understand their students' health and their role as health educators.

What do teachers draw on to understand the health of their students?

A tendency (indicated above) to draw heavily on experiences with particular students infuses much of Wendy's testimony. It is what she 'sees' in front of her, what she 'knows' as a parent, what she concludes from conversations with health professionals (like the school dental nurse), and what she understands about parents within the Toroa community that fuels her approach. However, on the flipside, her personal parenting experiences, in particular, informed a scepticism around some of the health promotion practices being foisted on schools. The parental culpability (Burrows, 2009b) evident in her talk about the physical health issues which students face was tempered when she discussed her view of nutrition-centred health promotion practices:

> At one stage we discussed banning little chippie packets. But those of us that are parents turned around and said 'It's all very well for you, but when you've got to make the kids lunches, you know if you can throw in a couple of things that are already wrapped well, that's time saving'. (Interview, Wendy)

While regarding nutritional knowledge as a key constituent of her teaching, she eschewed some of her colleagues' attempts to ensure their students' lunch-boxes were 'healthy' ones:

> Interviewer: So how would you go about encouraging them around the healthy eating thing. Is that something that you find yourself regularly talking about or...?
>
> Wendy: Not me in particular, um, I'm not sure. I don't know if it comes from being a parent and just having this fight every day with my own children and not having to bring it in here. But certainly Sandra next door, she used to have competitions, the kids had competitions about who brought the healthiest lunch. I can't remember if she had a chart or what she was doing. They had their 5+ a day, this was with her last year class. And, she got into it in a really big big time. I find that I don't tend to stress the kids too much about it. I think, being a parent, I have more understanding of the fact that they have very little say over what gets put in their lunch box. (Interview, Wendy)

Rather than cast aspersions on the food choices of her students, she recognises their desires as ones most young people have, including her own children. As a parent, she 'know(s) the amount of effort to make a healthy meal and then listen(s) to the children moan and moan about how much they hate eating it...'. In reference to her own children she says:

> I've got my kids who are relatively well educated. First thing they want when they go to the shop is either those powerade drinks, or they want fizzy drinks, or they want lollies. (Interview, Wendy)

Further, rather than adopt a developmental argument that ascribes irrational behaviours exclusively to young people (Mayall, 2000), she recognises that adults too do not always do what is in their best interests. She suggests, 'I don't think it changes that much as you get older ... we do tend to not think of the future'.

Wendy's perspectives on obesity, too, are markedly influenced by her experiences parenting her two children. When asked what she thought about the current level of governmental concern about childhood obesity, she replied:

> I find it really really hard, mainly I think because my 11 year old is quite overweight. And he gets teased all the time, just constantly. And I have the opposite end of the stick, I have a 9 year old daughter who is a stick, who's just rake thin. (Interview, Wendy)

In her extended commentary below Wendy points to the personal conundrums this raises for her as nutritional guide and mentor for her family:

> I have the two issues because, OK, we talk about half your plate needs to be fruit and vegetables. And I bought them, when they had that DownSize Me programme. They had those portion plates. I bought them both portion plates; just simply so they could be aware of how big each portion of food should be on their plate. But then I have to be very careful because I've got to – the awareness that my 9 year old can't ever get into her head to go on a diet because she's already according to the doctor; she's the 60th percentile for height and the 30th for weight. If the disparity gets any wider, then she's hitting danger point. And I'm thinking, Well I've got to be aware that she can't, she's got to eat, you know. I'm trying to push her milk and all this sort of thing to make sure that she stays healthy. Where at the same time trying to explain to my son that when we get fish and chips he can't just have the whole lot of the chips, because that's what he wants. And at one stage I found jelly crystals hidden in his top draw and you know, his whole attitude to food is kind of very difficult for him to see. (Interview, Wendy)

Keenly aware of the correct portions of food her children should be having, having two children at distinctly different ends of the 'BMI' scale, means that 'normative' notions of what counts as too much or too little are troubled. The high doses of asthma steroids her son is on mean that even when he exercises intensely, his weight does not necessarily change. The injustice of this does not escape Wendy, nor does the potential for humiliation carrying extra weight can yield for her son:

> He was in one class, where in his maths lesson, the teacher weighed everybody in the class, and then they were categorized or lined up. Well, I mean he just, he didn't get over that for quite a long time. (Interview, Wendy)

All of these experiences have contoured Wendy's approach to health teaching, yet not necessarily in predictable ways. Despite watching her own child struggle with the sense of shame attached to being publicly weighed in a maths class, and acknowledging the risks posed by her daughter being too thin, the healthy eating messages are ones she regards as vital for students to know about in the context of formal and informal curriculum. As she puts it:

> It all comes down to that healthy body, healthy mind, and food, is certainly something that we can influence a lot in terms of what they're allowed to bring into a school. (Interview, Wendy)

Helen was troubled by the degree of influence schools should/do have in monitoring and regulating children's health. Acutely aware of the ways her school is regarded as a superlative site for health improvement, the ostensibly benign initiatives and programmes reaching into her school environs (such as fruit in schools) are reconceptualised in her testimony as phenomena that potentially override the interests/needs of parents and families. Indeed, as is evident below, she is also not overly comfortable with the role teachers are expected to play in implementing the plethora of policies and programmes embraced by her school:

> I've had concerns for quite a while with the initiatives that have come to the school. Because sometimes they've required me to be the food police or the water police or... And that doesn't sit well with me. I know all the arguments for and against. OK, well, if you're not going to do it, nobody is, and all that sort of stuff. But the lunch box checking and enforcing rules about healthy lunches. I didn't always feel comfortable with those. And, OK, the school's done really well. It's the gold heart thing school, but I felt like I was overriding what parents had chosen for their children. And I guess I was thinking: Well, they know the issues, they know, and you know. In the end it's their choice... So yeah, and just some of the other things seem to be a little bit heavy handed. They had to be if the school wanted to achieve the goals that it's trying to achieve. But I felt, you know, I didn't feel entirely comfortable with being the enforcer with some of those. (Interview, Helen)

As is illustrated above, Helen has no desire to intervene in parents' decisions about what constitutes healthy eating. While fully cognisant of the arguments for and against a surveillant stance in regard to students' food and beverage choices, for her, parents have the right to feed their children as they wish. While Wendy believes parents are unaware and potentially negligent, Helen thinks parents are knowledgeable and 'it's their choice'. While she did allocate a student to record lunch boxes each day, her motivation was to make sure every child had a lunch, rather than to instruct her students on the constituents of a 'healthy' one. Clearly uncomfortable with enforcing some of her school's nutrition policies, this discomfort was compounded in relation to a planned introduction of a fitness initiative in her school. As her narrative (below) illustrates, the nuances of her school's context, an understanding of what her students need and how public health messages and programmes may potentially denigrate rather than enhance young people's sense of themselves as 'healthy', assisted her and her colleagues in a decision to reject what at first blush, may have seemed like a prime opportunity to introduce an outside agency's fitness initiative into the school. Helen describes the process of resisting this outside initiative as follows:

> We had a group of people who were offering to come to this school and do a fitness programme with our kids. And they were offering to do baseline data then run the programme, and then do a summative assessment at the end. They gave the children, you know, these individual fitness plans. And there was a local school doing it, and we rang them and said well 'What's it like? Ah, it's fantastic... the kids' fitness levels have... blah blah blah... they've got better. It did cost a bit of money but there was some funding available. We were (asking) 'Shall we? Shall we? Because we think maybe

our kids' fitness levels aren't so good. Then we had a very wise and thoughtful PE advisor who came, and we said, What do you think about this fitness programme? So why were you wanting to do this? Maybe our kids aren't so fit. She said, How do you know this? What does fitness mean to you anyway? OK, right, we won't be doing that. It was great because we've heard for a lot of schools PE is fitness. It's pounding the pavement. And we had to re-think ... And we came up with this thing: if you could do the physical activity that you wanted to do, and enjoy what you're doing, then your fitness levels are OK. (Interview, Helen)

When asked what she thought about current concerns around childhood obesity, she responded as follows:

I don't think it's positive at all. I'm thinking there'll be a whole lot of spin-offs with the anorexics and the bulimics ... I think there's a whole lot of really healthy really strong fit large people out there, and this is all wrong ... And, you know, to me the whole thing is: Can you do what you want to do with your body shape? And if you can't, well OK. Maybe there's some things that you need to work on. But all the reality shows, DownSize Me; this is the messages in them. And I think we're really going to have a whole lot of problems with mental health if we keep just putting this sort of pressure on people. That's not positive. We've just got to look at other places where you know food is not the enemy. The food is just this nice thing that you enjoy ... I don't know, [I have] got that French model in my head, sitting in the café and just enjoying food with friends .... (Interview, Helen)

Helen's recognition of the potentially pernicious effects of prevailing nutrition and physical activity messages informs her approach to teaching. In physical education, she avoids a focus on exercise for health purposes. Rather, her belief that exercise is something young people enjoy, something positive and fun; it informs a pedagogical approach that is inclusive, that focuses on teamwork, joining in, learning skills and strategies rather than 'pounding the pavement'. She embraces events like festivals where children share food in the context of promoting cross-cultural understanding and fostering a love of eating.

Pete, too, was adamantly opposed to the notion of bringing an outside fitness motivator into the school. For him, it was not the activities per se that were problematic, but rather the notion that this agency would measure children's capacities, their weight, their progress in ways that potentially diminish rather than enhance their sense of themselves as 'healthy' children:

No, well, what they wanted to do was come in. They wanted to measure all of the children's fitness using this particular range of fitness measures. Then they were going to develop an activity programme, and then re-measure and so they could say: Right, this was your starting point, now you've been doing these eight weeks of physical activity so many times a day every day ... dah dah dah ... This is where your physical fitness is, here measured against these certain markers. And we said, No, we don't believe those markers are appropriate for primary school children. It wasn't that we were rejecting the activities, but we rejected the markers. We didn't think we needed to put children down in the hall and measure their ability to run up and down a certain number of times against the clock, and so on, and so forth ... And what message does it send? I mean we could bring them in and start doing fat tests and ... dah dah dah ... I mean what messages are we sending? If somebody wants to take themselves off because they recognise a problem, and they want to do something about it, that's different. For us to line everybody up, and put body mass indicators on each one and so on. Um, I don't think that's the right way to go personally. (Interview, Pete)

His own feelings about exercise inform what he thinks is important for the children he works with:

> I suppose . . . I kind of want them to enjoy what they do. You have fun while you're doing it. I mean, if we're going down there to slog – where's the fun in that? Why would you want to do that! I mean I've never felt, for instance, that pounding the pavement was running, that's never appealed to me. Just me personally, I can't speak for everyone. But I see people doing it and I think, well, why would you put yourself through that? Um . . . (Interview, Pete)

Pete's firm stance on outside intervention in monitoring of his students' fitness levels is contradicted in his support of lunch-box checks although, as is evident in his testimony below, this practice is motivated by a desire to ensure children have something substantial to eat in their box rather than a desire to cast aspersions on the contents of the boxes:

> Yeah, every now and again I'll surprise them a bit and first thing in the day – Right, lunches out! So we actually put it out on the table and have a look. Normally what I do is just wander round at lunch time and have a quick check, you know, sandwich, sandwich, yeah, making sure that they're eating something that's sandwich or roll or yoghurt or something that's you know substantial. (Interview, Pete)

Like Helen, Pete has a nuanced understanding of the physical, cultural and familial barriers children in his community face in any attempts to adhere to orthodox health messages. He repeatedly drew on wider issues like the extension of shopping hours into weekends, poverty and the cultural proclivities of families to explain why it is that his students recite healthy mantras but do not necessarily incorporate them into their daily lives:

> Some of it's money. I mean in the winter time the local shop the pies are $1. The kids are hungry. it's after school, it's cold, it's a hot pie, it's only $1, it's good value in terms of you're hungry . . . Yeah, it puts something inside you that fills you and makes you warm. So I'm certain myself that money is part of it. (Interview, Pete)

He also understands the ways his own personal history contours his contemporary concerns, draws on his experience as a parent, his understanding of how things used to be in his day, and recognises that the current climate, where health messages are pushed at every crevice potentially informs the judgements he makes of students and their behaviour. In the following statement, the ways public messages reach into his psyche and with what effect is compellingly illustrated:

> Yeah, um, . . . I hear myself asking about breakfast, whether they've had breakfast, what they had for breakfast. I hear myself commenting about the cookies that they might have for morning tea, um, about the packets of chippies. I hear myself commenting about the snacky crispy stuff . . . Although I talked to my own kids – they're in their middle to late 20s now, but they used to knock off quite a few chippies and bits and pieces. I mean, they ate what they wanted to eat. It wasn't up to me. But I used to drill them a bit, you know, sort of this scoffing down the packs of chippies. Ah, that'll come back and haunt you later on. I hear myself making comments if I see the kids eating the pies or the fizzy drinks after school. Some of it's probably learnt . . . the school has a message, and some of it's probably just without really thinking, reiterating the school

message. So some of it's probably a comment without a lot of thought behind it, just rote kind of comment, if you like. (Interview, Pete)

Pete has a nuanced understanding of his students' needs and no desire to foist health messages upon them. Despite his knowledge of the 'local' he cannot necessarily shake off the imperatives in his day to day practice. His own history together with the ubiquity of health imperatives renders his pedagogical practices unpredictable. At times, he rejects health mantras outright, while at others, they 'slip out' unwittingly. His narrative complicates any easy equation between teacher disposition and pedagogy. Rather, it suggests that he draws on different sources at different moments, to inform his practice and make sense of his students' life worlds.

So what?

As the above testimonies indicate, even within a single school, and within a single teacher's testimony, priorities for health teaching are differently expressed. Each of the teachers' narratives point to a genuine lived and felt commitment to doing right by their students, yet their personal proclivities lead each to enact this 'right' in distinct, yet inconsistent ways.

Wendy, at first, seems to heartily embrace orthodox health imperatives. Yet, as other parts of her testimony suggest, her experience as a parent, of caring for two children – one overly thin and the other with a 'weight problem' – affords a lens through which the health messages pervading her school are filtered. As a parent she knows that simply telling a child what's good for them does not necessarily change thought or action – an understanding that critical health scholars (e.g. Colquhoun, 1990; Gard, 2007) have been advancing for some time now. As a parent of a thin girl, she worries that a preponderance of healthy food messages may compound her daughter's eating difficulties. This is a concern reiterated in much of the socially critical health research to date (e.g. Evans et al., 2008; O'Flynn, 2008; Rich, Evans, & De Pian, 2010). As a parent of a weighty boy, she knows that he can be fit but fat (Blair, 2010; Campos, Saguy, Ernsberger, Oliver, & Gaesser, 2006), that factors other than food and exercise (that is, asthma medications) influence his weight, yet she ponders the potential effects his size may yield in terms of self-esteem and social capital. She draws on this lived reality to enact in-school pedagogies designed 'not to stress kids out' about food, yet remains committed to the pivotal role of schools in improving children's healthy eating practices. In a sense, her private troubles fuel professional dilemmas – ones that mess up any expectations that she might translate school policies in a uniform way.

When read alongside prior research that points to the investments many teachers have in trimming down their student population, enforcing health policies, and 'making' the student body understand the vagaries of their practice (Burrows, 2010), Pete, Helen and Wendy's perspectives tell a different story. Helen's focus on fun, enjoyment and her vision of a 'french style approach to eating well' has little in common with dominant health promotion discourses that explicitly focus on nutrition and exercise as the keys to a healthy future. Indeed in Helen's world, children would connect eating and physical education to pleasure rather than 'work', learning rather than 'fixing' health issues. Pete's embodied understanding of physical activity as fun, together with his acknowledgement of the ways socioeconomic and familial priorities contour opportunities available to young people, leads him to accentuate the positive and rail against the 'do's and don'ts' that characterise much public health promotion emphases. As signalled above, however, at times he delivers 'rote' messages that encode precisely what it is he rails against. And Wendy, despite her embracing of the fruit in schools programme, and any initiative that may assist students to eat better, and therefore be healthy, is able, wittingly or not, to draw on her lived experience as a parent of a fat and a skinny child, to temper her perhaps otherwise desire to adopt some of the more 'heavy handed' practices her colleagues do in the name of student health.

Green et al. (2009) suggest that physical education teachers' understandings of their students' lives are characterised by a blend of 'myth and reality' (p. 401). With respect to the current study, given the ubiquity of public discourse on child health, we initially assumed that 'myth' would dominate. However, our analysis suggests that this assumption belies the reflectiveness and capacity to interrogate dominant discourses and understand what their purveyance might mean for their pupils, that these teachers display. Armour and Fernandez-Balboa (2001) suggest that the capacity to establish deep connections to selves, learners, curriculum and the context within which each exist are crucial attributes for teachers. It is this intimate knowledge of their school communities, together with a capacity to reflect on how personal knowing influences their public pedagogies that is particularly evident in each of the teacher's testimonies. They know what's out there – they know the ways others regard their school community, are concerned for what all of this might do to and for young people, who may come to envisage themselves as unhealthy when they are not (Aphramor, 2005; Campos et al., 2006).

The teacher perspectives canvassed in this article suggest that a shared orientation towards health teaching is most unlikely. Not only do health messages, programmes and policies change once they rub up against school cultures (Evans et al., 2010), but once teachers' own personal and political aspirations are added to the mix, it is multiple and uncertain effects that are yielded rather than normative ones. Our analysis points to the folly of over-determined views of links between health discourse, teacher subjectivity, and pedagogy (Evans et al., 2010). It would seem that at least at Toroa, there are spaces where discourses can play. Even a seemingly straight forward pedagogical device (Leahy, 2009) like monitoring lunch box contents is differently enacted by each of the teachers, morphed and moulded by their divergent understandings about who their students are and what they need. While health promotion agencies and policy makers may find this disturbing, we would counter that it is precisely this diversity that potentially yields productive rather than poisonous pedagogies in school contexts.

Children taught by Helen would likely receive the message that physical activity and eating are fun practices while those in Wendy's class may be prompted to understand nutrition and exercise as constituents of a healthy lifestyle. Students working with Pete may have their lunch-boxes surveilled and face the occasional 'weigh-in' for rugby, yet it is unlikely they would ever feel judged or blamed for any 'unhealthy' transgressions. For students who at various stages of their schooling may experience being taught by the Petes, Wendys and Helens, the diversity of health messages they receive may breed confusion, yet we would argue that exposure to certain prescriptions for their own and others' health is hardly a palatable educational alternative. It is the rich diversity of perspective evidenced in teachers' work that yields opportunities for students to think and do health otherwise – something 21st century teachers would undoubtedly embrace as a 'healthy' outcome.

References

Aphramor, L. (2005). Is a weight-centred health framework salutogenic? Some thoughts on unhinging certain dietary ideologies. *Social Theory and Health, 3*(4), 315–340.

Alton-Lee, A. (2003). *Quality teaching for diverse students in schooling: Best evidence synthesis.* Retrieved from http://www.educationcounts.govt.nz/publications/series/2515/5959

Armour, K., & Fernandez-Balboa, J. (2001). Connections, pedagogy and professional learning. *Teaching Education, 12*(1), 103–118.

Blair, S. (2010, February). The crucial role of physical activity in the prevention and management of overweight and obesity. Paper presented at The Big Fat Truth Symposium, School of Physical Education, University of Otago.

Burrows, L. (2008). 'Fit, fast and skinny': New Zealand school students 'talk' about health. *Journal of Physical Education New Zealand, 41*(3), 26–36.

Burrows, L. (2009a). Discursive dilemmas in New Zealand's Health and Physical Education curriculum. In M. Dinan (Ed.), *Health and physical education: Contemporary issues for curriculum in Australia and New Zealand* (pp. 147–164). Melbourne: Oxford University Press.

Burrows, L. (2009b). Pedagogising families through obesity discourse. In J. Wright & V. Harwood (Eds.), *Biopolitics and the 'obesity epidemic': Governing bodies* (pp. 127–140). New York/London: Routledge.

Burrows, L. (2010). Kiwi Kids are Weet-Bix kids: Body matters in childhood. *Sport, Education and Society, 15*(2), 235–253.

Burrows, L., & Wright, J. (2004). The good life: New Zealand children's perspectives of health and self. *Sport, Education and Society, 9*(2), 193–205.

Campos, P., Saguy, A., Ernsberger, P., Oliver, E., & Gaesser, G. (2006). The epidemiology of overweight and obesity: Public health crisis or moral panic? *International Journal of Epidemiology, 35*(1), 55–60.

Carr, M. (2001). *Assessment in early childhood settings: Learning stories.* London: Sage.

Colquhoun, D. (1990). Images of healthism in health-based physical education. In D. Kirk & R. Tinning (Eds.), *Physical education curriculum and culture* (pp. 225–251). London: The Falmer Press.

Curtner-Smith, M. (1995). The more things change, the more they stay the same: Factors influencing teachers' interpretations and delivery of the National Curriculum Physical Education. *Sport, Education and Society, 4*(1), 75–97.

Curtner-Smith, M.D. (2001). The occupational socialization of a first-year physical education teacher with a teaching orientation. *Sport, Education and Society, 6*(1), 81–105.

Davies, B. (1994). *Poststructuralist theory and classroom practice.* Geelong: Deakin University Press.

Ennis, C., & Chen, A. (1995). Teachers' value orientations in urban and rural school settings. *Research Quarterly for Exercise and Sport, 66*(1), 41–50.

Evans, J., Rich, E., Davies, B., & Allwood, R. (2008). *Education, eating disorders and obesity discourse: Fat fabrications.* London and New York: Routledge.

Evans, J., Rich, E., Davies, B., & De Pian, L. (2010, December). Understanding policy: Why policy is important and why it does not appear to work. Paper presented at the Australian Association for Research in Education Conference, Melbourne University, Melbourne.

Gard, M. (2007). Is the war on obesity a war on children? *Childrenz Issues: Journal of the Children's Issues Centre, 11*(2), 20–24.

Gard, M., & Wright, J. (2005). *The obesity epidemic: Science, morality and ideology.* London: Routledge.

Garrett, R., & Wrench, A. (2008). Connections, pedagogy and alternative possibilities in primary physical education. *Sport, Education and Society, 13*(1), 39–60.

Gavey, N. (1989). Feminist poststructuralism and discourse analysis: Contributions to feminist psychology. *Pscyhology of Women Quarterly, 13*(4), 459–475.

Green, K. (2003). *Physical education teachers on physical education: A sociological study of philosophies and ideologies.* Chester: Chester Academic Press.

Green, K., Smith, A., & Thurston, M. (2009). Busy doing nothing? Physical education teachers' perceptions of young people's participation in leisure-sport. *Sport, Education and Society, 14*(4), 401–420.

Ha, A.S., Wong, A.C., Sum, R.K., & Chan, D.W. (2008). Understanding teachers' will and capacity to accomplish physical education curriculum reform: The implications for teacher development. *Sport, Education and Society, 13*(1), 77–95.

Hendrick, H. (1997). Constructions and reconstructions of British childhood: An interpretative survey, 1800 to the present. In A. James & A. Prout (Eds.), *Constructing and reconstructing childhood: Contemporary issues in the sociological study of childhood* (pp. 7–34). London: Routledge Falmer.

Jenks, C. (2005). *Childhood.* New York, NY: Routledge.

Kirk, D., & Macdonald, D. (2001). Teacher voice and ownership of curriculum change. *Journal of Curriculum Studies, 33*(5), 551–567.

Leahy, D. (2009). Disgusting pedagogies. In J. Wright & V. Harwood (Eds.), *Biopolitics and the 'obesity epidemic' governing bodies* (pp. 172–182). New York and London: Routlege.

Leahy, D., & Harrison, L. (2004). Health and physical education and the production of the 'at risk self'. In J. Evans, B. Davies & J. Wright (Eds.), *Body knowledge and control: Studies in the sociology of physical education and health* (pp. 130–139). London: Routledge.

Lee, J., & Macdonald, D. (2010). 'Are they just checking on obesity or what?' The healthism discourse of rural young women. *Sport, Education and Society, 15*(2), 203–221.

Macdonald, D., Hay, P., & Williams, B. (2008). Should you buy? Neo-liberalism, neo-HPE and your neo-job. *Journal of Physical Education New Zealand, 41*(3), 6–13.

Martino, W., & Beckett, L. (2004). Schooling the gendered body in health and physical education: Interrogating teachers' perspectives. *Sport, Education and Society, 9*(2), 239–252.

Mayall, B. (2000). The sociology of childhood: Children's autonomy and participation rights. In A.B. Smith, M. Gollop, K. Marshall & K. Nairn (Eds.), *Advocating for children* (pp. 126–140). Dunedin, NZ: University of Otago.

Ministry of Education. (2007). *The New Zealand Curriculum.* Wellington: Learning Media.

O'Flynn, G. (2008). *Young women, health and the self.* Germany: VDM Verlag Dr. Muller.

Petrie, K. (2009). *Teaching physical education: Primary school teachers as learners* (Unpublished doctoral dissertation). University of Waikato, Hamilton, New Zealand.

Petrie, K., Jones, A., & McKim, A. (2007). *Evaluative research on the impacts of professional learning on curricular and co-curricular physical activity in primary school* (Ministry of Education publication). Retrieved from http://www.educationcounts.govt.nz/publications/schooling/25204/25331

Quennerstedt, M. (2010). 'Warning: Physical education can seriously harm your health!' – But it all depends on our health perspective! In S. Brown (Ed.), *Issues and controversies in physical education: Policy, power, and pedagogy* (pp. 46–56). Auckland: Pearson.

Rail, G. (2009). Canadian youth's discursive constructions of the body and health. In J. Wright & V. Harwood (Eds.), *Biopolitics and the 'obesity epidemic': Governing bodies* (pp. 141–156). New York and London: Routledge.

Rich, E. (2004). Exploring teachers' biographies and perceptions of girls' participation in physical education. *European Physical Education Review, 10*(2), 195–210.

Rich, E., & Evans, J. (2005). Making sense of eating disorders in schools. *Discourse: Studies in the Cultural Politics of Education, 26*(2), 247–262.

Rich, E., Evans, J., & De Pian, L. (2010). Obesity, body pedagogies and young women's engagement with exercise. In E. Kennedy & P. Markula (Eds.), *Women and exercise: The body, health and consumerism* (pp. 138–158). London: Routledge.

Robertson, J. (2005). *Making sense of Health Promotion in context of health and physical education curriculum learning* (Commissioned report for Minstry of Education). Retrieved from http://nzcurriculum.tki.org.nz/Curriculum-resources/NZC-resource-bank/Health-and-physical-education/Supporting-materials

Ross, B. (2004). Press ups, put downs and playing games: The meaning of physical education? *Childrenz Issues: Journal of the Children's Issues Centre, 8*(1), 22–25.

NEW HEALTH IMPERATIVES ON EDUCATIONAL POLICY AND SCHOOLING

Rovegno, I. (2003). Teachers' knowledge construction. In S. Silverman & C. Ennis (Eds.), *Student learning in physical education: Applying research to enhance instruction* (pp. 295–310). Champaign IL: Human Kinetics.

Sinkinson, M. (2009). 'Sexuality isn't just about sex': Pre-service teachers' shifting constructs of sexuality education. *Sex Education: Sexuality, Society and Learning, 9*(4), 421–436.

Smyth, J. (2001). *Critical politics of teachers'work*. New York, NY: Peter Lang Publishing.

Sparkes, A. (1990). *Curriculum change and physical education: Toward a micropolitical understanding*. Geelong: Deakin University.

Sparkes, A. (1999). Exploring body narratives. *Sport, Education and Society, 4*(1), 17–30.

Sparkes, A.T., & Templin, T. (1992). Life histories and physical education teachers: Exploring the meaning of marginality. In A. Sparkes (Ed.), *Research in physical education and sport: Exploring alternative visions* (pp. 118–145). London: Falmer Press.

Stainton Rogers, R., & Stainton Rogers, W. (1992). *Stories of childhood: Shifting agendas of child concern*. Hempel Hempstead: Harvester Wheatsheaf.

Stroot, S.A., & Willliamson, K. (1993). Issues and themes of socialization into physical education. *Journal of teaching in physical education, 12*(2), 337–343.

Templin, T.J., & Schempp, P.G. (Eds.). (1989). *Socialization into physical education: Learning to teach*. Indiana: Benchmark Press, Inc.

Tinning, R. (1994, July). If physical education is the answer, what is the question? Ruminations on the relevance of physical education in the 1990s. Paper presented at the New Zealand Association for Health, Physical Education & Recreation National Conference, University of Waikato, Hamilton.

Weatherall, A. (1992). *Gender, language and discourse*. East Sussex: Routledge.

Wright, J. (2004). Post-structural methodologies: The body schooling and health. In J. Evans & B. Davies (Eds.), *Body, knowledge and control: Studies in the sociology of physical education and health* (pp. 19–31). London and New York: Routledge.

Index

INDEX

For Product Safety Concerns and Information please contact our EU representative GPSR@taylorandfrancis.com Taylor & Francis Verlag GmbH, Kaufingerstraße 24, 80331 München, Germany

Batch number: 08158242

Printed by Printforce, the Netherlands